The Terrible We

ASTERISK: Gender, Trans-, and All That Comes After
A series edited by Susan Stryker, Eliza Steinbock, and Jian Neo Chen

The Terrible We

THINKING WITH TRANS MALADJUSTMENT

CAMERON AWKWARD-RICH

Duke University Press
Durham and London 2022

Printed in the United States of America on acid-free paper ∞
Designed by Courtney Leigh Richardson and Dan Ruccia
Typeset in Minion Pro, Fengardo Neue, and Trade Gothic by
Westchester Publishing Services

Library of Congress Cataloging-in-Publication Data
Names: Awkward-Rich, Cameron, author.
Title: The terrible we : thinking with trans maladjustment /
Cameron Awkward-Rich.
Other titles: Asterisk (Duke University Press)
Description: Durham : Duke University Press, 2022. | Series:
Asterisk | Includes bibliographical references and index.
Identifiers: LCCN 2021056766 (print)
LCCN 2021056767 (ebook)
ISBN 9781478016052 (hardcover)
ISBN 9781478018681 (paperback)
ISBN 9781478023302 (ebook)
Subjects: LCSH: Transgender people. | Gender nonconformity—
Psychological aspects. | Gender identity—Psychological aspects.
| Disability studies. | Queer theory. | Feminist theory. | BISAC:
SOCIAL SCIENCE / LGBTQ Studies / Transgender Studies | SOCIAL
SCIENCE / People with Disabilities
Classification: LCC HQ77.9.A95 2022 (print) | LCC HQ77.9 (ebook) |
DDC 306.76/8—dc23/eng/20220216
LC record available at https://lccn.loc.gov/2021056766
LC ebook record available at https://lccn.loc.gov/2021056767

Publication of this book is supported by Duke University Press's
Scholars of Color First Book Fund.

Financial support was provided by the Office of the
Vice Chancellor for Research and Engagement, University
of Massachusetts, Amherst.

CONTENTS

PREFACE/ACKNOWLEDGMENTS

I began thinking in earnest about what would become *The Terrible We* in 2014, a year that was shot through with Obama-era optimism, condensed in the much-discussed *Time* cover story that declared that we had, as a country, arrived at the transgender tipping point. Indeed, 2014 also marked the inauguration of *Transgender Studies Quarterly*, the notorious trans studies cluster hire at the University of Arizona, and the one-year anniversary of the *Transgender Studies Reader 2*, which together formed a decisive tipping point for the field of trans studies.[1] It's crucial to remember, then, that when the essays that make up this book were conceived there was not yet a journal of record, regular conferences, or more than a small handful of tenured/tenure-track faculty who worked primarily in the field. At the same time, it was not true to say that trans studies had not yet begun; indeed, announcements of its beginning have occurred iteratively since the 1990s. What happened in 2014 and after, rather, was the beginning of the field's more robust institutionalization in the US university.

As a graduate student in 2014, then, I felt caught between the profound and varied optimisms that circulated with *trans* as a political and intellectual horizon and the recalcitrant distress that marked the lives/writing of those people who constitute trans pasts and presents. It seemed to me that the version of *trans* that was on the precipice of inclusion—of having an official, institutional life—was one that simply could not accommodate the cognitive/affective divergences, black moods, and peculiar itineraries endemic to what I understood as trans life and thought. Further, the mainstream optimism of 2014 was discordant with what I understood about the way *trans* has, historically, cycled through moments of visibility and repression, possibility and foreclosure. Put another way, I did not believe that those optimistic conditions would prove durable, nor that trans studies as it was being constituted offered me tools for living and thinking with all that persisted, persistently, in optimism's wake. In fact, it seemed to me then—and still seems to me now—that the "disciplinary position" of trans studies as institutionalized in, alongside, and against women's/feminist studies and queer theory, and the concurrent incorporation of trans people into the disciplinary imaginary of neoliberal citizenship, actually intensified, rather than alleviated, the maddening experience of living in what Talia Bettcher calls, aptly, "the WTF."[2] *The Terrible We*, then, is a book-length inquiry into the "bad"—pathologized, painful, or politically impairing—trans feelings and habits of mind that linger on in (and threaten to undo) trans people's and trans studies' relatively newfound legibility. In particular, the book is interested in what one might learn by thinking with, rather than against, the mad and dismal images of trans life that had to be disavowed in order for *trans* to emerge as a name for a species of rational man who could be the subject, not merely the object, of academic inquiry.

Much has happened since 2014: the Trump administration demonstrated the ease of undoing many Obama-era causes for optimism; trans-exclusionary "feminisms" have resurged in the United Kingdom and the United States and have been shaping conversations about transness (and, notably, transmasculinity) in a variety of domains—cultural, legal, and academic; queer theorists of a certain kind have repeatedly and publicly waged generational and/or theoretical conflicts on the backs of their trans students; and on and on. At the same time, trans studies, trans literature, and trans thought have (thankfully, luckily, with much effort) expanded far beyond the terms of the formative, ongoing conflicts that *The Terrible We* traces, such that this book might be understood to be speaking to and from a different time. In a real sense, it is. I am.

Indeed, at *this* time, I can't help but worry that this book takes too seriously trans-antagonistic forms of thought that I should have, instead, simply ignored. But like so many trans scholars who came to trans studies in a place "before trans studies," I had to write the book in order to learn that, next time, I could.[3] Further, on this side of 2020–21 in the United States—on this side of the coining of "gender critical feminism" and "rapid-onset gender dysphoria;" the conservative desire and legal campaign to define "transgender . . . out of existence;" the killing of (mad/black/trans) Tony McDade (and Aja Raquell Rhone-Spears, Brian 'Egypt' Powers, Sumer Taylor, Tatiana Hall . . .); wide-scale attempts by the Republican Party to restrict the freedoms of trans youth under the cover of a pandemic; the emergence of venture-capital backed transition companies that nonetheless capitalize on structural trans isolation and abandonment through "the promise of happiness," Euphoria, and Bliss—the one thing I know on this side of all this and more is that times recur. [4] More than anything, therefore, *The Terrible We* is a record of an attempt—an often awkward, sometimes chaotic, but hopefully ultimately space-clearing attempt—to think with the terrible parts of the felt life of trans and trans studies under these conditions.

* * *

The writing and thinking that follows—with all of its partiality and faults and untimely movements—is mine but depends on the labor and living of so many others. This book began at Stanford University, where I benefitted tremendously from the mentorship of Paula Moya, whose intellect and care enabled my trajectory through graduate school (and everything after). Likewise, I am grateful for the time, encouragement, and formative lessons in creativity and capacious thought provided by my other committee members, Sianne Ngai and Lochlann Jain. I owe thanks, too, to Jennifer DeVere Brody, Michele Elam, Mark McGurl, Sharika Thiranagama, Stephen Sohn, and Yvonne Yarbro-Bejarano, other faculty who, in one way or another, helped me along. My life and work at Stanford were enriched and enlivened by time and conversation with innumerable other students across campus, perhaps especially: K. J. Cerankowski, David Stentiford, Ben Allen, Corey Masao Johnson, Laura Eliasieh, Rebecca Wilbanks, Annika Butler-Wall, Luz Jimenez Ruvalcaba, Melanie Leon, Jonathan Leal, Calvin Cheung-Miaw, Vanessa Seals, Aku Ammah-Tagoe, Annie Atura Bushnell, Jess Auerbach, and Kate Turner. Thanks also to Mel Y. Chen for inviting me along to a University of California, Berkeley, Center for Race and Gender/Center for the Study of Sexual Culture dissertation retreat, and to the other faculty and students in that nourishing space.

I'm so grateful to have landed in Women, Gender, Sexuality Studies (WGSS) at the University of Massachusetts, Amherst, particularly, and among wonderful colleagues and friends across the Five Colleges more generally. Thanks especially to Angie Willey, Banu Subramaniam, Kiran Asher, Svati Shah, Miliann Kang, Laura Briggs, Laura Ciolkowski, Kirsten Leng, Fumi Okiji, Jina Kim, Britt Rusert, Ren-yo Hwang, Elliot Montague, Samuel Ace, Sonny Nordmarken, Sony Coráñez Bolton, Andrea Lawlor, Jordy Rosenberg, and Ocean Vuong. Also, thank you to all of the program administrators of every department/program I have passed through—particularly Karen Lederer, Linda Hillenbrand, Monica P. Moore, and Rachel Meisels—without whom nothing would happen.

The Terrible We was also enabled by fellowships from Duke University's Program in Gender, Sexuality, and Feminist Studies and the American Council of Learned Societies, as well as the generous support of Dean Barbara

Krauthamer and the College of Humanities and Fine Arts at the University of Massachusetts, Amherst. A portion of chapter 1 was originally published as "'She of the Pants and No Voice': Jack Bee Garland's Disability Drag," *TSQ: Transgender Studies Quarterly* 7, no. 1 (2020): 20–36; and an earlier version of chapter 2 appeared as "Trans, Feminism: Or, Reading like a Depressed Transsexual," *Signs: Journal of Women in Culture and Society* 42, no. 4 (2017): 819–41. I thank these editors for giving these essays their first homes. Further, individual chapters of *The Terrible We* benefited from brilliant audiences, interlocutors, and event organizers at the 2019 Alliance to Advance Liberal Arts Colleges funded Queer/Trans* of Color Critique (AALAC QTOCC) Summer Writing Workshop at Mt. Holyoke College, the English Department of the University of Virginia, the University of Mt. Union, Duke University, the 2019–20 Five College Crossroads in the Studies of the Americas (CISA) Seminar, the Pennsylvania State University's Transforming Feminist and Gender Studies Colloquium, and the University of Cambridge's Queer Cultures Research Seminar. Aside from these scripted appearances, I am for better and for worse something of a trans recluse, which means that many of the intimacies that have enabled my thinking here are mostly (or entirely) virtual and/or one-sided. But for varied reasons, this book would not exist without Trish Salah, Aren Z. Aizura, Hil Malatino, Susan Stryker, Alison Kafer, Cáel Keegan, Amy Marvin, and Kai Green, among many others. I am also tremendously grateful for the keen eye and ranging intellect of Zoe Tuck, who helped ready *The Terrible We* (and me!) for review, and for the insight, enthusiasm, and helpful reorientations of my three anonymous reviewers. More generally, I have been lucky to find myself buoyed by the hard-won infrastructures of trans studies, up to and including the ASTERISK book series at Duke University Press. In a profound way, I owe the present form of my life to all of those involved in trans studies' institutional maintenance. This includes all of the workers at Duke University Press, especially the wonderful Elizabeth Ault and Benjamin Kossak, who saw this project through.

Finally, I would like to thank Nicholas Clarkson for his sustaining and intimate friendship; Cassius Adair for returning pleasure to thought; Nora Hansel for being there through our growing pains; and my friends from the world of poetry, my family, and the cat, Bean, for putting up with me for all these years. Also, of course, thank you to Frances Choi—our *we* makes everything else possible, bearable, and even (despite myself) a joy.

INTRODUCTION

On Staying with the Terrible *We*

But the old Frankie had had no we to claim, unless it would be the terrible summer we of her and John Henry and Berenice—and that was the last we in the world she wanted. —**CARSON MCCULLERS, *THE MEMBER OF THE WEDDING* (1946)**

How much goodness, after all, must one attribute to her identity objects of study to withstand what it means to both represent and be represented by them? —**ROBYN WIEGMAN, *OBJECT LESSONS* (2012)**

In the years leading up to the 2013 publication of the fifth edition of the American Psychiatric Association's *Diagnostic and Statistical Manual of Mental Disorders* (DSM-5), gender identity disorder (GID) became a concentrated site of contestation. Although freeing transgender identities from the grasp of medical regulation and the stigma of pathology had long been a goal of transgender activism, the revision process made the contents of the DSM again unstable, up for debate, prompting a flurry of discussion about whether, how, and why the GID diagnosis should be revised. It was in this context that I found myself participating in a workshop focused on the preliminary draft revisions to GID that were, at the time, available for public review and comment. The workshop, part of the 2010 Transgender Lives: The Intersections of Health and Law conference held annually at the University of Connecticut, was intended to equip participants with the tools to engage in this conversation that would ultimately affect our lives.[1] While I didn't walk away from the hour-long session with any clarity as to what I believed an adequate revision might be, I did leave with a bad feeling, one that, retrospectively, became the seed of this book.

During the workshop, a white woman sitting near the front of the room stood up and, through tears, told us that she was the mother of a happy, well-adjusted transgender teenager. Illuminated by the projection of a proposed revision that would continue to describe her son in the language of psychiatric disorder, she insisted, "My son is not sick!" In my memory, this was her only contribution to the workshop, but it opened up what seemed then to be a very strange space of shared pathos. Momentarily, divergent lines of thought and argument were brought into accordance with one another around the "fact" of not-sickness. Before, it had been clear that everyone in the room had a slightly different set of stakes in the conversation, that there was no obvious answer to the GID problem. Suddenly, however, here was the one thing on which everyone in the room seemed to agree: this woman's son was not sick.

If this anecdote feels familiar, it's likely because it echoes the one that Susan Stryker uses to introduce *The Transgender Studies Reader*, the anthology that "gave a name to the field."[2] In her story, Stryker herself attended a panel at a conference, fifteen years earlier. The scene opens with Stryker standing in line to "register a protest" that the panel, on various forms of racialized and otherwise queer gender nonnormativities, featured no transgender panelists and seemed to collapse gender diversity into sexual desire. Before she can articulate this critique, however, she finds herself thrust into "in a fog of righteous anger" by another conference-goer's opposing and "all-too-familiar diatribe," imploring the panelists to reject "the disturbing new trend" of trans politics and interpretive practices "because everybody knew that transsexuals were profoundly psychopathological individuals who mutilated their bodies and believed in oppressive gender stereotypes." From within her fog, Stryker reports that she "leaned into the microphone on [her] side of the room and said, interrupting, 'I'm not sick.'"[3] In 1995, Stryker was, quite literally, interrupting "a line of thinking that passed at that time for a progressive point of view" that sought to exclude transsexuals from queer/feminist politics and knowledge production. In this story, *I'm not sick* functioned as a powerful speech act that cleared the room, literally and figuratively, of those who would dismiss trans people's authority to "be taken seriously on our own terms," a precondition for the existence of what has become transgender studies.[4] Indeed, in a second anecdote, Stryker returns to the scene of the conference ten years later, and when the same man stands to register his same complaint, he is promptly told by several of the numerous trans people in attendance to "shut up and sit down," indexing the profound success of the trans intellectual project in the United States. A feel-good ending.

And yet. Something about the durability and persuasiveness of the space opened by (and the reflection of) *I'm not / my son is not sick* made me—still makes me—profoundly uneasy. Two things, really. First, how quickly a complex conversation with multiple stakeholders—including incarcerated trans people who have relied on the GID diagnosis to make claims, albeit curtailed ones, to gender-affirming treatment—resolved into something like consensus because of the righteous invocation of a well-adjusted, well-supported, white trans child. Or, in the Stryker anecdotes, how quickly various forms of racialized gender are eclipsed by *trans* through the righteous anger of a white trans woman. And, second, that both of these moves toward consolidation could be produced only in direct opposition to the word *sick*. Thus, while this book shares much with Stryker's introduction—a deep investment in the flourishing of the intellectual project of trans studies as something distinct from (though proximate to) queer and feminist studies; an effort to map the field's origin stories in relation to its present trajectories; and ultimately, a commitment to ways of knowing developed in and by trans life—it works against the strategy of securing trans authority through the disavowal of *sick* on which, in Stryker's account and elsewhere, trans studies is founded.

Retooling this habit of trans thought is perhaps particularly necessary in this long moment in US culture, in which a range of trans bodies, lives, and narratives has become, again, newly visible and affirmable, prompting a relatively widespread liberal announcement of the incorporation of *trans* as yet one more form of minority difference. At the same time, the still-suspect health and sanity of transgender people undergirds everything from mid-pandemic legislative attempts to strip health care and other basic freedoms from trans kids, to hand-wringing about mundane and nonmedical aspects of transition in the pages of the *New York Times*, to the reversal of Obama-era policies regarding the enlistment of transgender service members. Much trans-affirmative discourse responds to this state of affairs by reaffirming the sanity/health of trans people by pointing to, for example, studies that link supported social transition to lower rates of depression and anxiety in trans youth, demonstrating that "being transgender is not synonymous with [mental health] challenges."[5] The incorporation of *trans*, that is, seems to hinge on whether it can be effectively decoupled from pathology, mental illness, and feeling bad.

In many ways, *The Terrible We* responds to this extended *right now*, to the disorienting trans 2010s (and now 2020s) in the United States. However, while it is only within the terms of *right now* that "a trans person can . . . be considered able-minded" within (some) dominant discourses in the first place, the pervasive undergirding assumption that knowledge, politics, and a worthwhile life depend on "distancing ourselves from disabled and mentally suspect others" has been a recurring ableist conceit of progressive movements and thought.[6] While narrowly focused on white trans[masculine] contexts, *The Terrible We* works generally against the premise that sanity/health indexed by the absence of bad feeling should be necessary to secure the authority of minoritarian subjects and thought in the first place, given that the horizon of health and happiness is itself a "promise that directs you toward certain objects" and ways of knowing, a normalizing technology.[7] Against the imperative of happiness, disciplinary discourses of health, and adjustment to a murderous given—and inspired by work in "the introspective turn" of feminist and queer studies—*The Terrible We* gathers tools from disability studies, queer and feminist studies of affect/emotion, and an archive of trans[masculine] writing to argue for and model a version of *trans* that thinks with, rather than against, what I call *trans maladjustment*.[8]

Trans Maladjustment

In the 1970s manifesto depicted in figure Intro.1, members of three trans liberation groups came together to lay out a list of demands that, from the vantage of the present, articulate a startlingly familiar (if more forcefully utopian) trans politics. Toward the goal of trans liberation, they demand the end to the policing of gendered clothing and comportment, the end to anti-trans discrimination in general and "within the gay world" in particular, the end to exploitative extraction of knowledge and capital from trans bodies (free hormones and surgery on demand), the ability to change one's identification documents "with no difficulty," the end to incarceration in prisons and mental institutions on the basis of trans status, and so on.[9]

Indeed, in addition to foreshadowing contemporary trans activism, the manifesto anticipates the terms of my opening anecdotes as, in the second sentence, its authors insist: "we reject all labels of 'stereotype' 'sick' or 'maladjusted' from non-transvestic and non-transsexual sources and defy any

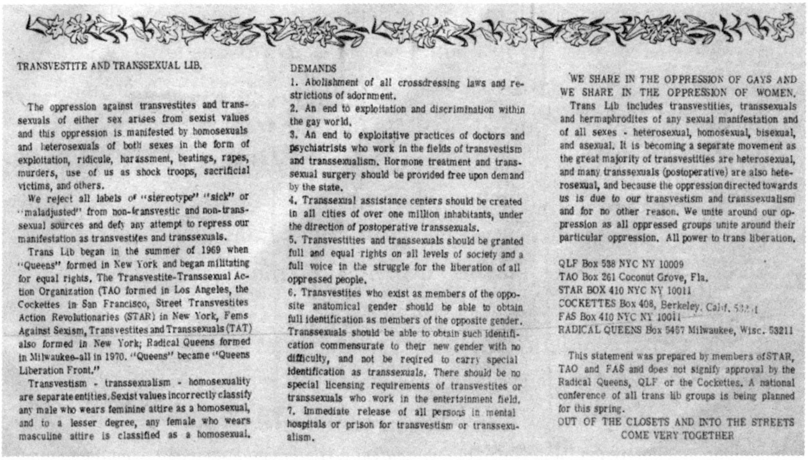
TRANSVESTITE AND TRANSSEXUAL LIB.

The oppression against transvestites and transsexuals of either sex arises from sexist values and this oppression is manifested by homosexuals and heterosexuals of both sexes in the form of exploitation, ridicule, harassment, beatings, rapes, murders, use of us as shock troops, sacrificial victims, and others.

We reject all labels of "stereotype" "sick" or "maladjusted" from non-transvestic and non-transsexual sources and defy any attempt to repress our manifestation as transvestites and transsexuals.

Trans Lib began in the summer of 1969 when "Queens" formed in New York and began militating for equal rights. The Transvestite-Transsexual Action Organization (TAO formed in Los Angeles, the Cockettes in San Francisco, Street Transvestites Action Revolutionaries (STAR) in New York, Fems Against Sexism, Transvestites and Transsexuals (TAT) also formed in New York; Radical Queens formed in Milwaukee—all in 1970. "Queens" became "Queens Liberation Front."

Transvestism - transsexualism - homosexuality are separate entities. Sexist values incorrectly classify any male who wears feminine attire as a homosexual, and to a lesser degree, any female who wears masculine attire is classified as a homosexual.

DEMANDS

1. Abolishment of all crossdressing laws and restrictions of adornment.
2. An end to exploitation and discrimination within the gay world.
3. An end to exploitative practices of doctors and psychiatrists who work in the fields of transvestism and transsexualism. Hormone treatment and transsexual surgery should be provided free upon demand by the state.
4. Transsexual assistance centers should be created in all cities of over one million inhabitants, under the direction of postoperative transsexuals.
5. Transvestities and transsexuals should be granted full and equal rights on all levels of society and a full voice in the struggle for the liberation of all oppressed people.
6. Transvestites who exist as members of the opposite anatomical gender should be able to obtain full identification as members of the opposite gender. Transsexuals should be able to obtain such identification commensurate to their new gender with no difficulty, and not be reqired to carry special identification as transsexuals. There should be no special licensing requirements of transvestites or transsexuals who work in the entertainment field.
7. Immediate release of all persons in mental hospitals or prison for transvestism or transsexualism.

WE SHARE IN THE OPPRESSION OF GAYS AND WE SHARE IN THE OPPRESSION OF WOMEN.

Trans Lib includes transvestities, transsexuals and hermaphrodites of any sexual manifestation and of all sexes - heterosexual, homosexual, bisexual, and asexual. It is becoming a separate movement as the great majority of transvestities are heterosexual, and many transsexuals (postoperative) are also heterosexual, and because the oppression directed towards us is due to our transvestism and transsexualism and for no other reason. We unite around our oppression as all oppressed groups unite around their particular oppression. All power to trans liberation.

QLF Box 538 NYC NY 10009
TAO Box 261 Coconut Grove, Fla.
STAR BOX 410 NYC NY 10011
COCKETTES Box 408, Berkeley, Calif. [illegible]
FAS Box 410 NYC NY 10011
RADICAL QUEENS Box 5457 Milwaukee, Wisc. 53211

This statement was prepared by members of STAR, TAO and FAS and does not signify approval by the Radical Queens, QLF or the Cockettes. A national conference of all trans lib groups is being planned for this spring.

OUT OF THE CLOSETS AND INTO THE STREETS
COME VERY TOGETHER

FIGURE INTRO.1. Transvestite and Transsexual Liberation Manifesto, as printed in *Gay Dealer: The Rage of Philadelphia* (October 1970). Accessed in Gale's Archives of Sexuality and Gender.

attempt to repress our manifestation as transvestites and transsexuals." On the one hand, this statement seems to confirm Jasbir Puar's observation that "historically and contemporaneously, the nexus of disability and trans has been fraught," at least in part because trans people have often "resist[ed] alliances with people with disabilities in no small part because of long struggles against stigmatization and pathologization that may be reinvoked through such affiliations."[10] On another hand, rather than refusing the affiliation outright, the manifesto leaves an evocative space for precisely the kind of politics and analysis that Puar calls for, in which critical trans and disability theory/politics "each acknowledges and inhabits the more generalized conditions of the other."[11] That is, the manifesto's authors leave open the possibility that, when made *from within trans life*, the association of *trans* with *sick/maladjusted* might be commensurate with trans "manifestation" and liberation.[12] They remind us in advance that trans liberation need not rely on stigmatophobic claims that cut trans off from a broader minoritarian *we* (trans ≠ sick); rather, they contest the use of *stereotype/sick/maladjusted* to deauthorize trans lifeworlds. Further, insofar as a primary object of the authors' critique was the power of medical practitioners to describe, contain, exploit, and otherwise regulate their nonnormative bodyminds and modes of living, their demands articulate the link between trans and gay liberation and contemporaneous disability and mad liberation movements.[13] Of course, by retaining an identitarian focus—by demanding, for example, the "immediate release of all persons in mental hospitals or prisons *for tranvestism or transsexualism*"—this particular manifesto does not take aim at medicolegal regulation per se; it merely contests that the trans subject is its proper object.[14] However, by leaving open the possibility that claims of trans sickness and maladjustment might not always be hostile to trans manifestation—might indeed be commensurate with trans liberation—they leave open the possibility that this book pursues; namely, that trans maladjustment might, in fact, still be a resource for trans thought.

Briefly, *trans maladjustment* is my shorthand for the tight, durable association between trans identity and particular bad feelings and mad habits of thought that show up again and again in transphobic and trans-affirmative discourse alike, things like depression, social withdrawal, unruly post-traumatic identity/affect, suicidality, dysphoria, feeling haunted, and so on. Insofar as I understand these forms of cognitive/affective divergence as endemic to trans experience, my attention to trans maladjustment resonates with—though does not exactly answer—Alexandre Baril's call to develop a "conception of transness that includes its debilitating physiological, mental, emotional or social aspects" that are not necessarily reducible to oppression.[15] That is, while the predominant version of contemporary trans-affirmative thought encourages us to read these forms of trans maladjustment only as outcomes of oppression, "symptomatic of the destructive forces in which these infelicitous subjects [are] caught," I read them as (also) integral to trans epistemology and cultural production: they point toward ways of knowing (and not-knowing), of living (and not-living) that arise from within being so caught.[16]

The term *maladjustment* means simply "imperfect or faulty adjustment" or, more dismally, "failure to meet the requirements for social life."[17] One can track in the *Oxford English Dictionary*'s illustrative quotations the drifting of *maladjustment* from a more general and neutral use as, roughly, *misfit between two or more things*—a relation—into a sociological use in which this relation was narrowed to be the one between the social and the individual, and finally, into the realm of psychology, where in the early twentieth century it came to take on a sense of being (or being evidence of) an incapacity of a person or organism to adapt to life, rather than strictly a relation. Grammatically, this entails a shift from "maladjustment between" to simply "maladjustment," a loss of preposition that in turn was (and is) used to rationalize intervention into or elimination/abandonment of racialized, feminized, gender nonconforming, mad, neurodivergent, or disabled people who trouble and are troubled by the requirements for officially sanctioned social life.[18] As one salient example, George Rekers justified his infamous, career-launching, devastating "treatment" of a gender-nonconforming five-year-old child, who appears in Rekers's writing under the pseudonym "Kraig," using the framework of maladjustment. A psychologist and cofounder of the Family Research Council—classified by the Southern Poverty Law Center as an anti-LGBTQ hate group—Rekers insisted that intensive, emotionally and sometimes physically violent intervention into Kraig's "rigidly feminine" bodily comportment, clothing and toy choices, style of play, vocal inflections, and so forth was "ethically and psychologically appropriate" because it corrected maladjustment in the present and warded off "more serious maladjustment" (i.e., transsexuality) "in the future."[19] Specifically, Rekers claimed that such interventions developed Kraig's capacity to flexibly adjust to a world where he was, as he was, marked out for "social isolation and ridicule."[20] That is, although Rekers and his mentor Ivar Lovaas (who in the 1960s and 1970s engineered the applied behavior analysis method of "treating" autistic kids using identical, if often more obviously abusive, methods) recognized that Kraig's "suffering" was relational—the result of others' responses to his way of living—they at the same time located maladjustment as what arose from *within* Kraig, specifically his "deeply ingrained, chronic maladaptive patterns of behavior," feelings, and thought.[21] A relation came to be understood as a condition.

Throughout this book, I use *maladjustment* in a way that is inflected by both "expert" and colloquial uses. However, as this book is not a genealogy of the term there are many others—bad feelings, madness, and so on—that I might have foregrounded instead.[22] But my use of *maladjustment* in particular emerges, in part, from an affinity for disability studies, sharing much with Rosemarie Garland-Thomson's concept of misfit, as what occurs when an "environment does not sustain the shape and function of the body; that enters it" and has the consequence of producing misfitting bodies as social misfits.[23] But *maladjustment* also names a particular, fraught relationship to "disability" as a legal and political category that promises access to the full range of rights and benefits of citizenship through antidiscrimination law and social services, even if only symbolically, contingently, and as an ever-receding horizon. Indeed, while the word has largely fallen out of use, one area in which it continues to have currency is in the administration of accessible education as the Individuals with Disabilities Education Improvement Act (2004), the current federal law that claims to ensure that students with disabilities have access to public education and that expressly excludes from this assurance students who are "socially maladjusted."[24] *Maladjustment*, therefore, marks the space where (physical, psychic, or social) impairment cannot become protectable disability, where difference does not or cannot become officially recuperable by these means. In fact, as discussed in chapter 1, this is precisely the status of *trans* in the post-1990s United States, as it is a category that is likewise included in federal disability law in the form of an exclusion.

Embedded in *maladjustment*'s definition, then, as well as in its present uses, is an emphasis on the way in which personhood is premised on the capacity to cultivate certain forms of feeling, habits of thought, and styles of relating—on meeting certain requirements. Although my opening anecdotes might have suggested otherwise, my conception of trans maladjustment therefore shares much with one of Susan Stryker's other founding documents: her endlessly generative theorization and performance of trans madness as trans monstrosity and rage. Framed as it is by Transgender Nation's protest of the pathologization of trans identity at the 1993 American Psychiatric Association's annual meeting, Stryker's "My Words to Victor Frankenstein" can be read as a maladjusted theorization of the conditions that produce trans rage—conditions that include feminist and queer transphobia; compulsory gendering; and the discipline and regulation of gender nonconformity through deeming its subjects disordered—that simultaneously regards that rage as enabling trans ways of thinking and being. Specifically, Stryker's essay is *mad* in at least four interrelated senses of the word: it records and thinks with the phenomenological experience of breakdown; it privileges felt life over and against enlightenment rationality; it is, plainly, furious; and it rages, in part, against the regulation of gender variance by psychology, specifically the political, epistemic, and psychic effects of being subject to diagnosis.[25]

While trans monstrosity animated by rage is certainly one recognizable form of trans maladjustment, in *The Terrible We* I am more interested in figures and feelings endemic to trans life that cannot easily be understood as politically enabling or as "mobilize[d] . . . into effective political actions."[26] What "My Words" and the introduction to *The Transgender Studies Reader* share, after all, is a narrative of righteous trans anger that moves things along by puncturing trans-antagonistic conditions. But, despite the literal and metaphorical association of transition and transness itself with travel, mobility, and movement, trans life under racial capitalism is at least as much about stuckness, waiting, "lag time," and recurrence—about living indefinitely, in Hil Malatino's terms, "in interregnum, in the crucial and transformative moments between past and future, between the regime of what was and the promise of what might be."[27] Accordingly, the forms of maladjustment I think with—depression, dissociation, and asociality/withdrawal—are less like Stryker's rage and more like Sianne Ngai's "ugly feelings," insofar as each offers a mode of investigating and perhaps bearing "ambivalent situations of suspended agency."[28]

Finally, although I certainly use the language of feeling, I tend toward the word *maladjustment* to retain the associated negativity and baggage and to foreground constellations of feeling, thought, style, and habit. Further, unlike feeling, forms of maladjustment might be understood as chronic, marked by long durations, persistent enough that they can become the ground of identity—a relation comes to be understood as a condition. This is the crucial difference between, for example, feeling social anxiety and being a recluse, feeling depressed and being a depressive, trans desire/dysphoria and trans identity, and so on. Thus, forms of maladjustment, in my usage, contain, cause, or coincide with bad feelings—feelings that are experientially painful, understood as potentially pathological in a diagnostic setting, or politically impairing—but are not reducible to them.

In the remainder of this introduction, I set out to do three things. First, I lay out a brief account of how and why the "methodological distancing" from *sick* has shaped the intellectual and affective horizon of trans studies.[29] Second, I offer an alternative entry point into the project—which is as much about trans literature as it is about trans thought—through a reading of Jack Halberstam's reading of Carson McCullers's *The Member of the Wedding*. I do so both because Frankie Addams's plot and the way Halberstam took it up in the late 1990s serve as an apt allegory for the dynamic within trans thought that I seek to address and because Frankie herself helps me to clarify what, in this text, I take *trans* to mean. And, finally, I sketch the project in full, including an outline of its individual chapters and a primer on its (sometimes idiosyncratic) vocabulary and grammar.

Feeling Trans, Trans Authority

"Transsexuality," Lucas Cassidy Crawford writes, "is a matter of affect at least as much as it is a matter of certain procedures of gender transition."[30] And while Crawford writes here against the harnessing of trans feeling into a single trans narrative, it is true that, over the course of the late twentieth century, we have witnessed the production and consolidation of what scholars have called the transnormative subject. *Trans*, that is, has become widely legible as a particular set of feelings (gendered unease, restlessness, suicidality) that necessitate a particular set of narrative movements (self-discovery, coming out, transition) for the health and persistence of the trans protagonist/subject within the terms of the liberal-imperial state. In this rendering, *trans* is a feeling that precedes, requires, and so justifies the project of medical or social transition, of living a trans life; for this reason, much ink has been spilled over the question of "what transsexuality feels like."[31] Although this book is undoubtedly another entry into that record, I conjoin it to a related question. Namely, "What does trans studies feel like?" After all, fields are a matter of affect, feeling, and desire at least as much as they are a matter of certain procedures of knowledge production.

As a book that adds to the objects of trans studies only insofar as it takes the emotional habitus of trans studies as its object, *The Terrible We* is most closely aligned with recent work in feminist and queer studies that has taken stock of how the institutionalization of the political desires called *feminism*, *queer liberation*, and *antiracism* has shaped the knowledge projects of women's/gender studies, queer theory, and black feminism. Notable among these are Clare Hemmings's account of the political consequences of the stories that Anglo-American academic feminism tells about itself; Heather Love's attention to how present desires for *emotional rescue* shape approaches to the queer past, and to what queer studies might teach us about "living with injury—not fixing it"; Jennifer Nash's diagnosis of black feminist defensiveness about *intersectionality*, what it enables and what it forecloses; Kadji Amin's argument for, and modeling of, a queer studies driven by *deidealization*; and Robyn Wiegman's taking very seriously that "objects of study are as fully enmeshed in fantasy, projection, and desire as those that inhabit the more familiar itinerary of intimate life."[32]

Wiegman characterizes the psychic life of what she terms *identity knowledges* as being driven by the desire for critical practice to produce justice and the belief that our objects—and our relations to them—might deliver it. The institutionalization of this disciplinary structure of desire places an enormous burden on our objects to be "adequate to the political commitments that inspire" us and to, therefore, be good—desirable, politically enabling, conduits of good feeling, and so forth.[33] Further, one of the ways that justice is routinely "figured" within such fields is "by claiming for minoritized subjects the right to study themselves and to make themselves the object of their study."[34] This definition of justice, in turn, produces a closeness between critics and our objects that, Wiegman suggests, makes it "harder to bear the psychic burdens" of the inevitable failure of our objects—of ourselves—to live up to our desires for them: "how much goodness, after all, must one attribute to her identity objects of study to withstand what it means to both represent and be represented by them?"[35]

Taking this account of the psychic life of identity knowledges for granted, it is easy to understand the assertion "I'm not sick" and the conversion of trans rage into enabling political and subjective movement as defenses of *trans* as a good object in Wiegman's sense. *Trans*, Stryker insists, does not name the delusional, medicalized, politically retrograde "[dupe] of gender"; rather, it names a subject from whom and for whom we might produce justice.[36] Indeed, although *transgender* appears within Wiegman's book primarily as an object on which other critics have pinned their hopes, Andrea Long Chu and Emmett Harsin Drager have since applied Wiegman's insights to account for what they see as the founding "disavowal of the transsexual" at work in trans studies.[37] In their story, in order to understand *trans* (and therefore ourselves) as a "good object" capable of delivering justice, trans studies scholars have abandoned the figure of the transsexual and repeatedly perform this abandonment in order "to prove that we are no longer the medicalized transsexual," who is, we all know, too desirous of normativity to be a theoretically viable political subject.[38] Out of a desire to be resistant and radical, that is, trans studies has abandoned its proper object—"the only thing that *trans* describes that *queer* can't"—and "severely limited our ability to fully understand trans pasts and presents."[39]

While I share with Chu and Harsin Drager the sense that trans studies has been structured by a series of disavowals of trans pathology, bad (painful, pathologized, and politically retrograde) feeling, and mad thought, and although this project is, like theirs, an attempt to ask after what would happen if we thought with these disavowed figures and feelings, it is insufficient to understand the present of trans studies as only the outcome of our own political and affective attachments.[40] Among other things, what Chu and Harsin Drager do not admit into the story of identity knowledges writ large is that such knowledge projects inevitably unfold in political and material contexts in which minoritized subjects' speech is constrained from the outset by the necessity to appear as subjects capable of authoritative speech at all. Only very recently, that is, has it been possible to speak as trans in nontrans contexts—though still, certainly, not all—without that speech being dismissed out of hand as "the confused ranting of a diseased mind."[41] If identity knowledges are, at least in part, projects of securing for minoritized people the authority to be subjects, as well as objects, of knowledge, then we cannot ignore that there are many concomitant factors—chiefly, the uneven distribution of life chances under racial capitalism, the animating context of scholarly desires for radicality—that influence the shape that such fields take. Put another way: while at the outset I, too, set out to understand trans studies' disavowals as the outcome of intimate and collective desires animating the field, I am mindful of the fact that those founding disavowals, both for better and for worse, enabled trans subjects to emerge into the academy in the first place.

* * *

In an essay collected in the 1999 anthology *Reclaiming Genders: Transsexual Grammars at the Fin de Siècle*, Stryker notes: "While it remains impossible to speak of a single unified transgender movement with clearly articulated goals, it is certainly true that one aim of many activists is to do for gender identity disorder what gay liberation did for social scientific accounts of pathological homosexuality—that is, to make transgender people themselves, rather than their self-appointed clinical caretakers, the ultimate authority about transgender lives."[42] As with other knowledge projects linked to minoritized identities, the goals of early work in trans studies were bound up with the goals of the transgender movement. Indeed, in Stryker's articulation of trans politics here, the transgender movement and transgender studies might be indistinguishable, given that "the aim of many activists" was precisely to establish a discourse in which it would be possible for trans people to be regarded as the "ultimate authority about transgender lives." While this demand for authority arguably animates all minoritarian scholarship, it is a particularly fraught issue in institutionalized forms of trans studies, given that trans identity has been and continues to be described in the language of psychiatric disorder in particular and of madness more generally.

As mad and critical disability studies scholars have noted, there is a way in which the conjuncture of madness and intellectual authority—and, therefore, "mad" and "studies"—presents a clarifying contradiction.[43] To the extent that having rhetorical/interpretative authority "means *making sense* and a [mental] diagnosis is in many ways to be labeled as speaking nonsensically or with the wrong kind of sense," then, within the protocols of rationality that organize the university, speaking from the position of one so diagnosed undercuts one's ability to speak.[44] Speaking madly risks literal and rhetorical confinement or, at the very least, the dismissal of one's sense as nonsense. Especially in the early stages of the field's formation, then, when trans identity was much more universally regarded *as* a form of madness, trans scholars' rhetorical claims to authority were caught within a persistent double bind. How, after all, does one stake a claim to know through a category that renders one's knowledge about oneself and one's world suspect? Under these conditions, to make claims as a trans person was simultaneously "an act of complicity with our own erasure, for no one need listen when we claim a place for our voices in theorizing about us."[45]

In response, trans studies proceeded largely by dismissing pathologizing discourse about trans lives altogether.[46] The first academic performance of this dismissal—one that models, perhaps even generates, a particular set of rhetorical moves that have since been taken for granted—can be found in Sandy Stone's pathbreaking essay, "The *Empire* Strikes Back: A Posttranssexual Manifesto." While Stone's essay is primarily a response to anti-trans strains of radical feminism—which I will take up in chapter 2—the essay also functions as a repudiation of psychiatric discourse in order to legitimize knowledge produced by trans people. Indeed, before the manifesto reaches its most obvious and most often remembered target, Stone takes on psychiatric texts that link trans identity to mental illness and characterize transsexuals as a class of "depressed, isolated, withdrawn, schizoid individuals."[47] By pointing to irregularities in the research subjects represented in the pre-1980s studies that produced this and similar claims, she then immediately undermines the studies' validity: "In each paper, though, we find that each investigator invalidates his results in a brief disclaimer. . . . In the first, by adding 'It must be admitted that Lothstein's subjects could hardly be called a typical sample, as nine of the ten studied had serious physical health problems' . . . and in the second, with the afterthought that '82 percent of [the subjects] were prostitutes.'"[48] Undoubtedly, a sample that isn't representative of a population should never stand in for that population, and such studies have had lasting negative effects on trans life. That said, there are several assumptions underlying Stone's argument that have subsequently been incorporated into much (especially mainstream) trans-affirmative discourse. First, that sex workers—likely poor, perhaps nonwhite—and disabled trans people are not and should not be considered representative, should not appear at the center of discourse about trans lives. Second, and relatedly, that *if* the transsexuals represented in these studies are "depressed, withdrawn, schizoid individuals," it is *because* they are sex workers or disabled—*trans*, that is, has no relationship to *sick*, but these other marginalized social positions might. And, finally, that depression, withdrawal, and a (too-)rich inner life are characteristics that cannot be incorporated into forms of agential and authoritative personhood, that in order to do work that affirms trans people as living viable lives, forms of maladjustment must always and only be seen as coming from the outside.

My point is twofold. First, and simply, in moving away from such dismal accounts of trans life altogether, we risk doing away with the people whose lives both far exceeded and provided the raw material/data for them. And, second, relying on a concept of authority that *requires* disavowing any relation between trans identity and mental illness paradoxically works to reproduce the logic of the medicolegal system in the moment that trans thinkers try to escape its purview—insofar as this strategy consents to the equation of the production of usable knowledge with medicolegal norms of emotion, cognition, or sociality. Stone's essay, therefore, represents both an indispensable founding gesture of trans studies and also a way of "working to become non-disabled" that "reinforce[s] the idea that there is something wrong with those disabled people [that trans people] are trying to distance themselves from."[49] While I'm certainly sympathetic to the desire to wholly repudiate self-appointed caretakers' claims to describe trans lives, the form and effects of this repudiation often too closely resemble the mother's insistence that her son is well-adjusted and, therefore, not sick. That is, in Stone's essay, too, the white (post)transsexual emerges as a viable political/academic subject through the reduction of and distancing from racialized/disabled lives via the insistence that trans ≠ sick.

* * *

By the 2010s, transgender studies had extended far beyond the terms of these founding scenes. Now, the steady proliferation of anthologies, journals and special issues, conferences, and so on is testament to the fact that trans scholars are no longer primarily tasked with producing ourselves as subjects, as well as objects, of knowledge. To the contrary, the interdisciplinary field has produced a range of inquiries that foreground *trans* not primarily as a coherent category of people but, rather, as a lens through which to ask and answer questions about governance, aesthetics, the history of science/medicine, digital culture, geopolitics, political economy, literary history, and so on.[50] The preoccupations of scholars in the field, therefore, decreasingly involve questions about what or who *trans* names and increasingly involve ones about what the production and regulation of gender-nonconforming lives, practices, and perspectives allow us to know.

My somewhat obsessive return to what is often taken to be the beginning of trans studies, then, is not an attempt to deny or downplay the sheer bulk and variety of work that has since been produced under its name. However, as trans studies is increasingly institutionalized—and, concurrently, as trans bodies, lives, and narratives increasingly circulate in mainstream representation—it is vital that we think critically about the effects of the stories about *trans* that undergirded trans studies' often para-institutional emergence. Returning to "the beginning" of the field is necessary because, following Stone's example, much work has been done that argues for a productive nonidentity between diagnostic standards of gender and trans self-knowledge, but we have yet to fully take stock of how diagnostic standards of emotion and cognition similarly shaped, and continue to shape, trans discourse.[51] In particular, founding scholars' disavowal of *sick* both enabled transgender studies and produced a particular mood—an emotional habitus, a space of shared pathos—that has delimited the horizons of the field.

I borrow the term *emotional habitus* from Deborah Gould's extension of Pierre Bourdieu's notion of *habitus*. *Emotional habitus* is also a phrase that describes the juncture of the social and the bodily, how it is that social norms and structures come to be embodied, to reproduce themselves through human action that nonetheless feels innate, like common sense. However, Gould extends the concept of habitus in order to register that, in addition to providing individuals with a shared understanding about action and bodily comportment (what to do and how), social groups also provide members with habits of feeling (what and how to feel, how to name feelings, and how to interpret them). "An emotional habitus," Gould argues, "contains an emotional pedagogy . . . in part by conferring on some feelings and modes of expression an axiomatic, natural quality and making other feeling states unintelligible within its terms and thus, in a sense, unfeelable and inexpressible."[52] In turn, what is feelable and expressible shapes political and intellectual horizons, what kinds of actions, aims, and modes of interpretation are collectively understood as "possible, desirable, and necessary."[53]

Further, Gould's focus on social change, rather than on social reproduction, causes her to emphasize that habitus "are dynamic and always subject to alteration. For their reproduction, habitus must be reinstated [and therefore] . . . are historically contingent, requiring us to investigate the practices that generate, stabilize, reproduce, and sometimes transform them."[54] Indeed, there are numerous examples within trans scholarship of the reproduction of the emotional habitus of trans discourse that I describe above, in which justified anxiety and rage about the delegitimization of trans authority using the idiom of mental illness leads to a wary watch for and reflexive repudiation of pathologized forms of feeling and habits of thought. For example, counter to the view of trans people as "helpless and afflicted," Dean Spade wonders, "What would it mean to suggest that such desire for surgery is a *joyful affirmation* of gender self-determination?"[55] Several essays collected in *The Transgender Studies Reader 2*—which, if *The Transgender Studies Reader* gave the field a name, could be said to be the anthology that records what trans studies became—likewise frame their interventions, explicitly, as movements away from stagnant bad feelings imposed on trans people toward better ones. Julian Carter frames a meditation on trans movement and relation by doing away with the "depressive figuration" of embodiment as a trap; Jeanne

Vaccaro's articulation of a transgender "politics of the handmade . . . put[s] pressure on so-called negative emotions or bad feelings like 'feeling trapped in the "wrong" body' as foreclosing of certain affective possibilities"; Eliza Steinbock closes an essay on the film *Dandy Dust* with a call for "groping theory," which, driven by curiosity, might help us gain some distance from "horrible things"; well, you get the picture.[56] Further, the anthology includes an essay—written by a transgender physician who specializes in trans health care—that takes this emotional habitus as one of its objects, critically examining the arguments surrounding the GID debate; notably, the editors introduce the essay with the caveat that its model of trans identity is insistently "dissonant" with the rest of the reader.[57]

While *The Terrible We*, of course, does not set out to contest the critical value of potentially good trans feelings—euphoria, curiosity, hope, earnestness—nor to mire trans studies permanently in the well of loneliness, it does contend that the emotional habitus undergirding much trans[masculine] discourse is structured around a series of disavowals, and the thing disavowed in each case is a proximity to forms of maladjustment associated with the clinic, the dime museum, the madhouse, and the dissociative rhythms of some trans childhoods. Although distancing *trans* from these sites has been important for authorizing trans voices, each disavowal contains within it a familiar body onto which bad feelings are repeatedly pinned—the girl, the disabled or mad person, and the person of color. Importantly, the structure of disavowal guarantees that these figures will perpetually haunt the version of trans discourse that I have described, because disavowal is premised on recognition; precisely by attempting to disavow an attachment, the attachment is foregrounded, sticks around. In thinking through this set of problems—how the attempt to narrate *trans* through a disavowal of sick produces others as not-subjects, and how we might think with trans maladjustment to avoid this effect—I am arguing for a version of trans studies that can acknowledge and think with a more expansive *we*, terrible though it might feel.

The Terrible *We*

One way to understand this project, then, is as one that is interested in the relatively stable emotional habitus that has structured trans studies—one that allows for some questions, some ways of interpreting, and disallows others—and that follows this interest by investigating how old questions might be rethought if they are approached in a different state of mind. In this way, it is a metacritical project; its object is, ostensibly, a set of conflicts about who/what *trans* names that frame the field of transgender studies. However, there is another, equally valid way to understand this book: as a project whose objects are a set of (mostly text-based) cultural artifacts—novels, films, poems, newspaper articles, polemics, biographies, and scholarship—by and about transgender people, primarily in the twentieth- and twenty-first-century United States, and that uses the above metacritical framing in conjunction with the method of close reading in order to offer a more or less unified interpretation of those objects. In this version, I argue that, rather than only impeding or confining trans life, thought, and creativity, forms of maladjustment have also been central to their development. More concretely, in one version of the story, this book begins with a feeling of unease generated by the goings-on at conferences. In another, it begins with a quibble over an interpretation of Carson McCullers's 1946 novel turned play, film, and (briefly) musical, *The Member of the Wedding.*

The Member of the Wedding follows the flights of fancy and circumscribed movements of twelve-year-old white tomboy Frankie Addams. When we meet her, Frankie is dressed in a tomboy uniform of "blue black shorts, [and] a B.V.D. undervest," has her hair "cut like a boy's," and understands herself to be "an unjoined person" who "belonged to no club and was a member of nothing in the world."[58] Although the clubs to which Frankie longs to belong are various and far-flung—ranging from the group of neighborhood children that she has outgrown, to the US military, to "the world"[59]—the most pressing is the neighborhood girls' club, made up of girls just slightly older than Frankie. The film version of *Member*, in particular, emphasizes just how pressing the girls' club is, as their clubhouse is located right next to Frankie's house, and we must watch alongside Frankie as this group of composed young women cross her yard, signaling to us and to her that this group is both the one to which she most nearly belongs and one for which she sorely lacks many of the necessary credentials. Notably, this is one of the few scenes that takes place outside of the cramped confines of the Addamses' kitchen; the girls' refusal to grant Frankie a place within their association effectively flings Frankie back into the kitchen, a space she experiences as a nonplace.

Unable to join the girls' club, or to "be a boy and go to war," or to donate blood and circulate in the veins of soldiers, or to fit beneath the arbor with the neighborhood kids, Frankie sets her heart on an unusual site of affiliation; for the majority of *Member*, Frankie schemes, fantasizes, and announces her intentions to join her brother's wedding, not simply as a member of the wedding party but as a member of the marriage itself.[60] Daydreaming about jet-setting about with the newlyweds, and momentarily changing her name to F. Jasmine (to indicate her belonging to the couple, Janice and Jarvis), Frankie falls in love with the wedding, understanding the couple as the site of her belonging, her "we of me."[61] Importantly, her attempts to belong to the wedding induce Frankie to change her gender presentation—she swaps the boyish moniker Frankie for F. Jasmine and her tomboy uniform for an orange organdy dress, high heels, and silver bow. And even after she is ejected from this "we"—literally dragged from the wedding car—Frankie does not, cannot, return to her prewedding way of inhabiting the world. The novel closes with a coda in which, months later, F. Jasmine is now Frances and has substituted a neighborhood girl named Mary Littlejohn as her love object; she has taken on Mary's interests—Michelangelo, "poets like Tennyson"—and now uses knives for cutting sandwiches into fancy shapes, rather than exclusively for throwing and picking splinters from her tough feet as Frankie once had.[62] Consequently, many have read *Member* as a quintessential female coming-of-age plot: in order to grow up, the adolescent Frankie must accept "her identity as female, [even though] she already suspects that her gender will be confining."[63]

Even though she occupies relatively little space in the book, Frankie Addams is central to the project of Jack Halberstam's *Female Masculinity*, a foundational work in the study of trans and (cis) lesbian masculinities; in at least two ways, Frankie drives Halberstam's book along. First, Frankie provides Halberstam with a political/theoretical stance concerning how best to affirm female masculinities, "not by subverting masculine power but by turning a blind eye to conventional masculinities and refusing to engage."[64] That is, Halberstam's project does not theorize female masculinities as being in a necessarily resistant relation to dominant masculinities or normative configurations of sex/gender; rather, he takes a page out of Frankie's book in order to assert "that power may inhere within different forms of refusal: 'Well, I don't care.'"[65] Second, and more significant for my own project, is that even though Halberstam mimics Frankie's posture, the thrust of *Female Masculinity* moves in opposition to Frankie's plot. In Halberstam's reading, Frankie's is the prototypically pessimistic tomboy tale: first "mired in a realm of unbelonging" and, finally, compelled into normative hetero-femininity, a club whose terms of membership the tomboy "cannot fulfill."[66] Thus, for him, "*The Member of the Wedding* emphasizes the tragic nature of the tomboy quest and quietly confines the tomboy to a past better forgotten and left behind as the girl blossoms into a quiescent young-adult femininity."[67] In contrast, Halberstam frames *Female Masculinity* as a text that "refuses the futility long associated with the tomboy narrative and instead seizes on the opportunity to recognize and ratify differently gendered bodies and subjectivities."[68] In doing so, in attempting to make adult female masculinity "plausible, credible, and real," Halberstam is thus attempting to make a world to which the tomboy might belong, in which she might be allowed to grow up.[69] If, when we meet Frankie, she is someone who "hung around in doorways," then—foreshadowing the *Transgender Studies Reader 2*'s preference for joyful, curious movement, set in opposition to the trap of bad feelings—Halberstam would like to make it possible for her to go fully outside.[70]

While I can't quite disagree with Halberstam's interpretation of Frankie's plight, his insistence on Carson McCullers's pessimism—her "sense of the overwhelming 'order of things,' an order that cannot be affected by the individual"—overlooks the strangely utopian, collective feeling embedded in nearly all of McCullers's fiction.[71] Put another way, there seems to be little reason to take Frankie's word for it that she is an unjoined person; even though, or more precisely because, she is excluded from membership to the worlds of soldiers, weddings, and normative female adolescence, Frankie is a member of a much queerer collective. When she is flung back inside by the neighborhood girls' refusal, Frankie finds herself in good company, as she occupies the sweaty summer kitchen with the Addams family housemaid Berenice (an unmarried black woman with one blue glass eye) and Frankie's cousin John Henry, a curious child who can sometimes be found in women's clothing, unambivalently desires and identifies with the "Pin Head" girl employed by the local freak show and importantly is "not a bit lonesome"—does not experience his queer proclivities as excluding him from membership.[72] Periodically, this trio is joined by Honey—Berenice's "sick-loose," "lightskinned, almost lavender," horn-playing foster brother—as well as a cast of queer/crip characters who come to the table via the stories that the three tell to each other: the Pin Head girl and the other "freaks" she is employed alongside; "a boy with his whole face burned off"; a cat named Charles who answers to Charlina; two black boys leaning against each other in an alley who, in Frankie's eye, "reflected the sudden picture of her brother and the bride"; and Lily Mae Jenkins who "fell in love with a man name Juney Jones . . . [then] changed his nature and his sex and turned into a girl."[73] So, while the kitchen is certainly a site of confinement and exploitation, it is also the place where a vast, uneven collective assembles; further, it is the scene of the primary trio's ongoing life and utopian dreaming.

Utopian dreaming is featured in much of McCullers's work, but in *Member* it is explicitly so. One of the trio's rituals, which occurs in the time "nearing twilight," is to sit at the kitchen table and "criticize the Creator. They would judge the work of God, and mention the ways how they would improve the world."[74] While each member offers a different, even conflicting, vision of how things ought to be, the important thing is that this is an iterative practice that creates the collective: "At home," Frankie notes, "there was only Berenice Sadie Brown and John Henry West. The three of them sat at the kitchen table, saying the same things over and over, so that by August the words began to rhyme with each other and sound strange."[75] This description of collectivity as a practice that allows separate visions to "rhyme with each other and sound strange" is instructive because it suggests that, as with words in a poem, the kitchen brings these three quite different figures into correspondence, which, in turn, produces an excess of meaning.[76] But Frankie cannot recognize this meaning as meaningful. For example, at one point in the novel, she fantasizes about speaking on the radio—which is always on in the background, the main way "the world" enters into the world of the kitchen—with Janice and Jarvis, insisting "we will be asked to speak." When Berenice misunderstands this "we" as Frankie, John Henry, and herself, Frankie viciously retorts: "When I said *we*, you thought I meant you and me and John Henry West. To speak over the world radio. I have never heard of anything so funny since I was born."[77] That is, Frankie locates all that might be meaningfully said in the other trio, the wedding *we*. Thus, if we recognize the narration as not entirely trustworthy because it is focalized through Frankie—if we refuse to take Frankie's feeling about herself as descriptively true—then it would seem that the pessimism of *Member* is not only located in Frankie's being coercively compelled into white femininity (although she is) but also in the way that, in being so compelled, she cannot acknowledge the club of which she is a member as legitimate, as productive of its own worlds and rhythms, as anything but a temporary and "terrible . . . we."[78]

While the project of theorizing female masculinity so that it is possible for Frankie, not Frances, to leave the cramped kitchen is an admirable one—and while it has certainly made my own work possible and thinkable—I approach the problem that Frankie's plot seems to pose differently. I want to stay with the imperfect, even terrible, we long enough to understand it as a world that contains its own possibilities. That is, *Member* serves as a useful allegory for the problems that arise alongside *trans*'s desire for—and theorization as—forms of joyful, felicitous movement. Frankie is the center of a story about a refusal to sit with bad feeling—and to stick with the disabled and racialized elements of her world—that has the effect of dissolving a capacious nonnormative *we*. Her trajectory, therefore, helps to illuminate the ways in which trans studies' trouble with bad feeling underlies, and works alongside, its trouble with race and disability—namely, the tendency of trans to stick to certain kinds of exceptional white individuals, who can be interpreted as "not sick." This trouble is often framed as a problem of the archive, a persistent entrenchment of the authorized medicolegal frames that have made a particular story about trans life visible, even as those frames are objects of trans critique. All this is true, but I suggest that what Frankie can teach us, as a fictional example of just such an exceptional white individual, is that this trouble is also and simultaneously a problem of emotional pedagogy.

In truth, this way of approaching the problem is more in keeping with McCullers; far from providing evidence that she was a social pessimist, McCullers's own life was one lived in opposition to—or, perhaps, in willful ignorance of—the idea that childhood boyishness, queerness, and freakishness must be outgrown.[79] Further, her fiction repeatedly returns to the queer, the tomboy, and the freak—as well as to strange, improbable collectives as sites of dreaming—as evidence, however fleeting, that the world might be other than the unbearable order of things. The trouble for McCullers, in both her life and her fiction, is that these collectives require emotional work—both work on emotions and work that raises emotions—to be maintained, and this is work that McCullers's characters, lovers, and friends (as well as McCullers herself) often find themselves unwilling or unable to do. In large part, this inability and unwillingness is derived from the painfulness of the feelings that tend to both bind together and, ultimately, undo these collectives.

Still, McCullers knew as well as anyone that pain, both physical and psychic, cannot be thought of as *only* hostile to life because it is often the medium in which life unfolds. Indeed, McCullers's own life was marked by chronic and recurrent illnesses, and by the time she was thirty, she had experienced three strokes and was partially paralyzed; "discomfort and pain" writes her biographer Virginia Spencer Carr, "had been a way of life since [her] early childhood."[80] But whereas McCullers's own gendered and sexual ambiguity has been, and is increasingly, read as central to the content of her fiction, her disability is most commonly presented as simply what "limited her productivity."[81] That is, while McCullers's reliance on disabled characters is often read, in universalizing terms, as symptomatic of her fixation on problems of isolation and loneliness that characterize the human condition, her own experience of disability—her pain as a way of life—provides another way to understand McCullers's particular fixation on the relationship between confinement and freedom, between being "caught" and being "loose."[82] She herself lived much of her life confined to bed or to a single room but, from that location, did a great deal of world making. Both her life and her art insist on recognizing—without romanticizing—various kinds of injury and impairment as productive of their own worlds and rhythms. Doing so, in turn, requires a method of thinking with, rather than fleeing from, Frankie's fearsome, lonely feeling.

Frankie Addams Made Me Trans; Or, Reading the Whitened Transmasculine Archive

Admittedly, there is another, somewhat more idiosyncratic reason for Frankie Addams's appearance in this introduction. In addition to being the center of a story about a refusal to live with bad feelings that dissolves a minoritarian *we*, Frankie was also my first lesson in the difficulty of narrativizing *trans*. To explain, I need to tell one more story.

When I was a young tomboy, I grew up alongside another tomboy; eventually, we both became adults who inhabit the pronoun *he*. But before that, sometime in junior high school, this friend of mine, let's call him J., played Frankie in a local production of *The Member of the Wedding*. For this role, J. had to get his hair cut like Frankie's; specifically, as indicated by the stage directions, he had to get his hair cut "like a boy's."[83] While I can't say whether J. interpreted this change in precisely the way that I did, it seemed to me that this haircut—which he has maintained ever since—marked a shift in how J. publicly identified and was identifiable. To say it more plainly, this haircut was a decisive moment in J.'s movement from tomboy to trans boy. For J., inhabiting the character of Frankie allowed him to make this move not through the differentiation that marked much intragroup conflict at what has been called the butch/FTM border, but through similarity, imitation. In turn, witnessing J.'s trans life enabled my own. J.'s story, my story, and Frankie's story, then, depend on one another, even as the selves produced by and in those stories might be said to exist on either side of various fissures of race and gender.

However, precisely because the tomboy and the trans boy—and, by extension, the transgender, feminist, gay/lesbian, and queer discourse that have been produced by and around them—share histories, psychic resources, aesthetic practices, and so on, the emergence of transgender as a discrete discursive field has necessitated a seemingly endless defining and redefining of *trans*. Hence, ever-expanding glossaries of "trans-related terminology" are often included in academic and lay publications, even if only as exasperated footnotes directing the reader to one of the "many glossaries . . . [that] already exist."[84] In lieu of writing yet another glossary, let me just say that I use the terms *trans* and *transgender* more or less interchangeably and largely in line with Susan Stryker's definition of *transgender* as a word referring to:

> people who move away from the gender they were assigned at birth, people who cross over (trans-) the boundaries constructed by their culture to define and contain that gender. Some people move away from their birth-assigned gender because they feel strongly that they properly belong to another gender in which it would be better for them to live; others want to strike out toward some new location, some space not yet clearly defined or concretely occupied; still others simply feel the need to get away from the conventional expectations bound up with the gender that was initially put upon them. In any case, it is the *movement across a socially imposed boundary away from an unchosen starting place*—rather than any particular destination or mode of transition—that best characterizes the concept of "transgender."[85]

Still, while Stryker's definition is a useful one, my insistence on staying with the terrible we is an insistence that there is, embedded within this definition of *trans* as movement away, a capacitating story that has some unsettling effects. In particular, as in Frankie's flight from the kitchen, movement away in white trans stories is enabled by—and often necessitates—a movement away from forms of maladjustment, routinely figured as movements away from sickness and blackness that leave the racialized/disabled body mired in fixity or rendered as spectral, "shadows . . . that disrupt the teleology" of trans movement "as corporeal freedom."[86] Put more strongly, the universalization of *trans* as movement away is a capacitating story that is also a racial/ableist one.

It is true, that is, that I can tell the story of Frankie enabling J.'s trans life, which, in turn, expanded my own sense of who it was possible for me to be. However, it must at the same time be said that my identification with Frankie was troubled by my simultaneously being identified with Berenice, Honey, and, especially, Lily Mae Jenkins, a black transfeminine character who appears in the story only to be immediately cast outside its narrative bounds. Appearing as a piece of gossip that Berenice brings to the kitchen table amid an inventory of "many a queer thing," Lily Mae is the only character in *Member* whose trans potential is actualized; according to Berenice, Lily "to all intents and purposes" "turned into a girl" out of love for a man.[87] As a condensation of the blackness, queer desire, and trans flight that must be abjected in order for Frankie to take up her place in the social order—and as someone who reportedly crosses with ease from m to f, as both John Henry and Frankie cannot—we might read Lily Mae as a figure of black ungendering. Lily Mae, that is, provides a "context" for Frankie's "understanding [of] sex and gender as mutable and subject to rearrangement," of gender's mutability as a potential way out of her predicament of gender, while simultaneously casting Lily Mae as a person outside the boundaries of consideration and care.[88] "You don't need to know Lily Mae Jenkins," Berenice tells Frankie. "You can live without knowing [Lily]."[89]

Two decades after its publication, José Esteban Muñoz's *Disidentifications* still aptly describes the "obstacles in enacting identifications" that marginalized—especially multiply marginalized—subjects must navigate in undertaking the work of making a self, given that "minority identifications are often neglectful or antagonistic to other minoritarian positionalities."[90] Muñoz's insight that disidentification is a strategy that minoritarian subjects—artists, activists, and theorists among them—use to craft habitable selves and usable theories from discourses that are at once solicitous of and hostile to them informs my reading practice here, which is in many ways a project of disidentifying with white trans studies and discourse, "work[ing] on and against" this terrain.[91] Therefore, while a growing body of trans of color scholarship—most notably work by C. Riley Snorton, Matt Richardson, Kai Green, Treva Ellison, Jules Gill-Peterson, Jin Haritaworn, Dora Silva Santana, and Jacob Lau—have provided me, have provided us, with critical concepts for pursuing Lily Mae's rumored life, this book takes up adjacent questions posed by this scene. In particular, what are the conditions in which Frankie might understand and desire Lily Mae as a member of her we?

Importantly, this is a question that black feminists, not only Carson McCullers, taught me to ask. Written in 1977, "The Combahee River Collective Statement," for example, is a document that trained me to, among other things, linger on the importance of the emotional work that might ultimately enable our political/theoretical analysis not only to diagnose the world but also to create the conditions in which it is possible to change it. "The Combahee River Collective Statement" insists on speaking as we. Although individual black women appear as citations, as members, as predecessors, they are folded into the work of the we who *believe*, who *feel*, who *question*, who *have a politics*, who *are*. Certainly, the first-person plural is a feature of many manifestoes, and bringing into being a we is, arguably, the function of the genre. But what I have always found remarkable about this particular statement is that it is committed simultaneously to speaking as an existing black feminist we, to bringing that we into existence, and to revealing to its reader how fragile that pronoun is, how much work goes into its maintenance, especially in the context of a group avowedly "damaged" by the psychic toll of living under a racist, sexist, capitalist order.[92] A full quarter of the statement is dedicated to documenting the problems of maintaining a collective voice; *we* is sometimes rendered inactive and split by "internal disagreements." It loses its political focus and lapses into an "emotional support" function. It has been made up of "hundreds," though individuals come and go. *We* is held together through, and because of, "success and defeat, joy and pain, victory and failure."[93] Working with its content, then, the form of "The Combahee River Collective Statement" underscores that an essential component of their black feminist work was developing practices of sociality, interpretation, and composition that allow *us* to hang together in the first place.

Admittedly, this minoritarian we is terrible and vexed and the work of maintaining it often distracts from working against the material conditions that necessitate it. And yet, the essays that make up this book are my own attempts at thinking with and against my own formative and terrible *we*, white(ned) transmasculinity, in a way that takes seriously that "trans normativity and trans exceptionalism are aspirational fantasies that very, very few trans subjects are able to live out phenomenologically"—that reads with the maladjustment of even this most normative form of trans life.[94] Certainly, there is another project composed of another archive, one that prioritizes texts that are erased or displaced in trans studies' present institutionalization. Ultimately, however, I decided to focus on well-worn (read: white, transsexual) texts, cases, and debates because, while alternatives can certainly be found by looking just to the side of what has been positioned as central, it's often equally true that there are alternatives imminent to the objects that have accrued—or are in the process of accruing—all the power. Thinking these central alternatives is particularly vital for trans thought given the persistent tenuousness of trans life and the fact that dominant trans narratives have been, for many, profoundly life affirming and life enabling, so it is nothing short of cruel to *only* critique or deconstruct those narratives. One wants the living to go on but also for it to remain attached (emotionally, financially, politically, discursively) to the forms of unlife that it is being rehabilitated from and that it produces, which requires locating the places within the dominant frame that suggest what *trans* could have been and also is.

Organization of the Book

One last word of explanation. You'll notice that, sometimes, I bracket the masculinity of transmasculinity. Within the text, I have tried to limit the use of this construction, *trans[masculinity]*, to places where I am trying to indicate that I am making a statement about *trans* generally but that it especially concerns transmasculinity. However, I encourage you to read that masculinity as if it were always in brackets, as if it were always a provisional term, a clarifying interjection not in the original text. I encourage you to read this way because the terms *transmasculine* and *transfeminine*—though often useful as descriptors and necessary to indicate the divergences of transmasculine and transfeminine histories and presents—are more or less self-defeating, in that they simply reinscribe the binary sex/gender system in a trans context, linking trans maleness with masculinity and trans femaleness with femininity. In doing so, these terms are both simply inadequate descriptions and also pose a serious theoretical problem. To illustrate, it seems imprecise to call prominent trans activist Lou Sullivan (discussed in chapter 1)—whose deepest, earliest identifications tended to be with fags and drag queens—masculine. When we do, implicitly, we are saying that he was masculine relative to his presumed womanhood and are, therefore, reenacting the founding violence of sex/gender (mis)assignment that *trans* attempts to problematize, evade, or undo. Still, I use *transmasculinity* and *transfemininity* because they are, for now, the best words I have to communicate that trans genders are always inevitably articulations of available gendered forms. The bracket, therefore, is meant as a visual reminder that trans people, like everyone else, "can be simultaneously identifying with and rejecting a dominant form."[95]

With this caveat in mind, I focus on transmasculinity because, to date, academic monographs within and around trans studies have largely taken transfemininity as their object or collapsed transmasculinity and femininity under the sign of trans. I do not mean to suggest, however, that transmasculinities are more marginalized—quite the opposite. In the past decades, trans men and other transmasculine people have come to occupy prominent places within spaces of trans cultural and knowledge production—the academy, the arts world—where social and other forms of capital accrue. At the same time, the trans woman has continued to operate within the public and critical imagination as the paradigmatic trans-figuration, reinforcing the harsh hypervisibility of trans women. This discrepancy creates a particular set of problems for transmasculine narration. In particular, because accounts of transfemininity have defined what is often understood as a universal trans narrative, transmasculine people—and those writing about us—continue to rely on these accounts for producing intelligible selves. For instance, some forms of trans discourse have long relied on one kind of proximity to pain to make claims on the state—the threat of murder and other forms of spectacular violence. However, the vast majority of those murdered are poor, black trans women, whose deaths must be understood as the outcomes of antiblackness, the criminalization of sex work, transmisogynoir, and so on, not only or even mostly "transphobia."[96] Most trans men are simply not subject to violence in the same ways but remain attached to this narrative for lack of other viable ways to articulate how—given that, for instance, studies have shown that transmasculine people are affected by sexual and intimate partner violence in numbers that are comparable to other feminized people—our lives (and the imaginaries that shape them) are structured by trans-antagonism, misogyny, and resulting forms of feeling bad.[97] Thus, I chose to focus on the transmasculine archive in particular in order to dredge up some examples of the problem of transmasculine narration and to suggest some ways it might be addressed that do less of a disservice to our sisters and ourselves. In particular, I read with forms of maladjustment that pervade the transmasculine archive in order to argue for and model a version of transgender studies that does not begin with the premise that a commitment to doing justice requires the wholesale disavowal of transgender's historical association with madness. Doing so, I wager, offers new vantage points on—or perhaps might simply help us to bear—old, recurrent conflicts that structure the relationships among queer, trans, and feminist discourse. More than this, however, unlinking trans authority from discourses of emotional adjustment and cognitive coherence is crucial for the work of staying with the terrible we.

To this end, chapter 1 traces the coproduction of disabled and transgender as categories of people at the turn of the twentieth century in order to put forward maladjustment as a resource for doing trans theory. In particular, I focus my analysis on newspaper representations of three transmasculine people who found themselves caught up in a multisited regulatory system—which included the law, the asylum, and the entertainment industry—that attempted to contain disabled, trans, and other "problem bodies" in spaces outside of the properly public sphere.[98] While this system produced a series of constraints—and while contemporary trans and disability activism have, for this reason, attempted to disarticulate these categories—I demonstrate that the coproduction of disability/transgender also allowed for unexpected freedoms. For example, I linger on the life of Jack Bee Garland, whose performance of gender, for a time, relied on a performance of disability; this performance, in turn, granted Garland a profound access to authority and allowed them to maneuver beyond the boundaries imposed on gender-variant and female (both cis and trans) lives.

Just as maladjustment was a resource for Garland's life and livelihood, each subsequent chapter meditates on how contemporary, disavowed figures of trans maladjustment—the depressed transsexual, the sexually traumatized transgender man, and the trans recluse—might likewise allow for new perspectives on, and imaginative routes around, old impasses. Chapter 2, for example, takes up the central challenge of the work by analyzing popular and scholarly discourse produced by the continually reiterated "conflict" between trans and feminism. Because this conflict largely concerns the perceived incompatibility of trans and feminist theories of gender, scholars and activists have, for decades, tried and failed to build an integrated theory of gender that can accommodate both. Sitting alongside a strain of disability studies scholarship on pain and mad epistemologies, I explore how thinking with bad feelings can be useful for reevaluating the terms of this debate, as its rhetorical force is undergirded by a conflation of "bad feelings" and "bad knowledge." In doing so, I make a case for living with the lack of trans feminist integration, even though it does not feel good.

Chapter 3 extends my treatment of the conflicted relationship between trans and feminist studies by considering transmasculine narratives of sexual harm. Due to the risk of pathology, trans-affirmative scholarship often actively suppresses any connection between sexual violence and trans identity; however, in so doing, I suspect that we have overlooked the centrality of something like a dissociative poetics to transmasculine writing and thought. Reading, among other things, the Brandon Teena archive and the fiction of contemporary writer Elliott DeLine, this chapter explores the possibility that dissociation in transmasculine thought describes at once a response to feminized forms of degradation and a formal/psychic strategy for the inhabitation of trans[masculine] forms of life.

In chapter 4, I read with the enduring figure of the trans recluse in order to reframe debates about the place of the social in the development of trans subjectivity. Insofar as it names a social category defined by a contestation of overdetermination from the outside, *trans* has long been marked by a certain measure of trouble with the social, which manifests as trouble theorizing the relation between, on one hand, the self and the social discourses that produce it, and on another, the self and the others it relies on. This trouble, in turn, gets *trans* in trouble. It is forever having to ward off charges of naïve individualism, gender essentialism, and a lack of understanding of gender's location and function in "the social map of power."[99] Rather than trying to make *trans* properly extroverted, this chapter takes an interest in the forms of sociality to be found in withdrawal. Framed by the life of mid-twentieth-century trans man Michael Dillon, I examine the function of solitary acts of reading in trans projects of world- and self-making, as well as the formal pressure that trouble with sociality has exerted on trans writing. Ultimately, I argue that Dillon's life and writing offer an alternative, lyric model of trans subjectivity that recognizes the importance of social anxiety to the development of trans thought.

The book concludes with a brief, failed meditation on the ghostly transgender child and representations of trans suicides and suicidality. Ending with a consideration of suicidality is necessary, both because it marks the limit of my own ability to think with maladjustment and because it dramatizes the problem at the heart of my project, namely, the affects and effects of the inevitable failure of the politics of affirmation, love, and legibility to fulfill their promises.

What follows, then, is a series of thought experiments that attempt not to invert the value of but to really think with maladjustment. The goal of not simply revaluing will be felt in the fact that none of the essays that make up this book neatly resolve or point toward a coherent theoretical program. Instead, each chapter returns to the scene of trans studies' terrible we in order to ask what might be found there if it is inhabited in a maladjusted state of mind.

1

Disabled Histories of *Trans*

She was afraid of all the Freaks, for it seemed to her that they had looked at her in a secret way and tried to connect their eyes with hers, as though to say: we know you. —**FRANKIE, IN CARSON MCCULLERS, *THE MEMBER OF THE WEDDING* (1946)**

In November 1989, *Renaissance News*—a Philadelphia-area trans community newsletter—published an opinion piece titled "Who's Disabled? . . . I'm Okay but You're Not." The piece, unattributed though likely penned by *Renaissance* editor JoAnn Roberts, grappled with the implications of the recent passage of the Americans with Disabilities Act through the Senate. In particular, the dispatch narrates the moralizing drama whose outcome was, in its words, "troglodyte" Senators Jesse Helms and William Armstrong successfully amending the bill's definition of *disability* to specifically exclude a litany of more and less formal diagnostic categories, including transvestism, transsexualism, and gender identity disorders.[1]

The author's unequivocal stance about this mode of exclusion, which framed transness as an impairment but not a protectable disability, was that it harmfully reinforced "the notion that people who dress as the other gender, or who believe themselves to be of the other gender, are sick."[2] At the same time, the piece was more ambivalent about the titular question at hand, an ambivalence grounded in the fact that trans people had previously had some, albeit very limited, success bringing discrimination cases under existing federal disability law, a route toward securing employment protections that the ADA effectively shut down.[3] Retrospectively, in fact, it is possible to understand Helms's and Armstrong's deeply conservative amendments to the ADA as helping to cement the now seemingly commonsense view that trans people ought be protected under Title VII of the Civil Rights Act but not under the ADA. That is, it is now largely taken for granted that the answer to "whether or not we [trans people] are disabled" is *no*.[4] However, in the years surrounding the passage of the ADA, *Renaissance News* was one of a handful of trans community publications that devoted page space to debate over the costs and benefits of trans exclusion from the ADA in particular and the category of disability in general. The law's answer to the question of who is disabled, then, was understood as an event in trans history as it unfolded.

One potent strain of trans scholarship has been engaged in the work of granting *trans* a life before and beside the clinic, as well as residence in tenses other than "futurity itself."[5] However, while such projects have situated transness in relation to histories of science and medicine, nation making and imperialism, slavery and settler colonialism, and so forth, they by and large take for granted that to do trans history is to do the history of gender and, sometimes, sexuality. Put another way: due to the (uneven, tentative) institutionalization of trans studies within women/gender/feminist/sexuality studies, as well as the complicated and consuming entanglements between trans, queer, and feminist politics/theory, scholars tend to foreground the entanglements of trans with queer and feminist history. Substantially less attention has been given to the equally complicated entanglement of trans and disabled as social/political categories and modes of life.

Further, given that the withholding of rights and personhood from many groups has long been justified through imputations of impairment, incapacity, irrationality, and idiocy, "one might think of disability as the master trope of human disqualification."[6] As a result, disability studies scholars have long argued that many otherwise progressive social movements and schools of thought are premised on what David Mitchell and Sharon Snyder call a "methodological distancing" from disability: "As feminist, race, and sexuality studies sought to unmoor their identities from debilitating physical and cognitive associations" (female hysteria, black cognitive/emotional inferiority, and so forth) "they inevitably positioned disability as the 'real' limitation from which they must escape."[7] Thus, alongside the medicalization of gender nonconformity as transsexuality, gender identity disorder, and gender dysphoria, it is hardly surprising that gender nonconforming lives have also been delegitimized and regulated using various idioms of disability: transness as contagion, as mental illness, and so on. In turn, "Trans and other psychiatrized people . . . have set out to counter the stigma attached to disability and to build a rights movement by arguing that there is nothing wrong with them."[8] However, *trans* has never quite succeeded in gaining distance from disability. Unlike *queer* after the gay rights movement's contingently successful bid to officially depathologize homosexuality through suturing gayness to health, for example, *trans* remains bound officially to disability in diagnostic code and the practice of nondiscrimination law.[9] A trans/crip conjunction is, therefore, not a possibility that was foreclosed upon in the 1970s and again in the 1990s; rather, it is a live potentiality in the present.

Taking a brief detour through the longer history of gender nonconformity in the United States, this chapter sets aside *The Terrible We*'s animating question in order to first clear a space, one in which it will be possible to have a different response to the drive to disarticulate trans from sick/maladjusted than was on display in *Renaissance News*. Notably, in my interest in holding onto sick/maladjusted I do not focus on legibly disabled trans people per se; rather, by focusing on spaces of constrained agency—the courthouse, the prison, the freak show, the asylum, and the sensational newspaper report—I offer a series of vignettes that remind us how trans and disabled as categories of people were produced together from the nineteenth through the midtwentieth century, the period during which contemporary understandings of both were being (but were not yet) solidified. In particular, I focus my analysis on newspaper representations of three transmasculine people—Evelyn "Jackie" Bross, Milton Matson, and Jack Bee Garland—who, in different times and places, found themselves caught up in a multisited regulatory system that attempted to contain disabled, racialized, gender nonconforming, and other "problem bodies" in spaces outside of the properly public sphere.[10] While this system produced a series of constraints—and while trans and disability activism have often, for this reason, attempted to disarticulate these categories—I demonstrate that the coproduction of disability/transgender also allowed for fleeting, unexpected freedom, defined not "as a point of arrival, or as a right that one possesses," but rather "as an ephemeral sense and a practice of becoming that is performed into being . . . within tight and constrained spaces."[11] That is, although my analysis is focused on admittedly dismal spaces of confinement and display, I linger on Garland whose performance of gender, for a time, relied on a performance of disability; while Bross, Matson, and Garland all arguably found ways to manipulate the system regulating disability/transgender to their own ends, Garland's cripped transmasculinity granted them profound access to authority and allowed them to (temporarily) maneuver beyond the boundaries imposed on gender nonconforming and otherwise feminized lives.[12] Garland's life and afterlife, I suggest, offer a compelling model of trans authority that leans into, rather than flees from, the potentially disqualifying "lumping" together of gender nonconformity and disability in general, and madness in particular.[13] With this in mind, the chapter closes by briefly returning to the near present in order to examine a key moment in the disentanglement of disability and transgender in the United States: the passage of the ADA in 1990.

Importantly, my turn to historicize the relationship between trans identity and disability does not have properly historicist motives. Rather, following the lead of queer historiographers like Carolyn Dinshaw, Heather Love, Elizabeth Freeman, and Kadji Amin, I begin from the assumption that our approaches to the past are always structured by desire, which both enables and limits the stories we tell.[14] Initially, historical work in and around trans studies and the study of trans phenomena was largely structured by a desire to locate oneself in the past, or otherwise, to narrate *trans* as a project of gendered liberation or a medical invention. My project, however, is structured by the desire to locate ways of engaging with the production of trans identity as maladjustment other than its disavowal. Such a way of thinking requires, I believe, not only an ambivalence regarding the answer to who is disabled, but also a refusal to consent to medicolegal norms of emotion and cognition as the basis for securing dignity and epistemic authority. That is, a crip/trans response to the *Renaissance* writer's observation that the ADA reinforced the notion that trans people are sick might be: So what?, a question asked with both flippancy and sincerity. I turn to the transmasculine nineteenth to mid-twentieth centuries, then, in an effort to inhabit this *so what.*

Finally, unlike many histories that read gender nonconformity in the archive as transness, I make no particular attempt to claim the figures I discuss as transgender men. That is, each of the people I focus on traveled in their lives, and now in the archives, under multiple public identities, including multiple names, pronouns, and gender expressions. While all accounts suggest that Matson regarded himself as a man, the cases of Bross and Garland are not so clear-cut. Rather than presuming to know, then, I refer to Bross and Garland using the pronoun *they* as a singular pronoun that allows for both/and as well as neither/nor. I do so not to relitigate or fix Bross's and Garland's identities, nor to strip them of their historical contexts. But, rather—and given that I am a poet, not a historian—I use this bit of language to insist on multiplicity, unfixity, and nonbinary life, on what exceeds constraint. I anticipate that my use of *they*—in this chapter and throughout—will feel jarring or awkward for some readers, both for those still not acclimated to the singular *they* and for those inside trans lifeworlds where, far from being a neutral pronoun, *they* designates a range of particular gendered inhabitations. However, it's my hope that this uneasy feeling might translate into a readerly inhabitation of transness as a form of generative maladjustment to the given.

Revision: Jackie Bross and the Intent to Conceal

In 1851, Chicago adopted an ordinance that made it illegal for a person "to appear in a public place . . . in a dress not belonging to his or her sex."[15] In fact, between the 1840s and the end of World War I, over forty US cities in twenty-two states incorporated similar laws prohibiting "cross-sex" dress, most of which did not begin to be overturned until the 1970s.[16] These laws often appeared on the books in close proximity to others intended to regulate the appearance of bodies in public space, including, notably, the so-called ugly laws that targeted disabled people, particularly those who had to make their living by begging on the city streets.[17] Mirroring the language of the cross-dressing ordinance, the 1881 Chicago version of the ugly law read: "Any person who is diseased, mutilated, or in any way deformed, so as to be an unsightly or disgusting object . . . shall not therein or thereon expose himself to public view."[18]

In Chicago and throughout the nation, these laws were part of a larger strategy of governance intended to manage the population during a time of rapidly shifting demographics, destabilizing social movements, and increased mobility, which resulted in the unfixing of previously fixed social categories. Ellen Samuels has offered the term *crisis of identification* to describe the anxiety prompted by this sense that the individual bodies that made up the body politic in the mid-nineteenth century were becoming less identifiable and, therefore, less governable. In *Fantasies of Identification: Disability, Gender, Race*, Samuels traces the rise of identification technologies—from fingerprinting to chromosomal "gender" testing—back to the cultural fantasy of identification that emerged to counter the anxiety of this moment. This fantasy underpins our persistent belief that "embodied social identities such as race, gender, and disability are fixed, legible, and categorizable" and can be validated "through a verifiable, biological mark of identity," no matter how many times this is disproven.[19]

Alongside the development of identification technologies that attempted to suture social identity to the biological body, other social apparatuses participated in the project of fixing identity by other means. The ugly law and the cross-dressing ordinance, for example, worked to produce social identity as "fixed, legible, and categorizable" by attempting to remove gender nonconforming and visibly disabled bodies from the public sphere, literally fixing bodies in place. In this way, as Clare Sears has argued, the cross-dressing and ugly laws were part of a nineteenth-century strategy of "spatial governmentality," which operated by manipulating city space in order to fix a wide array of "problem bodies"—including those of immigrants and other racialized populations, the unsightly disabled, the cross-dressed, sex workers—outside of the properly public sphere.[20] As a consequence, gender nonconforming, disabled, and racialized bodies were often made to appear together in set aside spaces that were not private but also not properly public: the freak show, the asylum, the courthouse, and so on.

In 1943, nearly a century after the city's cross-dressing ordinance was put on the books, a nineteen-year-old factory worker named Evelyn "Jackie" Bross was arrested in Chicago on their way home from work for being "dressed in blue flannel, a plaid sport shirt, a plaid mackinaw jacket and oxfords," while sporting a "mannish hair cut."[21] Because it was the middle of World War II, when women across the country were wearing pants and occupying traditionally male roles in the workforce, Bross's arrest prompted many people to speak out on their behalf. Ultimately, the affair led to a slight revision of the law. Motivated by Bross's testimony in court that they chose their clothes because they were "more comfortable than women's and handy for work," alderman William Cowhey proposed amending the ordinance to prohibit cross-sex dress only when a person harbored the "intent to conceal his or her sex."[22] While some local newspapers framed Cowhey's amendment as a concession to the "indignation . . . [of] prominent women in the fashion world, industry, society, and volunteer war work," who contended that "women's suffrage and slacks ought to go hand in hand," John D'Emilio points out that Cowhey was careful to frame the issue specifically as one of wartime patriotism. Cowhey insisted: "We're in a war . . . Today, with the war industries calling for safe dress, we should permit women to wear comfortable clothes. If slacks are comfortable, let them be worn!"[23]

D'Emilio interprets Bross's story as indicative of the war's lasting reorganization of American gender roles and as a step toward the ordinance's eradication in the 1970s when "challenges to enforcing gender-based clothing norms became overwhelming."[24] That is, for him, the Bross affair represents a break from nineteenth-century ideology insofar as the revision gave the law less authority to police gender norms. However, when read in the wider context of the ordinance's hundred-year history and close relation to other laws meant to fix the appearance of the body politic, it would seem that this narrative is more continuous than not with the nineteenth century: rather than signaling a radical revision to the law, the Bross affair worked to reveal its ongoing intent. After all, when anti-cross-dressing laws began appearing on the books in cities across the United States, many of them already included the deception clause adopted by Chicago only a century later.

Clare Sears has argued that the cross-dressing ordinance was part of a nineteenth-century strategy of "spatial governmentality," or governing by means of manipulating city space.[25] Though Sears's study focuses on San Francisco, where high rates of immigration intensified the regulation of what Sears terms "problem bodies," this general argument is instructive for thinking through the logic of the ordinance nationwide. While local ordinances were not identical—some specified deception as the illegal act and some didn't, and some, like Chicago's, were embedded in laws also regulating "lewd" or sexually indecent behaviors and some weren't—cross-dressing laws consistently made it illegal to *appear in public* in a dress not "belonging" to one's sex. The law, that is, didn't target "cross-sex" dress per se but rather the act of the cross-dresser appearing in the public realm, appearing to belong to the public. Sears argues that this removal of visible gender nonconformity from the public sphere "consolidated definitions of gender normativity by overstating the rarity of 'difference' and exaggerating the prevalence of the 'norm,'" binding proper citizenship to the performance of Anglo-American, binary, hierarchized gender norms.[26] That is, regulating the movements of bodies in space was a crucial strategy of the national project of fixing identity because spaces were *already* infused with social meaning. This means that the addition of "with the intent to conceal his or her sex" to Chicago's ordinance in 1943 didn't exactly restrict the law's ability to police gendered appearance; rather, it responded to the necessary changes in what constituted gendered space.

Despite the revision, which was a response to Bross's insistence that their clothes were practical and not intended to conceal their sex, the judge determined that Bross needed to be fixed. When Bross returned to court for sentencing still in their flannel trousers, a woman named Theodora Fitzpatrick, who was also wearing slacks and had been arrested on suspicion of prostitution, happened to be in court on the same day. Unlike Bross, Fitzpatrick is described in the papers as appearing distinctly feminine, despite her pantsuit: "a bit like a Hollywood star" and "wearing a blue ribbon around her wavy blond hair."[27] Judge Jacob Braude, who presided over Bross's case, took advantage of the situation, using Fitzpatrick to illustrate that women wearing pants—and, implicitly, entering into male spaces—need not unfix binary gender. Indeed, the judge is described as having "triumphantly" pointed to the contrast between the two, declaring, "There's a difference as you can see . . . Mrs. Fitzpatrick shows that there should be no objection to women wearing slacks or other masculine appearing apparel if the wearer does not intent to impersonate a male."[28] This "strange drama," as D'Emilio calls it, reveals a tension between the revised law's stated aim (regulating intent) and its actual effect (regulating appearances). Bross, insistent on their lack of intent until the end, is quoted as telling the judge, "If I dress like a girl, I'll look like a boy anyway and I'll be picked up more often. . . . The police will say I'm impersonating a girl." Judge Braude responded by ordering Bross to tie a scarf around their head to "look feminine." Though Bross complied, the effect must not have been very convincing because Braude merely "shrugged and ordered [Bross] held under the court's psychiatric supervision" for at least six months.[29] Because Bross could not, or would not, be fixed to a gendered category, the judge ordered them fixed in a space outside of the public realm—the psychiatric system—where they could presumably *be* fixed, as in rehabilitated.

The Bross affair, therefore, reveals a second sense of *fix* that animated the cross-dressing law. While D'Emilio interprets the judge's decision to put Bross under psychiatric supervision as a novel concession to public pressure not to convict, there was, in fact, precedence for his decision, because cross-dressing laws had long been enforced using the logic of rehabilitation. In fact, rates of incarceration in asylums increased dramatically at the turn of the twentieth century, when cross-dressing laws were being adopted nationwide; gender/sexual "deviants" were among those increasingly at risk of being declared insane.[30] The path from courthouse to asylum is one of the ways in which gender nonconforming and disabled bodies were coarticulated, made to occupy the same spaces, collected together under the broad rubric of insanity or incapacity. In her history of the ugly law, Susan Schweik argues that beginning in the 1880s the "ugly ordinances sp[oke] the language of regulatory care" in that they gave judges the option of punishment *or* discipline. While the law authorized courts to fine or imprison disabled beggars arrested for being publicly visible "disgusting object[s]," in practice these beggars were primarily sent to state asylums. In this way, "the ugly law of biopower identifie[d] an abnormal group in order to 'care for' them" just as the cross-dressing law was wielded, until at least 1943.[31]

"Miss Matson May Be a Freak"

Through the practice of relegating bodies that variously threatened notions of productive citizenship to spaces outside of the properly public sphere, spatial and medical regulation combined to fix disability to gender nonconformity and to fix gender-variant/disabled bodies in place. Unlike Bross, Milton B. Matson first found himself caught in this multisited disciplinary mechanism for committing what appeared to be check fraud, not gender fraud. However, once caught up, Matson's narrative illuminates another space in which contemporary notions of transness and disability were coproduced, as he moved directly from the jailhouse to the stage of a San Francisco freak show. Admittedly, the freak show seems paradoxical, as a coexisting alternative to the prison and the asylum, since the latter are spaces of confinement, captivity, and coercive "care," whereas the former is a space of display, captivation, and commerce. However, "despite their different modes of operation, cross-dressing law and the freak show performed similar cultural work . . . as techniques of normalization that strove to produce clear, recognizable boundaries between normative and non-normative gender."[32] In what follows I add to Clare Sears's analysis of the imbrication of cross-dressing law and the freak show by attending to how the freak show not only lumped together a range of others in order to give cultural meaning to their bodies but also sorted among them, constituting *white* or *whitened* gender nonconformity and disability as the same kind of difference.

Milton B. Matson was arrested in January 1895 on the charge of obtaining money under false pretenses. He was held as a male in the San Jose County Jail for two weeks until the arrival of a telegram raised questions about his sex. A British bank contacted Matson in an attempt to find a presumed relative, Louisa E. B. Matson, who had received an amount of money that was available for her to withdraw in Santa Clara. Matson, it seems, tried to convince the bank to let him withdraw the funds, but—because Milton was presently incarcerated and Louisa, presumably, was not—the district attorney and sheriff got involved, concluding, "Either Louisa Matson and Milton B. Matson were one and the same person or the orders were forgeries."[33] When confronted, Matson initially insisted on his male identity, declaring, "Then . . . the question is settled, for I am a man." Eventually, however, Matson was "compelled"—in at least one account by the threat of being forcibly disrobed—

to reveal that "she was a woman."[34] Soon after, Matson was released and went on "a big drunk" to celebrate, which only served to increase the sensational quality of the story, which appeared in newspapers across the country, as it placed him even further outside the boundaries of nineteenth-century womanhood.[35] Matson, reportedly, could "drink the best brands of whisky, let loose at times the artillery of profanity and could tell a risqué story with the best of the boys."[36] As a result of the spectacle of his public unveiling, Matson received several offers to exhibit himself as a freak, and finding himself unable to continue working as a man, Matson left San Jose only a few days later to work in a dime museum in San Francisco.

Dime museums were part of the rise of new forms of popular entertainment in the period after the Civil War. These museums displayed a variety of attractions and curiosities—from historical wax tableaus to taxidermy to human anatomy—but the inclusion of live performance truly differentiated them from other public museums of the era. As a form of live entertainment found at dime museums, freak shows—or the dramatic staging of "human anomalies" popular in the United States and Europe between the years 1840 and 1940—have had a lasting effect on how we figure human variation. Human anomalies tended to fall within at least one of three frequently overlapping categories: wonders, novelty artists, and ethnographic freaks. Wonders included a wide range of people whose bodies visibly deviated, or appeared to deviate, from the norm: congenitally disabled people, intersex and other gender-nonconforming people, people who were very fat or very thin, and so on. Novelty artists were those like the tattooed ladies, sword swallowers, and geeks who fashioned bodies and bodily performances to produce shock and awe. And, finally, the category of ethnographic freaks included all sorts of people of color (or white performers in blackface) billed as savages, missing links, cannibals, or the last remaining member of this or that tribe. In short, freaks could potentially be anyone who visibly deviated from the racial, gendered, aesthetic, or behavioral norms of nineteenth-century Anglo-American culture and were used to manage white anxiety in a time of cultural, racial, and economic shifts, since "for those anxious about their own status, exotic freaks . . . reaffirmed their self-worth and the civility of urban life."[37]

Although the freak show functioned, in part, to naturalize the distance between the freak and the "normate," the exhibitions themselves were conscious performances, staged in order to produce and exaggerate that distance.[38] Matson, too, was paid to perform an exaggerated version of himself; "faultlessly attired in patent leathers, a handsome dress suit, embroidered linen and a white tie," Matson's act consisted of him reclining in an easy chair.[39]

Billed as the Bogus Man, the spectacle of Matson in an easy chair relied on his prior arrest and public revealing: the simple and seamless performance of genteel masculinity was freakish only because the audience already knew "the truth" of Matson's sex. Additionally, the other component of Matson's performance was the answering of questions "for the benefit of the curious public," who were interested in the how and why of Matson's persistent masculine presentation and reported romances with women—in how and why a "woman" would persistently live as a man.[40]

While analyses of gender nonconformity in freak shows tend to focus on intersex bodies, bodies that manifested gender nonconformity primarily as narrative were also put on display; however, scholars have tended to not know what to make of the "women in pants included alongside more patently unusual figures" in old freak photographs.[41] In *Sideshow U.S.A.: Freaks and the American Cultural Imagination*, for example, Rachel Adams attributes the wide array of people constructed as freaks—particularly those like the "women in pants" who strike us in the present as unremarkable—to the performativity of *freak* and to the historical variability of cultural norms, which is of course an accurate assessment. However, Matson's story also suggests that it may have been less the pants that made the female freak and more the public interest in stories of "deception"—of people crossing the theoretically rigid boundaries of nineteenth-century racial, gender, and class lines—and of deceiving bodies unveiled and put back in place.

Matson, that is, was not one of a kind, though his proprietor fought hard to make him appear that way. Very soon after Matson moved to San Francisco, an article in the *San Francisco Call* reported that the proprietor of the dime museum where Matson was being exhibited had filed a suit against three other individuals in order to prevent them from "exhibiting a woman as the 'only genuine Miss Martson [*sic*] in male attire'" because their exhibit was hurting his business.[42] While there is a certain irony to the desire to have "just one authentic Bogus Man"—and as Sears argues, incidents like this potentially increased the regulatory function of the freak show by heightening the public's awareness of the possibility of being duped—the desire to have the only genuine illusion is also indicative of how white wonders functioned in the freak economy.[43]

In *Extraordinary Bodies: Figuring Physical Disability in American Culture and Literature*, Rosemarie Garland-Thomson notes: "Perhaps the freak show's most remarkable effect was to eradicate distinctions among a wide variety of bodies, conflating them under the single sign of the freak-as-other . . . freak shows traded indiscriminately in both cultural and corporeal otherness.

Hence a nondisabled person of color billed as the 'Fiji Cannibal' was equivalent to a physically disabled, Euro-American called the 'Legless Wonder.'"[44] However, the effort to secure the rights to display the "only genuine Miss Matson" underscores the way that the Legless Wonder and the Fiji Cannibal were precisely *not* equivalent: white freaks were generally staged as anomalous individuals, whereas freaks of color tended to be staged as fungible data, as representative rather than unique. Perceived authenticity was also vital to the staging of ethnographic freaks, but offstage, people of color were interchangeable—there could be only one "Miss Matson," but it sometimes happened that the black "cannibals" and "savages" on display were actually white people in blackface or African American people from cities nearby.[45] And while wonders were frequently, as Matson was, costumed and staged in formal dress, ethnographic freaks were usually staged so that they appeared entirely outside of Anglo-American cultural norms rather than as perverse deviations from, or inhabitations of, them.

Freaks of colonialism, not only the multiple characters called the "missing link," were persistently figured at the boundary of the human/animal divide. For example, Ota Benga—a Central African Batwa first brought to the United States to be a part of the Pygmy Village at the 1904 Saint Louis World's Fair—was infamously displayed in the monkey house at the Bronx Zoo. While Benga's is an atypical example of how staging was used to animalize ethnographic freaks, it was not uncommon for proprietors to draw attention to perceived anatomical similarities between people of color and apes through this kind of juxtaposition. Further, the techniques that thrust ethnographic freaks outside the boundaries of the human rendered them incoherently or ungendered "in the outcome."[46]

In one of the images of Ota Benga that continues to circulate, a five-foot-tall black figure stands bare-chested with a knee-length piece of printed fabric around the waist. The figure carries a baby chimp on the hip, as a human mother might carry a child. The figure does not smile. This image undoubtedly portrays Benga as nearer to chimp than human, but in doing so it also portrays him as feminized, petite, and maternal, a gendering that sits in uneasy relation to other images where he is portrayed as savagely masculine, smiling to display his sharpened teeth and/or posing with a spear.[47] Representations of Benga, like those of Saartjie Baartman and Tono Maria—women figured as excessively feminine in body and excessively masculine in desire—exceed and recede from the sex/gender system of the nineteenth-century United States and highlight how gender deviance was used to produce and secure racial otherness onstage, and vice versa, showing the shadowy underside of (white) trans fury that "a gendering violence is the founding condition of human subjectivity; having a gender . . . makes one's personhood cognizable."[48]

Ultimately, the display of both wonders and ethnographic freaks served to performatively produce the norm, but this operated in racially differentiated and differentiating ways. Indeed, for example, the differential logics of the white-gender-nonconforming individual versus racialization-as-gender-variance was also evident in the enforcement of cross-dressing laws. Sears notes that despite the "zealous prosecution of Chinese people through indecency and nuisance laws" in nineteenth-century San Francisco, the vast majority of cross-dressing arrests covered in the local papers involved "a person presumed to be white."[49] That is, while papers framed white gender nonconforming people like Matson as exceptions worth reporting on—spectacular, immoral, and/or pathological individuals—Chinese gender in particular, and racialized gender in general, was largely represented as itself "a foreign and pathological formation." Further, "cross-dressing featured prominently in these representations, but as confirmation of Chinese difference and danger, not as evidence of individual criminal acts."[50] Binary sex/gender, that is, was taken to be a "unique achievement" of white populations, which is what produced individual (white or whitened) gender deviants as objects of fascination/curiosity and people to be fixed.[51]

As many have noted, the rise of the medical model of disability contributed to the decline of the freak show because human variation was increasingly understood as the proper object of medical science, turning these bodies from profitable wonders into individual pathologies to be cured. Alongside (or as) disability, in the early to mid-twentieth-century United States, gender nonconformity increasingly entered into the purview of medicine, where the differential racial logics that structured the enforcement of cross-dressing ordinances, the circulation of spectacularized news stories, and displays of human variation reassembled in the practice of transsexual medicine, the discourse in which gender nonconformity was made to live. Indeed, as Jules Gill-Peterson notes of this transition, "The differential between the abstract whiteness of plasticity and the visual regimes of race and antiblackness . . . is a central feature of the modern medicalization of sex."[52] For this reason, as late as the 1980s, psychoanalyst Leslie Lothstein, who evaluated patients for the Case Western Reserve University gender clinic, went so far as to speculate that—despite the fact of black transmasculine people arriving at his clinic—"black women may somehow be 'inoculated' against" transsexuality by the relative undifferentiation of black gender.[53]

The tendency of *trans* to stick to exceptional, white individuals is often framed as a problem of the archive, a persistent entrenchment of the authorized medicolegal frames that have made a particular story about trans visible. Or, in L. H. Stallings's words, transness is often "theorized though material and physical articulations of gender authorized by medical communities with little concern for race or culture," a lack of concern that can be said to characterize both the theorizing and the authorized archives from which it is derived.[54] However, taking a wider view of trans history provides a glimpse of a story about the analytic separation of race (as fungibility, atavism) and [trans]gender (as particularity, plasticity) that extends before and beside the clinic. With this in mind, the next vignette will linger on the life and afterlife of Jack Bee Garland, the subject of Lou Sullivan's 1990 biography *From Female to Male: The Life of Jack Bee Garland.*

In what follows, I offer a recuperative reading of Sullivan's biography as not an impaired (but useful) work of historical recovery but rather as an aesthetic object marked indelibly by Garland's (and Sullivan's) cripped transmasculinity. In doing so, I hope to demonstrate that Garland's navigation of gender, labor, race, and authority for a time relied on a performance of disability, and that this cripped transmasculinity allowed them to maneuver around the physical and epistemic boundaries imposed on gender-nonconforming and female-assigned lives. That is, while the systems that produced what we now know as disability/transgender at the turn of the century, a series of epistemic and physical constraints that fixed Bross "under the eye of a psychiatrist" and Matson on a dime museum stage, the co-constitution of disability/transgender also sometimes allowed for fleeting access to authority and freedom.[55] In particular, Garland used the "disability con" as a technology that scrambled the codes of gender, race, and class, allowing them to live—briefly in life but indefinitely in the archive—a publicly nonbinary life.[56] Their narrative, therefore, offers a compelling model of trans agency and authority that leans into, rather than flees from, the potentially disqualifying "lumping" together of disability/transgender.[57]

Born in 1869 to José Marcos Mugarrieta, a former officer of the Mexican Army and San Francisco's first Mexican consul, and Eliza Garland, an Anglo-American daughter of a Louisiana congressman, Garland was "perhaps something of—to be *vulgarly* perversely presentist—a gay mixed-race Chicano transman" whose gendered passing relied on a form of racial/ethnic passing.[58] As Nan Boyd and Victor Mendoza have both argued, it's notable that Garland abandoned their Spanish last name in favor of a series of Anglo names, ultimately coming to be remembered by their mother's last name, Garland.[59] Garland's proximity to whiteness not only undergirded their ability to cultivate relationships with other white men, but we might speculate that it also accounted for some of the fascinated attention their gender presentation provoked. I focus on the role of disability in Garland's narrative because this is an aspect that has been largely underthought. However, Garland's ability to navigate the terrain of nineteenth-century gender must also be read as one story about how whiteness came to be overrepresented in the US trans[masculine] archive. That is, the paper trail Garland left behind and the authority they were able to garner through their disability drag were obviously enabled by their proximity to whiteness.[60]

"She of the Pants and No Voice": Jack Bee Garland's Disability Drag

I feel like I'm the only one with this problem—a gay man in a woman's body—and so alone, so left out. I gather Jack Garland's remnants with delight + think of his life compared to mine + it does make me feel better. But not much. —**LOU SULLIVAN, *WE BOTH LAUGHED IN PLEASURE***

In 1979, Allan Bérubé delivered a lecture at the San Francisco Public Library titled "Lesbian Masquerade," which gave an account of several people, presumed lesbians, who passed as men in nineteenth- and early-twentieth-century San Francisco. Lou Sullivan was in the audience of that lecture and found himself particularly moved by one of Bérubé's subjects, a character who went by various names and pronouns but lived the majority of their life as Jack Bee Garland. Sullivan was a prominent trans activist and writer in 1970s and 1980s San Francisco: he founded the support group that became FTM International; published the first guidebook for female-assigned cross-dressers and other transmasculine people; maintained correspondence with transmasculine people across North America, acting as a central node in a dispersed web of FTM life; and worked tirelessly for the recognition of gay FTM transsexuals among medical professionals. But although Sullivan's insistent life and work laid the ground for the proliferation of queer transmasculinities that populate the present—and although his life was populated by friends and lovers, mentors and mentees—he was often haunted by the sense of being utterly alone, the only one of his kind. Undoubtedly, this feeling sparked his pursuit of Garland who, despite Bérubé's interpretative frame, was not immediately legible as a lesbian. Unlike the female husbands who were their contemporaries, Garland evinced no particular interest in partnerships with women.

Instead, Garland seemed much more interested in the company of men and frequently formed bonds within male-only spaces: the military, the city government, bachelors' clubs, encampments of homeless and transient men, and so on. For this reason, Sullivan saw in Garland the glimmer of someone like himself, a gay trans man, in the historical record. Pressed on by this desire for history, Sullivan "resolved to learn more about . . . Babe Bean, also known as Jack Bee Garland."[61]

Learning more about Garland turned Sullivan into a public historian in his own right and, eventually, Sullivan's desire for history resulted in his writing and publishing Garland's biography, *From Female to Male: The Life of Jack Bee Garland*. The biography itself was greeted with mixed reviews, in part because Sullivan's desire to claim Garland as like himself struck many reviewers as ahistorical at best. Writing for the *Lambda Book Review*, Victoria A. Brownsworth in particular took offense at Sullivan's account of Garland's life, writing: "As a journalist and a historian, I found myself cringing at nearly every page, either from the thoroughly bad writing or the ludicrous historical liberties taken with what little research was done." While it's true that *From Female to Male* does not conform to the conventions of academic or journalistic writing, one gets the sense that what Brownsworth really finds ludicrous is that "Sullivan seems to claim that Garland was one of those people who wished to be a member of the opposite sex so as to be a homosexual in that sex," a claim she perceived as not only going against the standard notion that "women who crossdressed did so to camouflage their lives as lesbians," but daring to do so with very little evidence to back it up. Never mind that she simultaneously accuses Sullivan of being overreliant on primary sources, insisting: "Sullivan should have called himself 'editor,' [because] so little of the actual text is in his words."[62]

Even sympathetic reviewers shared with Brownsworth the sense that Sullivan's writing somehow simultaneously gives too much and too little access to his subject. In her review, prominent trans writer and activist Kate Bornstein celebrates the biography for beginning to give a history to the still-emerging female-to-male trans community. At the same time, Bornstein insists that there is something missing, which she calls the emotional or philosophical tone of the book: it's unclear, that is, what the author wants from his subject and who this subject might have actually been. "Perhaps," Bornstein suggests, "this is because Sullivan shows us solely the public Babe Bean, what the reporters wrote and what Bean wrote for the newspapers. I wanted to see more of the private man behind the writer."[63] Likewise, William A. Henkin praises the book as "a tribute to its subject" but "regret[s] . . . that Sullivan's approach does not let us see deeply enough into that public life to really grasp the nature of the private human being underneath."[64]

Certainly there is something peculiar about the form of this biography insofar as it is primarily an accumulation archival material. However, rather than interpreting what these critics identify as a lack—of inner life, of coherence, of clarity—as a failure of Sullivan's, I argue that the book's form should be read as the trace of Garland's successful manipulation of the regulatory mechanisms that landed their known contemporaries in courts, in asylums, and on stage as dime museum freaks. Indeed, to opine Sullivan's overreliance on newspapers is to miss how remarkable the kind and quantity of public-facing text devoted to Garland's life is in the first place. Bross and Matson, along with most of the other "cross-dressers" from this period that we know about today, only entered public discourse as the result of being exposed as "the other sex," either upon postmortem examination or upon running afoul of the law. Bérubé's lecture that inspired Sullivan, after all, emerged from his repeated encounters with stories of spectacular postmortem reveals in the archives. As a result, many of the available sources that document these individuals' lives are structured by the desire to locate an "authentic" self behind the public face and, in doing so, deny their subjects control over how their lives are narrated, containing gender nonconformity even as it is made public. This form of making gender nonconformity public functions in a way that is analogous to Matson's being displayed in a dime museum, answering the public's questions; this form of the public display of gender nonconformity is premised on his always already having been fixed as "the other sex." Publicity, that is, was usually attended by a loss of agency and authority, narrative and otherwise.

Though passing for a trans person commonly is taken to mean being publicly regarded as the gender one is, it could just as readily mean (nearly) the opposite. Possible strategies for navigating "the bathroom problem"—the architectural production of the binary gender system often invoked as *the* sign of trans people's reduced access to the public sphere—illustrates this point.[65] When faced with the choice between sex-segregated bathrooms, a trans person can enter the restroom that most closely matches their gender presentation and hope that no one questions their sex. In this case, identity is managed by passing as non-trans. Alternatively, they can choose the restroom designated for their assigned sex, whether or not this "matches" their gender presentation. For example, a transgender guy in the women's room can emphasize attributes that might allow him to pass as a non-trans woman. Or, in the same situation, he might emphasize his *transness*, making no move to pass as a non-trans woman and choosing instead to momentarily capitalize on the liberal trans-antagonism that positions trans men as "women-lite" in order to pee in peace.

There is, of course, a fourth option. Rather than occupying the space designated for "the normal," one can also retreat. In "The Butch Body," Sally Munt narrates her own threatened discomfort when occupying the women's room in a gender-nonconforming body, a discomfort that Munt resolves by retreating into the "disabled toilet," "a stress-free location, a queer space in which [she] can momentarily procure an interval from the gendered public environment, and psychically replenish."[66] Though Munt marks the contemporary distance between disability and gender nonconformity by worrying that she is not "worthily" disabled, the kind of public restroom Munt is talking about—single occupancy and gender neutral—extends the structure of the freak show and sensational newspaper report insofar as these are all spaces that, despite being in public, function to contain disabled and gender-nonconforming bodies, a way of accessing the public sphere without appearing to belong to the public. However, as Munt compellingly describes, precisely *because* these rooms "set aside for the disjunctive, ungendered, and strange" provide spaces outside of the proper public, they are also potentially sites of enablement.[67]

In late nineteenth-century California, Jack Bee Garland, too, recognized that the lumping together of bodies designated as disjunctive, ungendered, and strange could be manipulated to allow for forms of authority and freedom not generally granted to gender-nonconforming or female-assigned people of the time. During the period of their life that is most recoverable in the archive (because it generated the most text), Garland lived as a newspaper reporter in Stockton, California. While in Stockton, going by the name Babe Bean, Garland did not exactly attempt to pass strictly as a man or woman, male or female but, rather, engaged in something more like a masquerade by heightening and then manipulating the public confusion caused by their gender deviance, allowing them to control public discourse about themself.

There was much speculation about Garland's sex in the Stockton newspapers in the first months after they arrived in town. In *From Female to Male*, Sullivan cites an article that, fumbling for language, calls Garland "the mysterious girl-boy, man-woman, or what-is-it." While this article is written in the genre of the public spectacle that—like the freak show—is driven by the titillation of the revelation of sex, its failure to make this reveal illustrates how Garland was able to maintain their gender nonnormativity in public precisely by *not* withholding the "truth" of their sex. The article continues: "The mystery is still unsolved as to whether 'Babe' Bean is a boy or a girl, a man or a woman. It is true that this peculiar personage could be taken for a male or female. As a matter of course, people have used the pronoun 'she' in reference. Because of a certain feminine appearance she was arrested some days ago for masquerading in male attire. The girl-boy stated at that time that she was a woman. That, however, might have been done to deepen the doubt as to the truth of sex."[68] In this way, Garland encouraged the proliferation of public discourse about themself that could reveal nothing but what Garland was willing to reveal. Importantly, though, Garland's ability to control the content of public text relied on a very different kind of proliferation of text. Written about affectionately as "she of the pants and no voice," Garland claimed to be unable to speak and communicated solely in writing. In newspapers throughout the Bay Area, the mystery of the "truth" about Garland's silence generated just as much text as did the mystery of the "truth" of their sex. That is, while Garland made no attempt to pass as any particular sex/gender while in Stockton, they did attempt to pass as disabled, which was central to their ability to live out their gender nonconformity in public.

While numerous reporters speculated that Garland's muteness was a ruse intended to conceal a "feminine voice" that "would disclose her deception," this speculation was itself incoherent in the face of the facts—Garland announced their womanhood to the police and was disbelieved.[69] How, in this circumstance, would the reveal of a "feminine voice" disclose a deception? Further, Garland's explanation of their silence was somewhat incoherent, vacillating between something like a nervous disorder, the result of a physical injury, and an act of volition. Sullivan's biography includes this illustrative quote, attributed to Garland, explaining that their "affliction came on me on account of a fright, a fall which hurt me internally. Sickness followed. I could with an effort speak, but I grew so accustomed to write out my wants that even that power left me."[70] Rather than shoring up Garland's masculinity, these explanations—especially insofar as "fright" is the precipitating condition—conform to discourses of white female frailty and impressibility.[71]

However, the performance of this particular disability, regardless of whether Garland *could have* spoken, was crucial to their gendered performance, particularly because it was an excellent tool for managing information. In particular, we can speculate that Garland's disability drag allowed them to conduct their public life according to what Alison Kafer and others have called "crip time," which, by slowing things down or dragging things out, "requires reimagining our notions of what can and should happen in time, or recognizing how expectations of 'how long things take' are based on very particular minds and bodies." Kafer continues, "Rather than bend disabled bodies and minds to meet the clock, crip time bends the clock."[72] By conducting all of their communication in writing, Garland was able to slow down the flow of their social life; people—all eager for information—had to wait for Garland to think and then to write. Moving in crip time, that is, might have allowed Garland to evade some of the constant questioning that attended life as a gender deviant in nineteenth-century Stockton, California.

Further, remaining voiceless in their present paradoxically allowed Garland to have more say over how they would be represented in the future. While the papers certainly made wild speculations, it would have been impossible for a paper to skew Garland's words or misquote them in order to make salacious claims, as Garland, by necessity, had a written record of everything they said to the press, to anyone who might talk to the press, and so on. Additionally, by not speaking and therefore remaining a perpetually fascinating object of the local news, Garland was able to build relationships with the reporters, eventually allowing them to become an *author* for those same newspapers, and was helped along by the fact that these relationships were conducted in writing. One reporter noted that Garland "writes a large, round, masculine hand, and leaves a large space between the lines, as newspaper writers are required to do," and Garland's constant demonstration of their competence led many of the Stockton reporters to simply assume that they were there on business, writing a story for some out-of-town paper.[73] Living as a reporter aided Garland's gendered performance because it gave them reason to access spaces coded as male, including gambling halls, the hangouts of the homeless, a bachelor's club, and the male ward of the Stockton asylum, about which Garland wrote articles for the Stockton papers. But serving as a reporter also ensured that many of the records we have now about Garland's life are in their own words. Importantly, these are not texts along the lines of diary entries or even letters, which might have revealed the private man behind the public face that Sullivan's critics were after; rather, Garland left behind an archive of newspaper articles, which work to further solidify Garland's public performance of self *as* their self.

While the relationship between *trans* and *disability* is often thought of as a confining imposition of the medical system—and the coarticulation of disability and gender nonconformity has led and does still lead to literal confinement—Garland was able to work this connection to their own ends. A two-part exposé detailing the Stockton asylum that Garland wrote for Stockton's *Evening Mail* is perhaps the best example of this, particularly because it suggests that they were cognizant of how gender nonconformity was construed and regulated. The content of the article works to reinforce Garland's distance from "the insane," who are described throughout as "poor, helpless creatures [who] have no reason," as opposed to the rational subject that Garland proves themself to be through the act of writing. However, the article's title—"Babe Bean in the Asylum: First Woman Ever Admitted to the Male Department"—is clearly playing with expectation that someone like Garland would be in the asylum as a ward. In fact, the Stockton asylum *did* house at least one "male impersonator" at the time of Garland's article; Dick Ruble was declared insane after being arrested for masquerading in San Francisco in 1890 and committed to Stockton, where they died in 1908.[74] But just as Garland was able to manipulate their capture by the newspapers in order to avoid the narrative of the spectacular reveal, by invoking—not avoiding—the potentially confining equation of gender nonconformity and madness, Garland was able to spin even this life-and-death narrative in their favor.

Disability drag is used primarily to refer to the phenomenon of nondisabled actors playing disabled characters and is most often read as a form of performance that strips disabled people of authority. As scholars like Tobin Seibers have argued, this phenomenon tends to reinforce the stigma of disability and, importantly, keep "disability out of public view" by keeping disabled actors out of circulation and by transforming disability into "a sign of the acting abilities of the performer" rather than a lived reality with its own material and epistemological effects.[75] However, keeping these negative connotations in mind, disability drag is a useful framework for understanding Garland's time in Stockton precisely because of these multiple valences: dragging out the time of sociality, drag as an appropriative performance that reinforces the distance between the normal and the other, drag as an action that brings two or more categories into close proximity, drag as repetition with a subversive difference that produces spaces of freedom.[76] In fact, disability drag as a trans strategy is more common than one might expect. While Munt's elaboration of the disabled toilet as a queer space is one example, we need look no further than the life of Garland's biographer. Even as Lou Sullivan turned to the archive to find evidence of someone like him in order to write a history to which he belonged, there was a strange way in which the life of the biographer mirrored his subject's in ways he was not looking for. Like Garland, Sullivan also claimed his belonging to homosocial worlds (in the eyes of the officials) not through seamlessly passing as a man but through a performance of affliction.

Because he refused to conform to narrative expectations of trans lives—that is, because he didn't hide his life as a gay man—Sullivan was denied entry into Stanford University's Gender Dysphoria Program, which would have provided him access to counseling, hormone therapy, and surgery. Years later, Sullivan famously wrote a letter to the coordinator of the program, informing her that not only had he accessed medical care and staked a claim to belonging to the gay male community in 1980s San Francisco but that he had done this so well that he was now dying of an AIDS-related infection. In his own words, "So, Judy, even though your Program did not believe I could live as a gay man, it looks like I'm going to die like one."[77] While one cannot read this as an unmitigated gain of agency, it's also true that, like Garland, Sullivan became legible to "the experts" as the authority of his own self in part by embracing and overperforming sickness. This particular performance of illness—the speech act, the sending of the letter—granted him the authority to name his own gendered and sexual identity in a context where this authority had been previously denied him but was subsequently extended to gay transgender men in the future. Further, and more speculatively, while I've suggested that Garland's moving in crip time affected the shape of their biography, it's also true that Sullivan's manuscript was completed and published only after he had entered a crip temporality of his own: "When I got sick in December '86," Sullivan relates in his diary, "there were two things I wanted to accomplish before I died: to publish my Garland book, and to ensure that no other female-to-gay males would be discriminated against by the gender professionals because of their sexual orientation. This week I accomplished them both."[78]

In closing, let me reiterate that the authority garnered by Garland's disability drag was obviously enabled by their education and proximity to whiteness. That is, Garland's ability to work the connection between trans and disabled for their own ends—and their subsequent recuperation by lesbian and trans historians as a queer pioneer—was undoubtedly enabled by their ability to otherwise yoke themself to white, US imperial, pioneer masculinity. Meditating on their life trajectory, Garland writes: "Has love had anything to do with my present mode of living? . . . My first recollections of loving anyone is of a dark, handsome and noble face, with honor stamped upon every feature—a solider; to me a hero."[79] Importantly, Jack became Jack as opposed to Babe Bean, the man as opposed to the "boy-girl, man-woman," not in California but overseas in Manila, serving as a reporter, nurse, and solider in the Twenty-Ninth Infantry during the Philippine-American War. In securing their manhood, prompted perhaps by love of their dark father, Garland ultimately "served the same U.S. imperial, settler-colonial force that his Mexican Army father had fought against some fifty years earlier, during the Mexican-American War."[80]

Garland's mute months in Stockton, months in which they evaded capture by all manner of confining narratives and institutions, binary gender among them, were exceptional, not only in relation to other gender nonconforming people of the time, but also in Garland's own life. After returning from Manila, Jack, as Jack, lived out the rest of his days as a talkative, philanthropic man in San Francisco. And when he died, a new round of newspaper articles surfaced that finally pinned Jack down, revealing once and for all that "'Jack Bee' Was a Woman."[81] Thus, it's precisely the exceptionality of the Stockton episode that proves the point that a willingness to lean into, rather than flee from, the disqualifying associations between gender nonconformity and disability—and particularly gender nonconformity and madness—has the capacity to open up spaces of unexpected freedom and interpretative authority, however partial and fleeting.

Disability/Transgender Now

In *Feminist, Queer, Crip*, Alison Kafer highlights the work of a twenty-first-century campus activism group, People in Search of Safe and Accessible Restrooms (PISSAR), as an example of the productivity of crip/trans coalition. In particular, in light of the exclusion of trans from the ADA, Kafer suggests that disability studies/politics ought to "treat the public toilet as a site for undoing this exclusion, recognizing public inaccessibility as a problem that connects both those authorized to claim disability and those who are not" and, in so doing, keep "the meanings and parameters of disability, access, and disability studies open for debate and dissent."[82] However, in the midst of this argument, Kafer cannot help but take a lengthy pause to point out the ways in which trans and disability refuse to work together, in institutionalized spaces and individual minds alike:

> It remains rare . . . for issues of disability access and trans access to be raised concurrently on GLBTQ organizational websites or in the (often sensationalized) news coverage about trans campus activism. The frequency with which activists, administrations, and reporters use the language of "gender-blind," as opposed to "gender-neutral," "unisex," or "nongendered," suggests that critical disability perspectives are not at play here. By the same token, my own experiences with PISSAR suggest reluctance on the part of some disability activists to engage with trans and genderqueer issues: one of the disabled students initially opposed forming PISSAR for fear that addressing trans access would dilute the

struggle for disability access. The annual conference of the Society for Disability Studies has yet to consistently include gender-neutral restrooms as a required component of access, and too few disability studies scholars include attention to the relationship between trans and disability in our work on access, sexuality, stigma, or medicalization, only a few potential areas of overlap.[83]

Likewise, Isaac West begins his book's chapter on this same crip/trans activist group with a moment of rhetorical hesitation, noting that to suggest crip/trans as a site of solidarity "is not without risk. Many members of these communities, save those who live at the intersections of these identities, have labored to untangle the negative articulations of one with the other. . . . Therefore, to link the interests of people with disabilities and LGBTS may seem counterintuitive, regressive, and politically untenable."[84] While Kafer's and West's works are examples of the increase in thought invested in crip/trans coalitions, both are marked by doubt, hesitation, and worry. Despite their numerous sites of overlap, that is, *trans* and *disability* can feel like strange bedfellows in the present.

Kafer's story about the activist who fears that addressing trans issues would "dilute the struggle for disability access" suggests that these feelings are symptomatic of single-issue politics more generally; however, the hesitancy that marks crip/trans coalitions must also be understood as a historical production, not merely the inevitable affective residue of a general problematic. After all, *trans* and *disability* have not always felt like an odd couple. In what follows, I conclude by very briefly examining the contemporary disarticulation of transness and disability in federal US law. While West's narrative—in which activists "have labored to untangle" these two categories—suggests that this disarticulation was the product of progressive social movements, it can also be traced through the strange drama that attended the passage of the Americans with Disabilities Act through Congress. In this story, trans identity is untangled from disability not as the result of a progressive move, but rather through a conservative push to legally define transness *as* maladjustment—an impairment but not a protectable disability, a particularly immoral kind of madness.

* * *

In fall 2006, a white trans woman named Kate Lynn Blatt was hired as a seasonal stocker by Cabela's retail in Pennsylvania and subsequently encountered a series of predictable, transphobic obstacles: she was forced to wear a nametag that depicted her former name, even though she had presented legal name-change paperwork to human resources; she was prohibited from using the women's restroom; she endured harassment from coworkers and managers; and she was "abruptly" terminated in March 2007. All this resulted in Blatt bringing a discrimination lawsuit against her former employer, which was argued partially on the grounds of sex-based discrimination and partially on the grounds that Cabela's refused to grant the "reasonable accommodation" of Blatt's gender dysphoria required by federal disability law. While arising from an utterly ordinary instance of transgender workplace discrimination, Blatt's case has since led to a somewhat extraordinary court ruling: a federal district court denied a motion to dismiss Blatt's claims to discrimination under the Americans with Disabilities Act, which is "the first time a court has ruled that transgender people are not categorically barred from seeking relief" under the law (almost two decades old at the time).[85]

First passed in 1990, the Americans with Disabilities Act was intended to be a comprehensive civil rights law prohibiting disability discrimination in employment, access to public services, and access to the public sphere. The act's aspirational comprehensiveness is reflected in its definition of discrimination, which acknowledges that the problem is embedded in infrastructure as much as in attitude, as well as its broad definition of disability. That is, the act is written to protect any individual who has "a physical or mental impairment that substantially limits one or more of the major life activities . . . a record of such an impairment [*or* of] being regarded as having such impairment." However, at the same time that the ADA at least symbolically ushered a broad swath of disabled people into public belonging, it also worked to draw—or, at least, solidify—a line between the legal and political categories of trans and disability.

That is, while the ADA has not and cannot manifest its material promises, as a piece of civil rights legislation the act doubles as a kind of moral code, one that symbolically ushers some bodies into public regard and explicitly excludes others.[86] In particular, in order to gain enough votes to be passed into law, the ADA had to include specific exclusions of "certain conditions" to satisfy conservative senators: "transvestism, transsexualism, pedophilia, exhibitionism, voyeurism, gender identity disorders not resulting from physical impairments, or other sexual behavior disorders; compulsive gambling, kleptomania, or pyromania; [and] psychoactive substance use disorders resulting from current illegal use of drugs."[87] Many of these exclusions were justified based on their relationship to illegal activities, and while laws regulating drug use and sexual behaviors act as their own kind of moral code, they served as precedent. However, the exclusion of "transvestism, transsexualism, . . .

[and] gender identity disorders not resulting from physical impairments" could not follow this logic, nor was it justified on the grounds that gender nonconformity is not an impairment. Although this argument has certainly been made from within trans discourse, these excluded categories *were* seen by those who insisted on this clause as mental impairments, guided as they were by the *DSM*. Additionally, as Jennifer L. Levi and Bennett H. Klein have pointed out, "courts or administrative agencies in at least seven states have found that transgender people are protected under *state* civil rights laws that prohibit discrimination on the basis of disability."[88] That is, within the logic of twentieth- and twenty-first-century law, the construction of both disability and transgender is uneven, even contradictory, but reveals their ongoing entanglement.

Kevin M. Barry has detailed the drama that produced the ADA's definition of gender variance as impairment but not protectable disability. According to his account, "The ADA's exclusion of GID in 1990 was based on nothing more than the moral opprobrium of a small handful of senators, conveyed in the eleventh hour of a marathon floor debate and in the absence of an organized transgender lobby."[89] Before reaching the Senate floor, the language of the ADA did not exclude *any* impairment from the act; however, once up for debate, several senators—notably, Jesse Helms, William Armstrong, and Warren Rudman—contested the inclusion of various mental impairments on the basis that, as Senator Rudman put it, "in short, we are talking about behavior that is immoral, improper, or illegal and which individuals are engaging in of their own volition, admittedly for reasons we do not fully understand."[90] Consequently, Senator Armstrong initially proposed an amendment that would have excluded nearly all mental impairments from coverage, but by the end of the day disability rights activists had "whittled down Senator Armstrong's list [of excluded impairments] to approximately five conditions."[91] Though gender identity disorders were not originally included on this new list, by the time it went up for vote, they were back on the list of excluded impairments. In fact, the ADA excludes "transvestism" not only in the comprehensive list of excluded impairments but also in its own section.[92] This rhetorical overkill suggests not only the degree to which these senators wanted to be certain that transness was not regarded as a protectable disability but also how certain they were that it would have been if not for their action. That is, if the heated dispute to keep gender variance out of the original ADA signifies anything at all, it is that transness and disability were so linked in common sense that they might have legally been one and the same.

Barry's article was written after the 2008 amendment that offered a more expansive definition of disability and clarified that the law was meant to protect individuals with impairments not typically thought of as disabling, but that nonetheless failed to remove the GID exclusion. While Barry interprets this as a sign of an ongoing moral campaign against trans people, the benefits of pursuing protections for transgender people using disability law has long been—and continues to be—a site of controversy within trans thought. That is, the 2008 nondecision might be more properly understood as a sign of the ambivalence that marks the relation of transness and disability in the present. Indeed, if the late twentieth century was a period marked by an understanding of *trans* as a psychiatric impairment not protectable by disability law, then the present moment is, it seems, marked by an inversion of these prior terms. Now, increasingly, there is a profound ambivalence among the "authorities" like the American Psychiatric Association and the World Health Organization about trans identity's relationship to official taxonomies of mental illness, as illustrated by the move to *gender dysphoria* in the *DSM*-5 and the removal of *gender identity disorder* from the list of mental and behavioral disorders in the ICD-11. At the same time, transness and disability have been increasingly reconflated in the realm of law, as Blatt's case attests. That is, as this chapter has demonstrated, the trans exclusion from the ADA was only one moment in the long, uneven, ongoing relationship between disability and transgender in the United States, insofar as these categories are sometimes regarded as mutually exclusive, sometimes as odd or unfortunate cotravelers, and sometimes as one and the same.

Again, on Trans Authority

Rather than pursuing the moralizing disarticulation of *trans* from disability, this chapter has pursued the making of disability/transgender in the strange, set-aside space—the asylum, the freak show, the prison, the public toilet, and so on. In doing so, I have argued that not only were transness and disability produced alongside one another at the turn of the twentieth century insofar as they were caught up in similarly confining double binds with respect to law, medicine, and entertainment, but these constraints can and have been worked to create unexpected forms of freedom and authority premised on maladjustment. Admittedly, while Jack Garland exemplified this possibility, there was a certain undecidability that haunted my narration of their story: Could Garland have spoken in Stockton? Was their muteness volitional, or was it an impairment rooted in physical injury, in emotional injury? Is the question of Garland's silence actually equivalent to the question of their sex? And am I, committed to a trans epistemology that takes Garland's public gender as a truth, obligated to take their silence as similarly true?

As Abram J. Lewis has argued, this kind of undecidability fundamentally structures the transgender archive, "replete" as it is "with apparent psychosis, unverifiable and esoteric truths, supernatural and nonhuman agents, and myriad other bizarre experiences" that co-occur with, and perhaps even enable, the work of activism, philanthropy, and so on by "transparently rational, politicized, and agential historical subject[s]."[93] For the most part, this undecidability has been managed by bracketing the madness of the transgender archive altogether or interpreting it as strategic: in Garland's case, this has meant ignoring the significance of their muteness altogether or taking for granted that Garland was willfully "hiding his voice" in order to live as a white man.[94] Lewis puts forward a third, hauntological approach to the transgender archive; rather than ignoring or assimilating its unruly, peculiar, impaired, and mad elements, Lewis proposes to read them as hauntings, in Avery Gordon's vocabulary or, in his own, as "symptomatic of the destructive forces in which these infelicitous subjects were caught."[95] At the same time, he argues, doing so enacts its own kind of violence, as it works through "the deauthorization of [archival subjects'] lifeworlds" by putting the historian in the position to reconstruct "a truth about a visitation by aliens . . . as a truth about transphobia."[96] Put another way, our decisions about how to narrate the madness of the transgender archive are ultimately decisions about who is granted epistemic authority, under what conditions, and to what effect.

While all identity knowledges must, arguably, navigate similar issues of securing authority in the face of "destructive forces," it is a particularly fraught terrain within trans studies. Given that transness has been (and continues to be) described in the language of psychiatric diagnosis, founding trans scholars' rhetorical claims to authority were tinged with anxiety. How, after all, does one stake a claim to know through a category that renders suspect one's knowledge about oneself and one's world? Put more plainly, the necessity to ward off uncertainty about the status of trans persons as "sane" has produced, within trans studies itself, a defensive position analogous to the one occupied by the *Renaissance News* piece, whose author seems fine with a strategic alliance with disability, so long as it does not contaminate transness with the taint of sickness—understandably so, since "medicine's definition of [trans] identity as an emotional disorder" allows trans speech to be "summarily dismissed as the confused ranting of a diseased mind."[97] Being caught in this frame, in other words, has the capacity to reduce trans claims to authority.

However understandable, the defensive position taken up by *Renaissance* and by academic trans study poses serious problems for trans thought. The defensive position with respect to the question of madness/disability hampers our ability to fully describe trans life and its archives; it interferes with the ability of trans studies to meaningfully interrelate with disability studies, despite the structural entanglement of crip, neurodivergent, and trans lives; and it reproduces (through displacement) the medicolegal regulation of rationality, personhood, and interpretative authority. Further, while the defensive position does produce all three of these effects, it also and primarily undercuts our ability to fully know *trans*. That is, if, in Cáel Keegan's words, transness "is rooted in the desire to make perceivable a feeling of gender that others have not (yet) witnessed" and so "describes an inherently subjunctive relationship to what is considered real, to what can commonly be sensed," then transness by definition unfolds unreasonable questions about what is true and how we know it.[98] At the very least, knowing from a trans position ought to obligate us to take seriously phenomena not (yet) witnessed, which *requires* taking seriously orders of sense and ways of knowing usually cordoned off as mad.

Put another way, Garland's potentially hysterical muteness is obviously not severable from their voluminous presence in the transgender archive, nor from their successful negotiation of nineteenth-century Anglo-American gender as "a terrain to make space for living," nor from the trans-antagonistic conditions in which that living unfolded.[99] Perhaps, then, rather than continuing to resist—implicitly and explicitly—"popular notions of transgender people as at once insane, tragic, and absurd," we ought to ask a different set of questions: Might insanity, tragedy, and absurdity be integral, rather than only inimical, to trans life and thought? What might we learn by thinking with, rather than against, the madness and maladjustment that is everywhere evident in trans-antagonistic and trans-affirmative archives alike? And how might a trans studies, accountable to the world- and knowledge-making force of the maladjusted, the bad, the mad, the painful, and the "peculiar elements" haunting the archive, otherwise unfold?[100]

Holding Space

In a 2013 performance installation titled *72 Hour Hold*, Dylan Scholinski built and then lived in a replica of a hospital seclusion room for four seventy-two-hour periods. During their inhabitation, Scholinski was confined not only by the walls of the handmade cell but also by the surveilling eye of a webcam that recorded all of their activities, save for what might have gone on in a slice of space just out of frame. While inside, Scholinski slept; made their bed; journaled; created a series of daily self-portraits; ate; drew on the white walls in pencil and in charcoal; offered limited visiting hours for "current, practicing, and/or student therapists, educators, and social workers to take advantage of his 30+ years of experience as a 'client'"; got a massage; erased their drawings and began again; constructed a sculpture of Styrofoam cups turned inside out, the cups, vinelike, branching up the wall.[1]

According to the documentation available on Scholinski's website, "this piece was originally developed in response to a quote 'the patient has no sense of home' from the personal hospital chart from when Dylan was institutionalized as a teenager" for four years under a diagnosis of gender identity disorder, which had, at the time, been newly entered into the DSM-3.[2] While inside the carceral space of the psychiatric ward, Scholinski was subject to all manner of sanctioned abuse in order to cure them of a disordered gender that was regarded as cause and consequence of their depression, lack of future orientation, and "impair[ed] . . . social functioning."[3] As a performance and archive that emerge from the fallout of the official codification of gender nonconformity as mental illness, then, there is much that one might say about trans maladjustment in relation to *72 Hour Hold* and its companion exhibition, *After-Wards: Possible Side Effects Include*. But here I've limited myself to a brief reflection on Scholinski's aesthetic practice of return and reenactment, an aesthetic practice that has, in part, guided my critical one.

FIGURE HS.1. The scene of Dylan Scholinski's *72 Hour Hold* (2013). Used with permission of the artist.

As a white, mad/trans memoirist and visual artist, Scholinski's work returns again and again to the traumatic scene of their childhood in the hospital, meditating on the dis/figuring and dis/embodying effects of ideological and physical confinement, of being, as they have put it, "removed from the world."[4] At the same time, in returning to these scenes, Scholinski is working in a long tradition of asylum art that insists simultaneously on psychiatric institutions as spaces of profound violence and dispossession *and* as places of life—of isolation *and* potential "community that would refuse to leave even the most unresponsive, the most difficult, and the loneliest people behind."[5] In the durational performance of *72 Hour Hold*, for example, Scholinski reinhabits their memory of the space of the hospital and, in so doing, remakes it into a place marked by the daily rhythms of living, forms of sociality, and creative activity. In fact, because the recorded performance occurred four times over the course of two months, one can witness the transformation of the empty holding space into a place increasingly dense with life; each time Scholinski returns to the scene, each time the performance begins again, they begin someplace where the work has already begun. In this way, Scholinski rebuffs the premise of the report that spurred their confinement not by locating home outside the formative scene of the hospital—of being forcibly given "a new identity" as "the sick one"—but rather by working on and in this fraught space, claiming it as something terribly akin to home, with all of the violence home often entails for queer, trans, and disabled/mad youth.[6]

Importantly, the fraught space that Scholinski reinhabits is both the experience of institutionalization and the discursive space of the gender identity disorder diagnosis, the codification of gender nonconformity as mental illness that facilitated their removal from the world. Many trans critiques of medical/psychiatric models of trans identity that attempt to put distance between trans identity and mental disability do so precisely because of these models' past and present capacity to justify subjecting trans populations to such violent forms of "care." As a consequence, such critiques have long relied on a methodological distancing from disability, a refusal to inhabit their historical, phenomenological, and political interrelations. In recent years, however, trans and disability studies scholars have increasingly inhabited this fraught space in order to ask after what disability/mad studies and politics might offer to trans studies/politics and vice versa.[7]

Eli Clare, for example, has written critically about the tendency of some trans people to conceptualize transness as a disability, insofar as they understand it to be a medical condition that should, therefore, guarantee access to health care, "a defect" to be cured.[8] Clare argues that this framing, which relies on a medical model of both trans identity and disability, profoundly misunderstands the social and political situation of disabled people. Further, it reinforces the very terms by which ableist oppression and "curative violence" are justified by rendering disability as a necessarily negative bodily/mental difference and "an individual medical problem curable, or at least treatable, by doctors" rather than a site of political struggle and cultural creativity.[9] But rather than view this as a reason for neatly separating transness from disability, Clare calls for "a disability politics of transness," one that would encourage a loosening of trans investment "in the ways we're medicalized."[10] Like a disability politics that rejects medical and state authorities' capacity to define disabled bodyminds and instead cultivates knowledge about disability "from the inside out," a disability politics of transness would begin from the reframing of the trans bodymind as not a defect but a site of self-determination, a "bodily difference [that is] neither good nor bad, but . . . profoundly *familiar*."[11] Ultimately, as he asserts in his later *Brilliant Imperfections: Grappling with Cure*, Clare's disability politics of transness "imagine[s] dismantling the DSM itself, discarding the concepts of *disorder* and *defect*, and developing other means of accessing medical technology beyond white Western diagnosis."[12]

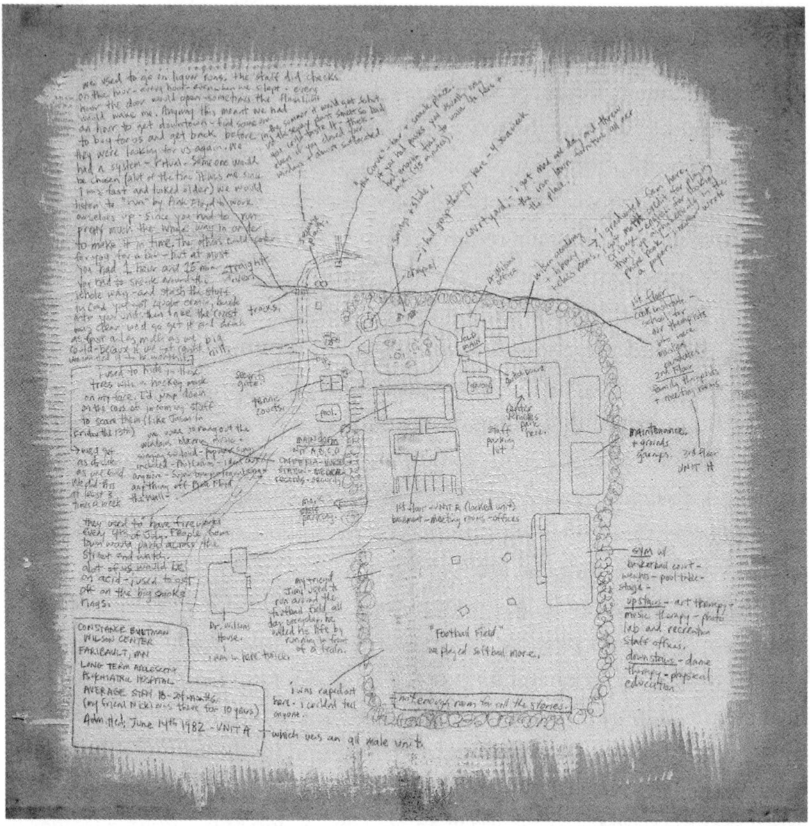

FIGURE HS.2. From Dylan Scholinski's *Home Sweet Home*, ca. 2009. Used with permission of the artist.

In some ways, Scholinski's aesthetic practice of return chafes against Clare's yearning toward an outside of diagnosis. Certainly, both are opposed to the pathologization of difference and the ideology of cure, but Clare's yearning and Scholinski's inhabitation are organized by different temporalities. Clare's thinking—here, at least—is future oriented, focused on how we might arrive at models of care and self-determination absent of violence, whereas Scholinski's work "feels backward" in its attempts to foreground and value the forms of creativity and knowledge they cultivated by being "crazy," including the skills they developed to bear their confinement (turning cups inside out and absorption in this task), insight into the workings of disciplinary power, and the particular ways in which they are "sensitive . . . to the world."[13] Scholinski's work, that is, puts forward a different mad/trans strategy, one of "living with damage in a damaged world."[14]

Scholinski's *Home Sweet Home* series, which consists of blueprint style images of spaces in which Scholinski has lived, exemplifies this aspect of their aesthetic practice. The images are full of text, meticulously labeled, as if to prove they had been there. At the same time, the drawings are uninhabited, empty of human bodies and other signs of domestic life. In their memoir, Scholinski describes drawing this series: "When I am drawing it is as if I am back in those rooms. But the wonder of it is, I'm looking down from above. All that practice in leaving my body has given me an aerial perspective."[15] In these retrospective drawings, Scholinski finds that dissociation—once a mechanism for surviving confinement, sexual abuse, and dysphoria—becomes a formal resource, a perspective from which to theorize, a strategy for "work[ing] the trap that one is inevitably in."[16]

While *The Terrible We* would not have been thinkable without the work of Eli Clare, Alexandre Baril, Marty Fink, A. J. Withers and so many others who call for and offer tools toward the assembly of a disability politics and analysis of trans life, this book should not be understood as an attempt to answer their call. *The Terrible We* is not a disability studies approach to transness, nor is it a book *about* the overlapping experiences of transness and disability/madness, though it insists on that overlap. Rather, it is a book that attempts to hold on to certain tools from disability studies—among other fields—in order to open trans studies itself up to different critical protocols. It is the record of my attempt to read with the forms of madness, distress, and maladjustment that are already endemic to trans literature and thought, to understand what they have enabled and might yet. As such, each remaining chapter does what Scholinski's *Home Sweet Home* and *72 Hour Hold* suggests by returning to a familiar, confining place using an officially deauthorizing but utterly familiar habit of feeling and mind. In particular, each chapter fixates on a figure of trans maladjustment that has been used to delegitimize trans[masculine] manifestation and puts them at the center of my reading practice. I do so, in part, to ask what these disavowed figures might help me to know about the impasses and unresolved conflicts that arise from *trans*'s institutionalization within and against women's/feminist studies and, to a lesser extent, queer theory, one aspect of the trap in which trans studies is inevitably caught.

Finally, and crucially, these forms of institutionalization—within the psych ward, within the university—name profoundly different situations. For that reason, the chapters that follow might seem to abruptly depart from, miss, or obscure the point—the real urgency of crip/trans coalitions in confronting the ongoing (if reorganized) life of the prison, the asylum, the clinic, and the epistemically violent media ecosystem that collude to snuff out, exploit, and limit trans/crip flourishing. In this context, my preoccupation with disputes between various trans/feminist/queer scholars and other writers might seem to be at best an indulgence and at worst a willful overlooking of the material realities of trans, mad, disabled, and otherwise minoritized forms of life. Certainly, to some extent, this is true. However, it is also plainly true that the university is itself a death-dealing institution, one with the power to extend or withhold resources from—and to discipline, exploit, and constrain the imaginations of—those within and without it, along predictable racial, ability, class, and gender lines. Also, and more to the point, certain forms of knowledge produced about transness within the women's studies departments, in which trans studies scholars now find ourselves, directly participated in producing the situation in which Scholinski and other trans youth found (and still find) themselves. More concretely, a year before the teen Scholinski was incarcerated in the hospital and subjected to conversion therapy, anti-trans feminist Janice Raymond—among the first tenure-line faculty members hired to teach in the Women, Gender, Sexuality Studies Department where I am currently employed—was writing a paper commissioned by the National Center for Health Care Technology.[17] Insofar as Raymond's opposition to trans medicine was couched in a larger opposition to the psychomedical disciplining of gender, she might have been opposed to Scholinski's treatment. And yet, the knowledge about transness that Raymond produced was put to use, then and now, in service of the ongoing project of "morally mandating [trans manifestation] out of existence" (via the withdrawal of public funding and support, the reduction of options for care, and intervention into youth's gendered educations) and of rationalizing this project as feminist.[18]

2

Trans, Feminism; Or, Reading like a Depressed Transsexual

In October 2014, the *New York Times Magazine* ran a cover story that positioned a group of transgender men at Wellesley College as a case study for thinking through how women's colleges have and ought to respond to "the trans question."[1] Should trans men occupy leadership roles on campus, or is this a reassertion of male dominance? Do transmasculine students' requests to be recognized within the school's imagined community—by, for example, changing the language of "sisterhood" to "siblinghood"—detract from the feminist ethos of the institution? Should students who do not identify themselves as women be allowed to gain entry to/remain in women's colleges at all? Although the debate about the place of trans people in historically women's institutions has had a long and multisited life, anxiety about trans men in women's colleges erupted in the second decade of the twenty-first century. Further, because of the history (and present) of the figure of the trans woman being central to such debates, what was notable about this iteration was the explicit focus on trans men, as men, as a problem. An institutional problem, to be sure, but also a problem for delimiting spaces marked as feminist more broadly. Are such spaces for all people marginalized by gender? Are they spaces for women? If so, what is a woman? On and on.

Trans and *feminism*, it seems, are caught in a continually reiterated conflict, driven by the search for an integrated theory of gender that is undermined by the political desires of each. That is, what was interesting, to me, about this article and similar conversations about transgender men in historically female colleges was neither the content of them nor the solutions that institutions came to, but rather their dramatization of the simultaneous promise and limit of what Robyn Wiegman calls "identity knowledges."[2] Wiegman's *Object Lessons* is interested in precisely this "conundrum" that follows from the desire for social justice, which propels us to endlessly reach for the "right discourse, object of study, or analytic tool" that will make our "critical practice . . . adequate to the political commitments that inspire it."[3] This commitment to the political differentiates "identity knowledges" from other fields, as adequate knowledge tends to be that which produces (forms of) social justice, often premised on the affirmation of the objects of knowledge as legitimate objects, legitimate producers of knowledge, legitimate modes of life, and, particularly, good ways of life. Focusing, in particular, on how transmasculinity has increasingly posed an un- or misrecognized problem for imagining trans-inclusive feminisms, this chapter suggests that work in trans studies and feminist studies—as well as mainstream accounts that claim these names—dramatizes the promise and limits of the obligation to do justice in these terms. However, rather than seeking new terms of resolution, I excavate the depressed transsexual as a position from which to think through living with the lack of trans(masculine) feminist integration, even if it does not feel good.

From the outset, it must be said that this chapter began its life in 2015 and was first published as an article in 2017. In the time between then and now, the mainstream resurgence of trans-exclusionary feminisms—or perhaps more accurately of transmisogyny under the guise of feminist concern—has moved from being a possibility that this chapter sensed on the horizon to an all-too-obvious fact. In turn, many of the things I had to actively argue in order to first write the chapter seem, now, utterly obvious. Among these now-unremarkable claims are that transmasculinity would become less peripheral to the rhetoric of trans exclusion and that we ought to pay attention to the force such rhetoric has and will exert in shaping the conditions of post-tipping-point trans life. While I have revised this chapter slightly from its article form, I've left intact its basic argumentative force, despite the fact that it is clearly speaking to and from a different time. After all, part of my point was that if the conflicted history of trans/feminism tells us anything, it is that times recur, so it might, therefore, be worthwhile to develop tools for bearing their recurrence.

* * *

My title is an evocation of an evocation: I am referencing Henry Rubin's "Reading like a (Transsexual) Man," which in turn gestures to a flurry of scholarship in the 1980s in which literary critics debated the politics and possibility of men reading "like (or as) women."[4] Like mine, Rubin's essay builds on this conversation about a kind of transgendered reading to ask after the relationship between transmasculinity and feminism. However, implicitly, I also invoke *reading* in the sense of queer/woman of color vernacular: the art of in-group critique, a practice of imaginative insult that both signifies and produces a shared world. In this spirit of reading, I linger on Rubin's essay both because it has made mine possible and because it illustrates the odd narrative tangle that attends a transmasculinity that desires to be feminist but that, because of the imperative of affirmation, disavows girlhood. In Rubin's case, this disavowal is relatively benign, but when carried through to the logical limit, transmasculine projects that disavow their attachments to girlhood tend to reproduce and reinforce m > f.[5]

In particular, Rubin's essay relies on the "hegemonic narrative construction of transsexuals" (*I always knew I was a boy*) at the same time that it works to model counterhegemonic, feminist transmasculinities.[6] For example, in order to debunk a narrative that grants trans men feminist status due to the shared experience of female embodiment, Rubin invokes the hegemonic trans narrative to insist that they never were women or girls and because of this "do not interpret their bodies like other female-bodied people. Instead transsexuals develop subjectivities that are specifically transgendered."[7] Therefore, experiences that might seem "eminently female" are interpreted through these trans subjectivities, leading to different outcomes. Rubin provides the example of a woman who encounters a stranger while walking alone at night and crosses to the lit side of the street to make herself less vulnerable to attack. According to Rubin, a trans man in the same situation would cross to the darker side of the street to avoid detection as gender nonconforming. While perfectly reasonable, to use this as a definitive example of "same bodies, different vulnerabilities, different courses of action" requires a series of disavowals of what constitutes transmasculine life history.[8] There is no space in Rubin's account for a transmasculine person who presents as a woman or girl, whose movements are conditioned by his once appearing to be a girl, who might want to cruise said stranger, whose racialization might decrease the salience of gendered threat in this scenario, and so on. Furthermore, although Rubin relies heavily on autobiographical evidence, he includes no scenes from before he went to college. Part of what allows Rubin to stick to the narrative of never having been something like a girl, it seems, is an impossible narrative of having never been a child.

Of course, the hegemonic construction is not the only available trans narrative. In fact, in an essay collected with Rubin's in *Men Doing Feminism* that also theorizes the relation between transmasculinity and feminism, C. Jacob Hale assumes that trans men "have lived parts of our lives as girls and as women."[9] Rather than trying to produce a coherent subject by means of narrative, he locates the source of incoherence in the linguistic structures in which narrative must be produced. To make this point, Hale offers a scene in which his father cannot find a way to tell a story about Hale as a child: "When Jake was a little boy . . . , I mean a little girl . . . , I mean a little child . . . , he . . . , I mean she . . . , I mean . . . , I don't know what I mean!"[10] While Rubin smooths over these narrative stumbling blocks, in Hale's essay, rather than being denied or displaced, the girl lives on as a "ghostly memory in [his] throat."

Here is where the unaccounted-for term, *depressed*, comes into play. Hale's ghost behaves remarkably like the not-quite-lost object incorporated into the ego of the Freudian melancholic: "the shadow" of the girl, that abandoned object that both is and is not the self, "[falls] upon the ego," leaving both open to scrutiny.[11] Importantly, a certain level of ambivalence toward the object defines both cases, and both Hale and Freud grant this condition an epistemological usefulness. In "Mourning and Melancholia," Freud wonders why "a man has to be ill" in order to develop a "keener eye for the truth" about himself.[12] Likewise, Hale develops the ghost metaphor through María Lugones's concept of world traveling, arguing that transmasculine people flit along the borders of multiple gendered worlds, which grants them a "better epistemological subject position . . . to engage this task of re-creating manhood."[13] Furthermore, while Hale does not use the language of melancholia, he does describe this better epistemological position as being necessarily linked to the "anguish" of unintelligibility.[14]

While I have no intentions of performing a Freudian reading of transmasculinity or even continuing this Freudian reading of Hale, I am taking the similarities between Hale's haunted transsexual and Freud's melancholic as an invitation. Hale has written the guide on how to do trans studies without replicating the structures that for so long rendered trans people mute objects of pathologizing discourses.[15] And yet, here, by figuring the trans body as haunted—and painfully so—Hale risks an association with what has been considered a pathological psychic process in order to produce a different kind of narrative ethics in order to produce a point of attachment between transmasculine lives and the production of feminist knowledge.

Likewise, in *Assuming a Body*, Gayle Salamon argues that the insistence on presocial, internal gender that Rubin's hegemonic narrative relies on denies the profoundly social and relational nature of the process by which all people come to have a body and a self. Although she approaches the issue tentatively and obliquely, it would seem that, for her, the high stakes of re-embedding the trans body in its social world have to do, in part, with the troubling status of the feminine within transmasculine discourse. During the course of a reading of Griffin Hansbury's article "The Middle Men: An Introduction to the Transmasculine Identities," Salamon observes: "It reads as significant that the structural positions occupied by the feminine in this text are quite limited. The feminine others that appear here—the lesbian partner of the butch who forbids transition and the homo- and transphobic straight-identified partner of the woodworker—are figures of denial and negation. . . . Does the voice of the other, particularly the feminine other, always only say no, replace a true identity with the prescription of a false one, hinder transition or threaten to leave because of it?"[16] Salamon worries that, although accounts like Hansbury's demonstrate differences among transmasculine identities—debunking the assumption that transition is always motivated by an aspiration to a single, heteronormative ideal—they do so by merely displacing sameness. Difference among transmasculinities, that is, appears most clearly in homosocial contexts that rely on the evasion or disavowal of the feminine other, whose own desire for self-identity threatens the transmasculine self with annihilation.[17] Thus, Salamon leaves us with a provocative question about transmasculine narratives that require the appearance of a stable self: "If the goal is to achieve a stable and enduring sense of self-identity, is there room for a transmasculine subject to encounter the other's desire without evacuating or annihilating it? Or feeling evacuated or annihilated by it in turn?"[18]

Annihilation, in Salamon's account, seems most nearly to mean a destruction of the self via having one's identity denied or substituted for another from the outside. In taking up Salamon's question, I also take up her psychoanalytic language of annihilation. However, while my use retains her meaning, it also includes the bad feelings and potential life-or-death consequences that attend being the object of this denial. Consequently, the term is slippery. While these meanings often work in concert with each other to limit some people's life chances, sometimes they do not. Hale's haunted trans person models one way of productively thinking from within the feeling of annihilation. However, although grounding feminist transmasculine discourse in a model of trans melancholia may provide a way to avoid relying on "a closed circuit of identity that runs the risk of eliding or evading difference rather than engaging with it," it is unclear how melancholia, if it is the inescapable process of ego formation by which the (trans) self is made, could be a position one can take up vis-à-vis the contest between (feminine) desire and (stable, transmasculine) identity.[19]

My use of *depressed*, then, bears some relation to Eve Kosofsky Sedgwick's use of Melanie Klein's *depressive position* insofar as it names a particular form of feeling and habit of thought that informs interpretive practice.[20] However, the depressed transsexual is specific to my interrogation, as they are a figure that emerges from the trans archive and against which many projects of trans-affirmative thought have been staged. That is, *depression* also marks this project's attachment to the field of disability studies. The preceding chapter explicitly theorized the attachments between transgender and disability as social/historical categories and sites of activism. Here, however, I am motivated by taking seriously a set of challenges that newer trajectories in disability studies—especially those that have, themselves, sought to address the disavowal of pain, (bad) feelings, and madness within disability studies—have issued to the desires animating identity knowledges in general and trans studies in particular.

For example, in *Disability Theory*, Tobin Siebers argues that much existing theory fails to adequately account for pain. Pain, according to Siebers, is theorized as either regulatory or resistant, a blunt effect of power or, otherwise, a resource for reconfiguring the body and its pleasures; it is never figured as an ordinary, albeit unpleasant, fact of being embodied.[21] His pursuit of theory that can account for the persistence of pain that does not give way to pleasure, that is certainly exacerbated by structural or ideological conditions but would exist nonetheless, is provocative largely because it requires rethinking what our commitments to our objects of study might actually be. What would it mean to do minoritarian studies without being driven by the desire to rehabilitate the subjects/objects of our knowledge? What kind of theories would we produce if we noticed pain and, rather than automatically seeking out its source in order to alleviate it or mining it for resources for perverse or resistant pleasures, we instead took it as a fact of being embodied that is not *necessarily* loaded with moral weight?

Although Siebers takes particular aim at queer theory—represented for him by Judith Butler and Leo Bersani—by foregrounding the "reality" of pain and the way that reality contravenes certain protocols of theorizing, Siebers should also be understood to be intervening in disability studies itself, which has long tended to contest the social devaluation of disabled people by foregrounding disability as a positive identity, a desirable condition, a fecund location of sociality and cultural production, and so on.[22] However, for the past decade or two, many scholars working in queer and feminist disability studies have also insisted that disavowing pain, distress, suffering, and debility narrows the range of questions that disability studies can ask and tends to (re)install a particular figure—white, cis, "healthy disabled," male—at the heart of the field.[23] And unlike Siebers, many of these scholars—Anna Mollow, Margaret Price, Alison Kafer, Mel Y. Chen, Alexandre Baril, and Merri Lisa Johnson among them—have asked the question "what shall we do with pain?" in order to admit the mental, the cognitive, and the emotional as proper subjects of the field.[24]

That is, the increasing salience of bad feelings to disability studies has coincided with an attempt to redress the fact that mental disability, madness, and/or mental illness have appeared much less frequently as primary lines of inquiry. One exception, Lennard J. Davis's chapter on "Depression and Disability," might offer some insight into why much early disability studies scholarship seemed to have such a hard time with bad feelings. Davis's essay performs a reading that spars with the medical model that defines depression as a biochemical imbalance to be corrected and insists instead that what is disabling about depression is a neoliberal society in which membership is premised on productivity and positive affect. Ultimately, Davis insists that reimagining depression outside of the medical model offers an empowering political stance to be taken up and that this stance will offer one route "out of the abyss" of acute sadness and despair.[25]

Herein lies the complication that things like depression pose to the emotional habitus that structures much work in disability studies. Davis is motivated to write this essay out of a deep suspicion of the "overcoming" narratives in popular depression memoirs and pharmaceutical commercials but, in the end, offers the disability studies model of depression as a possible route to, well, overcoming depression: "While I don't want to downplay the difficulties and pain of acute sadness and despair, and I don't want to minimize the pain and difficulty of having impairments in general, the overall message of disability studies is that there is a bright side, a very bright side, to being a person with a disability. Why cannot we shine that brightness onto the darkness of depression?"[26] Davis explicitly separates the "problems" and "bright sides" of impairment, where the problems are related to pain and difficulty and the bright sides are related to the modes of knowledge and relation that any given impairment make possible. But what if these two sides are not obviously separable? While Davis would certainly acknowledge that the two can never be separated in practice, depression marks a limit case for theory that depends on their separability. As Margaret Price asks of Davis during the course of a "Proliferating Cripistemologies" roundtable: "What do we do with depression? With panic attacks and borderline breaks? How do we desire disability when the condition in question is itself composed of pain?"[27] After all, depression fundamentally is feeling bad.

While Davis ultimately rehabilitates the depressive using the social model, it would seem that any value of a politicized depressive identity will require a different kind of orientation to bad feelings, one that lets "depression linger, [in order] to explore the feeling of remaining or resting in sadness without insisting that it be transformed" into hope or pride "or reconceived."[28] Developing such an orientation is no simple task because, of course, bad feelings are produced and exacerbated by social structures, and one must be able to attend to this. But also, one must expect that there will always be a residue of bad feeling, an unavoidable fact of being embodied, of being a self in a world inevitably split by difference. To read like a depressed transsexual, then, is to read from a position both committed to the idea that trans lives are "lived, hence livable" while also taking feeling bad as sometimes a mundane fact.[29] In particular, it relies on the depressive's habit of self-effacement and reproach, and knowledge of the fundamental fleetingness of self-sameness. These habits of thought are best exemplified in moments of transition, as in Andrew Solomon's question about the stability of his self after his first major depression, "What if tomorrow I wake up and I am not myself but a manure beetle?" Or poet Jane Kenyon's portrait of herself entering a depressive episode: "A piece of burned meat / wears my clothes, speaks / in my voice."[30]

Importantly, then, what follows is not about depression but rather makes use of it. In doing so, it risks using depression as a metaphor in a way that is reminiscent of earlier feminist uses of the figure of the madwoman.[31] However, I would stress that depression is resolutely not a metaphor for the conditions of trans life but rather a set of habits of thought and feeling that are endemic to it. And while I could set out to argue that trans depression is, at least in part, the product of life under trans-antagonism, racial capitalism, and so on (which it is), the chapter instead asks what reading with depressive habits of feeling and mind might reveal about the discourses and conditions that produce them. In this case, the depressing condition is the mainstream and academic circulation of trans-antagonism under the guise of feminist concern and the sense of living and thinking in the impasse that this circulation creates.

As Ann Cvetkovich remarks, "With its spatial connotations of being at a 'dead end' or 'no exit,' impasse captures the notion of depression as a state of being 'stuck,' of not being able to figure out what to do or why to do it."[32] Depressive reading, that is, has something in particular to say about what to do in an impasse, how to bear—or not bear—being stuck. Thus, the next section returns to the scene of transmasculinity and feminism by rehearsing an often-told story about the persistent conflict between trans and (a certain form of lesbian/radical) feminist theory, activism, and communities. In doing so, I ask what might be made possible by regarding the explicitly annihilatory portrayals of trans people in trans-exclusionary feminism and responding, "Yes, that is me. So what?"

Gender Hurts: "The TERF Wars"

> Discussions of political depression emerge from the necessity of finding ways to survive disappointment and to remind ourselves of the persistence of radical visions and ways of living. Rather than a paranoid watch for how forms of resistance are ultimately co-opted, it's more about noticing and describing the places where it feels like there is something else happening, and passing on strategies for survival. Survival also involves developing a higher tolerance for the conflicts that political life invariably produces—such as those between lesbian separatist and trans communities, gay marriage and antimarriage camps, or antisocial and utopian tendencies—so that groups don't implode or splinter into factions. —Ann Cvetkovich, ***DEPRESSION: A PUBLIC FEELING (2012)***

Ann Cvetkovich's *Depression: A Public Feeling* is largely driven by the keyword *survival*: how might refashioning our everyday lives, Cvetkovich asks, help us (queers, women, people of color, the Left) survive the bad feelings engendered by the violent past and the violent/disappointing present so that we can continue to dream of and work toward radical futures? What is being survived in the world of this book ranges from neoliberal subjectivity to political disappointments to writing a dissertation to the legacy of American colonialism and antiblackness. It's striking, though, how very different these situations are. While the demands of neoliberal subjectivity may not feel good, they depend on the continued existence of the subject on whom the impossible demands of productive citizenship are made. The legacy of American colonialism/antiblackness, however, is explicitly genocidal. Likewise, the kinds of conflict between "antisocial and utopian tendencies" and "lesbian separatist and trans communities" are profoundly different.[33] In the first, what is being survived is primarily an academic dispute that seems, in the end, somewhat disconnected from the material urgencies of survival. In the second—and as the rise of coordinated, state-level, anti-trans legislation in 2015–21 that often justifies itself using the idiom and talking points of "feminism" has made clear—what is at stake is the social existence of a category of people.

The stakes of the "conflicts . . . between lesbian separatist and trans communities" is perhaps best demonstrated by the conflict surrounding the publication of Janice Raymond's *The Transsexual Empire: The Making of the She-Male*. While Raymond was not the first to critique transsexuality in the name of feminism, her work has had significant effects on our cultural landscape insofar as it authorized transphobia using the idiom of feminism. For example, taken to be an expert, Raymond provided an evaluation of the social and ethical aspects of transsexuality that was used in the writing of a 1981 National Center for Health Care Technology report on transsexual surgery, which later became the basis of a national coverage determination (NCD) that officially made transsexual surgery ineligible for coverage from public insurance, a decision whose grounds did not come under investigation until 2013.[34] Thus, the amenability of Raymond's stance—what has since come to be imprecisely known by its opponents as trans-exclusionary radical feminism (TERF) to government policy contributed to a decades-long legal exclusion of trans health care from public insurance, inevitably leading to shortened life spans among trans people who were and are disproportionately impoverished. Because this history animates feminist/trans conflict—and provides the talking points for right-wing attacks on trans women and youth—in the present, trans communities look at the persistence of TERF discourse and correctly feel that our "living space is threatened."[35]

However, precisely because my aims diverge from Cvetkovich's in that I am less interested in how knowing depression differently might offer insight into how to survive the present, and more interested in how the habits of thought and feeling associated with depression might allow us to live together, I find Cvetkovich's flattening of the scales of conflict charming. It implies that, somehow, trans-exclusionary lesbian separatists and trans communities are always already part of a group that is at risk of splintering. What kind of group might that be? What might it mean to be in a group where some of the members are actively trying to make your very existence impossible? How does such a group hang together? Of course, the assumed and actual existence of such an unlikely group has been a condition of trans studies from its very beginning: nowhere else does separatist feminism so frequently stand in for what feminism *is*.

So, the story.[36] *The Transsexual Empire* was first published in 1979 and re-released in 1994 with a new preface that tried to account for transmasculinity and transgender politics. Three years before the initial book, Raymond sent a draft of what would become the fourth chapter of the finished monograph, titled "Sappho by Surgery: The Transsexually Constructed Lesbian Feminist," to the Olivia Women's Music Collective, which had, for two years, included trans woman Sandy Stone as their sound engineer. Olivia responded by denouncing Raymond's account of trans women in general and her depiction of Stone's effect on the collective in particular. Raymond published the chapter anyway, which resulted in the Olivia Collective coming under scrutiny and, ultimately, in Stone's departure from it. In the years following, Stone entered the doctoral program in the History of Consciousness at the University of California, Santa Cruz, and, during that time, penned "The *Empire* Strikes Back: A Posttranssexual Manifesto," which acted simultaneously as a direct response to Raymond and as a call for a transsexual counterdiscourse.

Stone's essay set the initial terms, goals, and methods of trans studies. In her vision, telling authentic stories about trans lives would allow us to move beyond the terms of binary gender that structured feminist and medicolegal discourse in a way that would not only do justice to trans experience but would also "make common cause with other oppositional discourses."[37] For Stone, affirming and representing the messy reality of trans lives necessitated a split from feminism that would, in the future, eventually be healed. Trans studies has continued to emerge through repeated performances of splitting from feminism, each time necessarily reasserting the prior existence of a group, often by staging a kind of family drama. For example, in a 2004 special issue of *GLQ*, Susan Stryker writes, "If queer theory was born of the union of sexuality studies and feminism, transgender studies can be considered queer theory's evil twin: it has the same parentage but willfully disrupts the privileged family narratives."[38]

Trans studies, or so this story goes, began in response to a particularly vicious, academically sanctioned expression of transphobic feminism that was then the "definitive statement on transsexualism by a genetic female academic."[39] Although this is no longer true, conflict between a form of "feminism" that relies on logic identical to Raymond's and a trans community that no longer exactly resembles the one Raymond levied her critiques against still animates popular and academic discourse about trans lives. In general, such arguments set out to demonstrate that trans lives, narratives, and practices are harmful to the goals of feminism insofar as they re-entrench *gender*—as a system of power and norms in which *woman* is the subordinate term—rather than subvert it. They tend to express "sympathy" for the transsexuals they study while, at the same time, advancing arguments aimed at eliminating trans health care, social support structures, and participation in the public sphere. Finally, such arguments rely for their emotional coherence on a rendering of *trans* as a particularly abject category of person. That is, they emphasize associations of trans life with pain, suffering, suicidality, (self) duplicity, and so on, in part to forward the claim that the research they are doing is important for trans people who, after all, represent a category of person that no one wants to be. In their accounts, feminist consciousness, on their terms, (not health care, employment, a living wage, social dignity, etc.) is the only way to alleviate the suffering of the trans person, which is produced by the fiction of gender itself, a fiction by which trans people are "dupe[d]" and through which feminism allows its author to see.[40]

The centrality of pain to the terms of this conflict is nowhere more apparent than in the flurry of activity surrounding the aptly titled *Gender Hurts: A Feminist Analysis of Transgenderism* by Sheila Jeffreys, a professor of feminist politics at the University of Melbourne. Just months after the book's publication, for instance, the *New Yorker* published an article titled "What Is a Woman? The Dispute between Radical Feminism and Transgenderism."[41] The author, Michelle Goldberg, was subsequently criticized for being too sympathetic to the TERF argument in that she failed to incorporate the reality of systemic violence against trans people (trans women in particular), refusing to incorporate stories of TERF harassment of trans women (but including instances of harassment in the other direction), and including outdated theories about the etiology of trans womanhood without also citing the counterarguments.[42]

While these critiques get at the transmisogyny of Goldberg's article, what strikes me is the disjuncture between the overt terms of the article and what Goldberg claims is actually at stake. In a supplementary podcast, Goldberg focuses on the voice of Alison Turkos, who ostensibly stands in as the representative young, non-TERF, nontrans feminist. Turkos is cochair of the New York Abortion Access Fund, a reproductive justice group that helps to provide access to abortions to those who cannot afford them.[43] "In May," Goldberg writes, the group "voted unanimously to stop using the word 'women' when talking about people who get pregnant, so as not to exclude trans men."[44] In the podcast, Goldberg explains that this shift in language is what really troubles her about contemporary trans-inclusive feminisms; in order to be on "the right side of history," young feminists are increasingly refusing to refer to their work as being for women.[45] This is the one point on which Goldberg and her correspondent, Margaret Talbot, emphatically agree. For both, to imagine reproductive justice activism, especially access to abortion, as for anyone but women is simply to deny reality in ways that are simultaneously "silly" and concerning.[46]

Here, then, is evidence of the limitations of collapsing transfeminine and transmasculine subjects under the sign of *trans*. At present, what is at stake when Goldberg and others insist on "reality" tends to be not only whether trans women are women but also how to understand the relationship between trans men and womanhood—and, implicitly, feminism—given that the precise arguments TERFs have used to justify excluding trans women would require them to include trans men. As the prominence and visibility of transmasculinities have steadily increased, contemporary feminisms have had to grapple with this incoherence. Still, many conversations about the tense relationship between *trans* and *feminism* continue to focus solely on how some forms of feminism—even those that are less overt about their reliance on biologically essentialist notions of sex/gender—fail trans women in particular. In doing so, however, we miss the way that transmasculinities have, beneath the surface, increasingly become a problem for imagining trans-inclusive feminisms, generating an anxiety that, in turn, reinforces the hypervisibility of trans women. That is, this article is evidence of the way that anxiety about transmasculine displacement of *women* as the imagined subject of feminism creates a feeling of bafflement that allows the TERF position to seem more closely aligned with reality. What Goldberg's informant, Turkos, calls the "discomfort" of incorporating nonwomen (and "women" in their account always means cis women) into reproductive rights feminism, Goldberg and Talbot experience as a kind of annihilation. It is this movement from baffled to threatened that allows Jeffreys to enter the scene as "a sympathetic, if eccentric, character" from whom young feminists might learn a thing or two about the reality of gender.[47] However, despite the fact that Jeffreys's book focuses explicit attention on the question of transmasculinity, I don't think her answers would leave Goldberg any less baffled, as Jeffreys seems to argue that, while it is true that trans men seem to be displacing women, trans men actually need feminism more than women do.

Jeffreys's argument is basically that, well, gender hurts. Because Jeffreys sees (masculine) power as utterly productive of the social world, gender simply is "the foundation of the political system of male domination."[48] "Transgenderism," claims Jeffreys, relies on an idea of gender that strips it of its function as a structure of power that subordinates one kind of body (f) to another (m), and the trans/queer insistence on gender transitivity and fluidity "disappears the fixedness of sex."[49] Because gender is always and only an expression of power, her explanation for transmasculinity has to do with the ongoingness of female (particularly lesbian) oppression, wherein transmasculinity is a side effect of the inability to cope with the pain of being female in a situation of m > f.

This is, I must admit, a generous reading of Jeffreys. *Gender Hurts* certainly does follow Raymond in making trans people out to be depressed, isolated, hyperlibidinous, narcissistic dupes. In her work, whenever Jeffreys encounters trans people, transmasculine people in particular, she is flooded with bad feelings—she is horrified by what the patriarchy dupes us into doing to our bodies, or she sees us and grieves the loss of a lesbian. Bad feelings produced by gendered oppression are also at the heart of her explanation of the etiology of transmasculinity. Not only does Jeffreys understand the trans man as the product of the mismanaged pain of the lesbian, she also repeatedly suggests that transmasculinity is a direct response to sexual trauma. While I by no means condone Jeffreys's arguments, my reading practice requires this generosity insofar as it requires being willing to lean into worldviews that might be hostile to my very life—to think in the feeling of annihilation, as it were. Additionally, and importantly, there is a tendency within trans-affirmative discourse to dismiss these forms of feminism outright, as outdated or merely hateful screeds based on bad science. Certainly, they are, and yet they persist and continue to structure mainstream representations of—and litigation around—trans life. For this reason, it seems to me that some of us too must take them seriously in order to properly understand the appeal.

Further, Jeffreys's rhetorical traffic in pain also works the other way around. For instance, Goldberg closes her article by quoting Sandy Stone in a way that adds to the overall sense of the TERFS as sympathetic: "Of the radical feminists' position, [Stone] says, 'It's my personal belief, from speaking to some of these people at length, that it comes from having been subject to serious trauma at the hands of some man, or multiple men.' She adds, 'You have to respect that. That's their experience of the world.' But the pain of radical feminists, she insists, can't trump trans rights."[50] Although Goldberg positions Stone's comment as a concession, it is also possible to read it as analogous to Jeffreys's repeated suggestions that transmasculine identity is a product of trauma. A worldview produced by trauma, in both cases, is one that is understandable but not, in the end, of any epistemic value. Feeling bad, they seem to say, obscures rather than clarifies, produces unreliable knowledge about the world. Curious. We seem to have found ourselves in familiar territory. You depressed transsexual. You traumatized white woman. You angry black woman. You melancholic homosexual. How can we possibly take seriously what it is you think you know?

When Salamon asks after the ability of a stable transmasculine identity to encounter the desire of the feminine other without either party being annihilated in the process, her examples of this other—the lesbian partner, the straight partner—suggest that she is asking after lived encounters between trans men and cis women. But because she is ultimately interested in trans-inclusive articulations of feminism and women's studies, Salamon's question is also relevant to the production of academic knowledge. Is it possible, she seems to ask, for lesbian feminist and transmasculine discourses to be in relation—say, housed within the same department—without annihilating each other? The encounter between Jeffreys and transmasculinity would seem to suggest no. Her grief and horror at transmasculinity mark, as Clare Hemmings has put it, "the extent of what can be incorporated within a feminist narrative of which she is to remain a coherent subject."[51] It's quite clear that for Jeffreys to recognize transmasculine discourse within her worldview would require her own annihilation as a feminist subject. And while Jeffreys is certainly not a representative lesbian feminist, even those who hold her up as an example of what they resolutely are not are similarly worried about the displacement of f (lesbian, femininity, femme) by m (gay male, masculinity, transmasculine) under the sign of *queer*. After all, doesn't Salamon ask the question because she is worried the answer might be no, even if she would like to think it is not?

Likewise, this threat of annihilation drives the split of trans and feminist thinking when Stone urges transsexuals to write themselves into existence in the face of medicolegal and feminist discourse that empties *trans* of its lived experience, a split that is continuously repeated in the story trans studies tells about its formation. Perhaps, then, a revision to Salamon's question is in order. Not, can trans and feminism engage without threatening the subjects arrayed underneath each with the feeling of annihilation, but is this feeling equivalent to actually being annihilated? Does the bad feeling that attends the relation necessarily negate it or render it always and only harmful? After all, reading like a depressed transsexual makes this possibility of annihilation much less, well, threatening. Put bluntly, one real tension in depression is that while the depressed person might not want to keep on existing (at all or, at least, as the version of themselves within a depressive episode), many do. The depressed transsexual, then, might assess this situation and determine that the problem is not so much that some feminists would like him gone. Rather, the problem is that he is here, and now we all have to figure out how to live with that.

Bobby Noble says something to this effect in his essay "Trans. Panic. Some Thoughts toward a Theory of Feminist Fundamentalism." His argument is that "*trans* bodies have always been present in feminism as a social movement, even as those bodies have been ghosted by a belief that such bodies have never been a part of feminism or women's studies" and that responses to trans bodies like those mentioned above—*what about (cis) women, what about (cis) lesbians*—are evidence of a kind of feminist fundamentalism, an unwillingness and resulting inability to reckon with the trans ghosts haunting her house.[52] I want to leave this here as an example of what I do not mean when I say that perhaps the first step in learning to live with each other is to recognize that bad feelings go both ways. I do not mean that of course trans studies will seem antagonistic to feminism as it is what has been ghosted and it is very rare to find a friendly ghost in your attic. This move, it seems, does little more than lift the mask of epistemological innocence from feminist studies and project it onto trans studies. And Noble, I'm certain, knows this, which is why he argues for an understanding of *trans* that isn't reducible to cross-gender identification or embodied gender nonnormativity. Instead, *trans* names a project of undoing (gender, disciplines, selves), a project that cannot be haunted because it never tries to build a house. Except, as Noble also knows, in practice the self—his self in fact—is resistant to being undone. For example, in the course of his argument, Noble suggests that his own women's studies department is guilty of such feminist fundamentalism, as evidenced by its exclusive use of she/her pronouns in its materials, despite his presence on the faculty. But what is this desire for language other than the desire of the self to be recognized? And doesn't asking that this desire be filled inevitably produce and then deny its own ghosts?

In particular, one familiar ghost emerges from reading Noble and Jack Halberstam, to whom Noble's work is indebted. In contrast to formulations like Jeffreys's, Jack Halberstam's *Female Masculinity* sets out to investigate female masculinities as distinct genders with their own histories rather than as (potentially pathological) imitations of maleness. Further, Halberstam argues, "If what we call 'dominant masculinity' appears to be a naturalized relation between maleness and power, then it makes little sense to examine men for the contours of that masculinity's social construction. Masculinity . . . becomes legible as masculinity where and when it leaves the male middle-class body."[53] The claim is not only that it is necessary to study "masculinity without men"—and nondominant masculinities more generally—but also that in doing so one will be able to know what masculinity *is*, unlinked from "power and domination."[54]

In addition, Halberstam clearly articulates a set of personal/political stakes, stating that "this book is an attempt to make my own female masculinity plausible, credible, and real," and by extension, it is an attempt to make female masculinities in the future plausible, credible, and real.[55] The violence of the persistent non- or misrecognition of female masculinity is especially evident in Halberstam's elaboration of the tomboy narrative, a coming-of-age story marked by the forced movement from the relative freedom of tolerated tomboy childhoods into the constraints of "compliant forms of femininity."[56] The inevitability of this narrative is precisely what Halberstam's project, in this book and in work that follows, seeks to refuse. At first, in *Female Masculinity*, Halberstam argues that pre-adulthood is the space where the tomboy is allowed to flourish; in his later work, *In a Queer Time and Place*, Halberstam makes "extended adolescence" synonymous with the resistant time/space of *queer*.

As opposed to Lee Edelman's infamous assertion that "queerness names the side of those not 'fighting for the children,'" Halberstam's *In a Queer Time and Place* suggests that queerness names the site of those who never quite left childhood behind.[57] Queerness, in this formulation, is "an outcome of strange temporalities" that "develop in opposition to the institutions of family, heterosexuality, and reproduction," which produce and define "straight time."[58] Because these institutions rely on a common narrative about maturation that "charts an obvious transition out of childish dependency through marriage and into adult responsibility through reproduction," interrupting this narrative allows for a proliferation of queer lives, genders, and futures.[59] While Edelman aligns a queerness outside of these logics as fundamentally against the future—figured, for him, by the likes of Scrooge, Captain Hook, and Voldemort—for Halberstam the queer refusal to grow up is what allows for the potential for other futures, aligning queerness more easily with Tiny Tim, the boy who did not die; Peter Pan, the boy (played onstage by an adult woman) who wouldn't grow up; and Harry Potter, the boy who lived.

Although this band of boys comes from Edelman, *In a Queer Time and Place* is characterized by a deep investment in and affirmative attachment to the feminist potential of the boy as an alternative to dominant and dominating masculinities. For example, in one of the book's closing scenes, Halberstam watches as a troupe of drag kings unlocks the heterotopia of queer time/space: "This is rather an intricate performance of butch masculinity, queer masculinity that presents itself to screaming girls as a safe alternative to hetero-masculinities. . . . When the Backstreet Boys croon 'I want it THAT way' and the girls scream, we think for a moment that it does not have to be *this* way and that just maybe girl and boy partial identities can be carried forward into adulthood in terms of a politics of refusal—the refusal to grow up and enter the heteronormative adulthoods implied by these concepts of progress and maturity."[60] Similarly, Noble writes that "the appeal of the boy is . . . the potential for its refusal of the teleological imperatives of manhood. . . . Boys paradoxically threaten to become men while categorically rarely materializing and, more often than not, refusing that identity outright," with the effect, again, being the possibility of refashioning politically viable (feminist) masculinities.[61] So the story that Noble and Halberstam tell about the boy as a "transed" masculinity—not necessarily female masculinity but masculinity without phallic power—is that not only does he have more fun, but he also refashions masculinity for the movement.

This is a nice story insofar as everyone involved walks away feeling good. Transmasculinity is rescued from both pathology and misogyny, and feminism has incorporated a new subject. But it strikes me that this story is obviously being told from the boy's perspective. Narrated from the perspective of the girl, who keeps popping up at the edges of the conversation, screaming as a mass from offstage, the boy's story seems to be yet another story of her displacement. In both Halberstam's and Noble's defenses of boyhood, non-trans female femininity is aligned with the static and decidedly unqueer time/space of adulthood.[62] Halberstam in particular, in an effort to affirm female masculinities, displaces the boy's bad feelings onto the girl, associating female femininities with "unhealthy body manipulations from anorexia to high-heeled shoes" and suggesting that "perhaps femininity . . . should be chosen later on."[63] Paralleling the activist language that troubles Goldberg, as the boy emerges as a feminist subject the girl is told it might be better if she all but disappeared. While I'm not the first to liken queer boys to Peter Pan, what everyone seems to forget is that Wendy effectively loses her childhood in Neverland. The boy, just like his most famous representation, gets all the attention while the girl misses out on all the fun.

Loving Transfeminism?

Which brings me, finally, to the point. There has been a serious ongoing effort to produce something called *transfeminism*, driven by the sense that if the bodies of knowledge arranged under the two terms *trans* and *feminism* sit together long enough at the same table—sometimes joined by *queer*, sometimes not—we will be able to produce some theory of gender, some political stance that adequately incorporates both. This sense is modeled in the introduction to the recent *Transfeminist Perspectives* anthology, which begins by noticing that, although they are "intimately connected to one another," *trans* and *feminist* "are far from integrated." The anthology's intervention "at the simplest level offers multidisciplinary models for *integrating* feminist and transgender theory, practice, and pedagogy."[64] As an alternative to striving for integration, I close by briefly sketching an answer to a question I posed at the beginning of this chapter regarding what might happen if we allowed ourselves to read with, rather than against, depressive forms of feeling and habits of thought. That is, what might our expectations for trans/feminist thought oriented to social justice be if we took pain—in this case the psychic pain produced in the encounter between competing theories of gender that seem aimed at each other's annihilation—as a given, not necessarily loaded with moral weight?

Perhaps the paradigmatic call for transfeminist integration comes in "The Transfeminist Manifesto," in which Emi Koyama defines transfeminism as "primarily a movement by and for trans women who view their liberation to be intrinsically linked to the liberation of all women and beyond."[65] In a postscript, Koyama concedes that her articulation of transfeminism centered the perspectives of trans women "at the expense of female-to-male trans people and others who identify as transgender or genderqueer" and that this "was a mistake."[66] I want to be clear that this straightforward version of transfeminism, one that understands trans women as and in league with women, is not what is at issue here. And while of course trans women must also deal with the added risk of both being seen as women and as failing to be so, antiracist, queer, and disability feminisms remind us that related forms of this double bind also structure the lives of disabled women, queer women, and women of color. Given that intersectional feminist scholars and activists continue to have to reassert the failures of feminisms that, like Jeffreys's, imagine woman as a monolithic category, perhaps this is not yet an obvious thing to say; still, it seems to me that Koyama's version of transfeminism might simply be called feminism.

Trans women, of course, do not exhaust the content of trans. But rather than setting out to correct Koyama's "mistake," I would like to suggest that her essay's straightforward articulation, backtracking, and pointing to a hole it does not then try to fill performs the structure of the relation between feminism and trans[masculinity]. In pointing to the "mistake" and "leaving the task to others" to correct it, Koyama repeats the deferral first performed in Stone's foundational manifesto, in which she promises an essay dealing with transmasculinity that, as far as I know, has yet to materialize nearly three decades later.[67] Likewise, as seen above, when the boy emerges as a feminist reworking of masculinity it is often through a story that conceals or displaces rather than alleviates the tension between transmasculine narratives and feminist ones insofar as it relies on the deferral of the girl.

However, this is certainly not to say that the stories transmasculinity and feminism tell are antithetical, do not need each other, or have no hope of living in constructive relation. Although I may have implied that Wendy gets nothing from her trip to Neverland, we all know that's not exactly true. The story of Peter and Wendy, after all, does not rely on Wendy embodying the clichés of early twentieth-century femininity as she does in J. M. Barrie's inaugural version. For instance, in the 2003 live-action film version, Wendy does not run away to Neverland because she has fallen in love with a boy who has broken into her bedroom. Instead, finding herself at the edge of puberty, Wendy senses that the specter of womanhood is unfairly closing down her life options—she is to be a wife and not a novelist.[68] Additionally, Wendy is the narrator of her own story, "knows a thing or two about pirates" (and momentarily becomes one), and is deft with a sword, actively participating in her adventures in Neverland, rather than simply standing on the sidelines "watching Peter with glistening eyes."[69] While it is certainly true that Barrie's *Peter and Wendy* (the novel's original title) accepts and amusingly enacts, as Susan S. Kissel argues, "the drama of gender," the enduringness of the story—its queer appeal and its ability to withstand multiple revisions of the content of gender—is a result of its enactment of the drama of desire: at its core it has remained a story about the promise and failure of love to anchor us to each other and to the world.[70] It is a fairy tale that, quite literally, cites *happily ever after* only to mark it as an impossibility, endlessly deferred.

"Love," writes Lauren Berlant, "is the embracing dream in which desire is reciprocated: rather than being isolating, love provides an image of an expanded self, the normative version of which is the two-as-one intimacy of the couple form. In the idealized image of their relation, desire will lead to love, which will make a world for desire's endurance."[71] This quotation is taken from *Desire/Love*, a dictionary entry turned short book-length meditation on how that primary self-interrupting drive, desire, is recruited into the self-stabilizing normative love plot. But in each iteration of Peter and Wendy, the closure that the love plot promises—the ever after—is deferred to Peter and Jane, and then Peter and Margaret, and on and on. This is because, although their desire for each other is reciprocated and their love brings Wendy to Neverland and, in the 2003 film, rescues Peter from certain death, there is no shared world, neither the fantasy of Neverland nor the dreary ongoingness of reality in which their desire can endure. Although misrecognition is a constitutive feature of desire—our objects never fulfill the promises we would like to think they have made—the promises Peter and Wendy would like the other to make are ultimately incommensurable. Even so, even though they cannot maintain their two-as-oneness, the love between them forever alters each one's story. But perhaps I have taken this analogy too far. All I wanted to do was ask a question: What if we think of the relation between trans and feminism as love? Halberstam's boys perform onstage for a crowd of screaming girls, and who could describe this as anything but a relation of mutual desire? Enke feels an intimate connection and, in compiling an anthology, hopes to initiate a merge. Salamon asks whether the lesbian feminist and the trans man can desire each other without annihilating each other in the process. Noble argues that *trans* and *feminist* were, in the beginning, not two terms but one, and who cannot hear Hedwig begin to sing in the background of his lament?[72] Finally, Jeffreys will not agree, but I suspect that a certain level of love underlies and drives her grief at the emergence of FTM transsexuality, an object that refuses to give her what she wants.

Love, that is, does not necessarily name a happy relation. Berlant, again, offers a useful definition: "To phrase 'the object of desire' as a cluster of promises is to allow us to encounter what's incoherent or enigmatic in our attachments, not as confirmations of our irrationality but as an explanation of our sense of *our endurance in the object*."[73] This is perhaps why the relation between *trans* and *feminism* remains so fraught: each sees in the other something that will ensure its own endurance. Incorporating transness as an object grants feminism interpretive power in a landscape where gender cannot be said to include only men and women, m's and f's. On the other hand, articulating feminism as a primary mode of analysis provides trans thought with an authorized language of power and a political stance to rescue it from accusations of, for example, being a sign of gender's ultimate commodification. Like my drawn-out analogy of Peter and Wendy, although trans and feminism want each other—need each other, even—what each wants from the other is not only not identical but may require the other to inhabit a world incommensurable with its own desires. TERFs aside, many forms of queer feminism seem to want from transness confirmation that there is no predictable, and thereby no fixed, difference between m and f. *Trans*, on the other hand, and despite protests to the contrary, seems quite attached to an expanded version of m/f but wants from feminism, in part, a way of interrupting the terms on which m/f has been naturalized and by which it reproduces m > f. *Transmasculinity*, in particular, wants this both because he loves feminism and wants her to get what he think she wants, but also because there is, as of now, no better discourse he can speak to articulate the harms he incurred for failing to be f.

If *love* describes the persistent sense that trans[masculinity] and feminism were once one and will be again, it also will always defer this merge until one accepts the other's "fantasy/realism as the condition of their encounter."[74] Until then, Peter will continue to return to the window, and *trans* and *feminism* will continue to produce monographs, anthologies, controversies, and so on, all the while "quizzically looking sideways-and occasionally winking-at each other. The sideways glance might be cautious, but it is surely born of a sense that, alone, neither feminist nor trans is living up to its most expansive vision and also that, at times, they fail us."[75] These relations, defined as they are by continual deferral, will likely leave no one feeling good, but isn't this, the depressed transsexual asks, a precondition for relating at all?[76] Desire, that which causes us to reach for something outside of ourselves, always arises from a wound that we would like the object of our desire to heal. And although desire always exceeds the object, although the wound remains open, we remain attached both because the promise of closure is not broken, merely and perpetually deferred, but also and most importantly because something usable is produced by the attachment.

3

Some Dissociative Trans Masc Poetics

To call dissociation a mere counter-structure of discontinuity or alienation would be to underassess the coherence of its profoundly social and historical character and to miss its utility in staying bound to life. —**LAUREN BERLANT, "SHE'S HAVING AN EPISODE: PATRICIA WILLIAMS AND THE WRITING OF DAMAGED LIFE" (2014)**

But tell me, if I start here by placing the issues of violence and neglect alongside my queerness, what will happen next? —**ELI CLARE, *EXILE AND PRIDE: DISABILITY QUEERNESS, AND LIBERATION* (1999)**

As the basis of the critically acclaimed 1999 film *Boys Don't Cry*, the story of the person who came to be known as Brandon Teena is perhaps still the transmasculine narrative most familiar to the general US public. While the film has dominated the retrospective production of the Brandon Teena story, Teena's life and death generated (and continue to generate) an enormous body of representation that tells often-conflicting stories. But here are the facts on which everyone agrees. On December 31, 1993, John Lotter and Tom Nissen shot and killed three other young people in a farmhouse in Humboldt, Nebraska: Lisa Lambert, a young white mother; Phillip DeVine, a disabled black man who was in town to spend Christmas with one of Lisa's friends; and a young white or presumed-white person who had recently been hanging out in nearby Falls City, going by the name Brandon. A week earlier, and fueled at least in part by jealousy/rage over Brandon's romantic involvement with Falls City local Lana Tisdale, Brandon was kidnapped and raped by Lotter and Nissen after questions about Brandon's sex had begun circulating in the small town that before, from the perspective of one city-dweller in *Boys Don't Cry*, wasn't "even on the map."[1]

In addition to the feature film, this story has produced a feature-length documentary; a true-crime novel; at least two spin-off novels; hundreds of academic articles and book chapters in feminist, queer, trans, and gay and lesbian studies; and countless newspaper articles, including near-annual retrospectives. As Jack Halberstam has pointed out, this sheer mass of representation—what he calls the Brandon archive—has proliferated in part because Brandon's violent death has been mobilized for multiple social and political projects. The figure of "Brandon Teena" has been used in the service of drawing attention to violence against women, violence against gays/lesbians, the lack of institutional support for trans youth, the need for queer community building in nonurban areas, and more. Each of these projects, however, has specific and conflicting requirements for Brandon's social ontology. Thus, in the service of political projects of which they were never a part, the person made in and by the Brandon archives has been posthumously named and renamed, dragged back and forth across various lines of gender and sexuality, has become a woman, a transsexual, and a lesbian, all as a consequence of having been raped and murdered. However admirable individual intentions, then, in more ways than one, the most widely circulated transmasculine narrative is one of violation.

In 2010, playwright Carolyn Gage added to the Brandon archive when she published an article titled "The Inconvenient Truth about Teena Brandon," which insists that we attend to another form of violation that haunts the story: childhood sexual violence. Gage argues that the trans narrative that has condensed into the Brandon Teena story is complicated by the often-ignored fact that, as a young person, Brandon experienced sexual violence at the hands of a male relative. "The inconvenient truth of Brandon's incest history," Gage claims, "causes trouble because incorporating information about child sexual abuse into the narrative of Brandon's life pathologizes the transgendered identity adopted by Brandon and for which she [*sic*] has become an icon."[2] Gage gets her information about Brandon's history from Aphrodite Jones's 1996 true-crime novel *All She Wanted*, which, as Gage hints, has fallen outside the acceptable archive for doing trans-affirmative or anti-transphobic work; however, it is arguably the account that offers the most complete portrait of Brandon's world. Gage processes the information presented in *All She Wanted* through Judith Herman and Janet Liebman Jacobs's work on incest in order to diagnose Brandon's gendered trajectory as the side-effect of abuse, a protective disavowal of the feminine and overidentification with masculinity. All the while, she insists that her intention is not to claim Brandon as a lesbian—though this is the piece's obvious rhetorical effect—but rather to simply restore the identity "incest survivor" to Brandon's narrative, an identity that she perceives has been posthumously attacked in the effort to appropriate Brandon for the trans movement.

Thus, Gage joined a decades-long line of transphobic arguments that diagnose transmasculinity as "really" a symptom of sexual and other forms of gender-based trauma. For example, in his 1983 treatise on female-to-male transsexuality, psychoanalyst Leslie Lothstein speculates that at least some female-to-male identifications are "a defensive solution to an established female gender identity" that has become psychically linked to weakness, passivity, and vulnerability to patriarchal violence.[3] Lothstein certainly wasn't alone in this "expert" speculation: Robert Stoller likewise diagnosed transmasculinity, unlike transfemininity, as originating in "a defense against trauma and the erection of identity structures to prevent identity destruction by recurrence of trauma."[4] More recently, Sheila Jeffreys's 2014 *Gender Hurts* repeatedly suggests that trans genders, and transmasculinities in particular, might be best understood as the product of unhealed or poorly healed trauma, especially sexual trauma, and Abigail Shrier's widely circulated 2020 *Irreversible Damage* takes as one of its premises that transmasculinity is a maladaptive response to the ordinary injuries of female adolescence.[5] These arguments are made in the context of differently discrediting projects. Jeffreys, for example, posits a traumatic etiology of trans identity to add rhetorical fuel to her argument that trans-affirmative politics are both antifeminist and misguided. Meanwhile, Lothstein writes against an understanding of transmasculine identifications as having any one cause, but does so in order to advocate for psychiatric rather than bodily and social interventions, against trans manifestation.

Given the durability of such trans-antagonistic projects, it is admittedly difficult to unlink the implication that gender-based trauma, understood broadly, and its attendant bad feelings are integral to many trans[masculine] narratives from projects that seek to discredit trans thought and life. At the same time, I, too, find the silence around such violence in Brandon's history in particular quite queer, especially because the sense that transmasculinity is a response to femininized and feminizing injury fundamentally structures

Donna Minkowitz's now-disavowed 1994 *Village Voice* article on Brandon Teena, an article that, in turn, inspired *Boys Don't Cry*.[6] But this history appears nearly nowhere in queer/trans discourse about Brandon, not even in the mediation on him that concludes Ann Cvetkovich's *An Archive of Feelings*, a book that foregrounds lesbian responses to sexual violence in general and incest in particular. This silence is all the more strange since the Brandon archive was *produced by* Brandon's violation; given that Brandon became an icon only *because of* his rape and murder, why should these other accounts of sexual violence be unspeakable? As in the displacement of the girl by the boy that I examined in chapter 2—and inverting the transmisogynistic talking point that figures trans women as perpetrators (or harbingers) of sexual violence against cis women—there is a curious way in which, in coming to signify extraordinary violence against trans[masculine] people, the Brandon archive must simultaneously conceal the ordinariness of violence against people designated as f. In part because of the difficulty of accounting for transmasculinity within the standard plotting of the "drama of gender," both of these stories, apparently, can't exist at once.[7]

Taking this impasse as a starting place, this chapter will, like the preceding one, meditate on the conflicted terrain of (white) trans, feminist, and queer thought. Whereas, in chapter 2, I was admittedly a bit harsh with respect to the revaluing of the boy in queer trans theory, in this chapter I aim to be much more sympathetic to his predicament, which is of course also my predicament. For this reason, whereas chapter 2 was loosely organized around the question of whether the habits of thought and feeling associated with depression might enable us to understand and to bear the irresolution of trans feminism, this one is guided by another, related question. Namely, might we approach dissociation not as the pathological root of transmasculinity but rather as something that has enabled transmasculine becoming and thought? Pursuing this question across multiple uneven domains—among them transmasculine autofiction and memoir, feminist and queer theory, and the film *Boys Don't Cry*—occasionally leads to a conflation of transmasculinity as a concept whose parameters have been intensely debated, transmasculinity as it is represented in varied genres, and transmasculinity as it is lived. Although this conflation makes me uneasy, it's also true that these registers are ultimately inseparable from one another, and the feedback loop between them is evident in one of the chapter's primary objects, Elliott DeLine's autofictional young adult novel *Refuse*.

Self-published by DeLine in 2011, *Refuse* is symptomatic of the tangled threads that I am attempting to bring into relief: (1) dissociation as a response to feminized forms of degradation; (2) dissociation as a formal and psychic strategy for occupying the absent presence of transmasculinity, particularly in spaces shaped by the 1990s "butch/FTM border wars" and attempts to solidify queer and feminist domains; and (3) dissociation as a sometimes necessary precondition for the inhabitation of trans[masculine] (and other "impossible") forms of life.[8] Inevitably, following these threads will lead to some unsettling places, which is one reason for the relative silence on the question of, as Clare puts it in the second epigraph above, "what will happen next?" In what happens next, then, I do not attempt to fill the silence—not exactly. Instead, I attempt to trace two of its component parts: the hard-to-discuss centrality of forms of feminized harm—especially sexual violence—to the narration of transmasculinity, on the one hand, and, on another, the hard-to-discuss centrality of transmasculinity to academic skirmishes around establishing the domains of queer and feminist thought. But for now I will begin where such an account must begin, with a return to the Brandon archive.

Dissociative Transmasculinity

"Dissociation," in Lauren Berlant's accounting, "is at least five kinds of thing."[9] Indeed, the history of the concept of dissociation is both long and fraught, such that well into the twentieth century there was little agreement on its reality and utility, let alone how it should be defined.[10] In everyday speech, for example, dissociation has come to describe the many ways in which we might recede from a scene while physically occupying it, how we might "space out" in a boring meeting or "lose ourselves" in a particularly absorbing book. However, what matters most to my account of transmasculine dissociative poetics is what contemporary students of nineteenth-century French psychologist Pierre Janet call "structural dissociation," or the posttraumatic disaggregation of consciousness (sensation, emotion, memory, sense of self) into discrete parts, parts that can, sometimes, take on a life of their own.[11] Of course, dissociation can feel like and accomplish and be caused by many nonidentical things—trauma, numbness, hypnosis, lost time, intrusive voices, fixation on moments of fracturing, being out of body, being beside yourself in fantasy for so long that nothing about your life feels "real."[12] But because I am trying to track and describe something across a series of incommensurate registers, it is useful to begin from the insistence that dissociation is this structure: divisions in consciousness, even as its feelings, effects, and histories multiply.

By this definition, Halberstam has more or less argued that the transgender gaze—and, paradigmatically, the transmasculine gaze—is fundamentally a dissociative one. During the course of his engagement with the Brandon archive, Halberstam reads *Boys Don't Cry* as a film that hacked existing cinematic techniques to "give the viewer access to the transgender gaze in order to allow us to look *with* the transgender character instead of *at* him."[13] To elucidate this gaze, Halberstam focuses on the narrative hinge of the film, in which Brandon's trans status is exposed and he is thrust into a chain of violent events that the viewer—perhaps especially the trans viewer—already knows in advance. In particular, Halberstam fixates on the scene in which Brandon is subject to "reality enforcement" by way of a violent genital exposure.[14] But rather than simply consenting to the "reality" of Brandon as f, Halberstam argues that the film appropriates the shot / reverse shot technique to instead divide—and so double—reality. Although this doubling of reality has been hinted at throughout the film, it erupts into view during the infamous scene in which Brandon is assaulted and exposed in the bathroom. Here Brandon's image is doubled: in the shot we see Brandon, unclothed, looking at the doorway, and in the reverse shot we see Brandon, clothed, among the crowd in the doorway, looking on. "In this shot / reverse shot," Halberstam argues, "the transgender gaze is constituted as a look divided within itself," a point of view that comes from (at least) two discrete places at the same time.[15]

Importantly, and as Cáel Keegan has argued, Halberstam here mistakes "the structure of cissexism itself" for a trans point of view.[16] Keegan, therefore, is right to insist that Halberstam's articulation of the transgender look cannot tell us anything about trans-specific image reception or about how trans people regard ourselves outside of the fracturing epistemology of the cis gaze. Still, given that trans life and thought presently unfold in contexts riven by cissexism, I can't help but be struck by Halberstam's insistence on what dissociation enables *for transmasculinity* given such conditions. Namely, although the remainder of the film forecloses on the possibility of Brandon's trans life, Halberstam's linking of the intact Brandon, who looks on and who no one but Brandon—and through him the viewer—can see, with the moments of nonrealist, imagistic flight throughout the otherwise "brutally realistic" film allows us to sense that there might be a time and place in which Brandon "survives."[17] Dissociation, by this logic, does what Keegan says it does—"insist[s]on the narrative possibility of only one body"—*and* introduces a split through which another possibility can briefly, fleetingly, if you need it be seen.[18]

In fact, this structure of dissociation features as a hinge in many trans[masculine] memoirs and works of autofiction, as a formal conceit of much trans[masculine] lyric, and is reported consistently in transmasculine accounts of lived experience. What differentiates such work from *Boys Don't Cry* is that what follows is not the foreclosure of trans[masculine] life but an opening out to the reality of it. During the course of conducting research for his landmark study of FTMs, for example, Aaron Devor found that over half of his study's participants reported experiences of intimate gendered abuse as children. Consequently, Devor speculates that "in some cases transsexualism may be an extreme adaptive dissociative response" to trauma.[19] To this end, Devor quotes one of his subjects—a practicing therapist—at length:

> I think that serious assault of a young child, especially sexual assault, might cause some children to dissociate and split in a way that establishes a sense of self different from one's biological sex. . . . I don't know whether there was a little girl that, fairly early on, through some abuse, disappeared. I don't know that. But I do know that even if that happened, and I were to try to identify that and work it through, it just seems like the way I've lived my life to this point, for forty-one years, says there's something to be said for that identity.[20]

Like Cvetkovich, who tracks lesbian cultural production in order to elucidate how "trauma can be a foundation for creating counterpublic spheres rather than evacuating them," Devor and his interlocutors gesture toward the ways in which dissociative responses to trauma might produce inhabitable selves and worlds rather than only destroying them.[21] Indeed, this gesture is made again and again in the transmasculine archive, in the form of narratives that contain scenes of splitting that are hinges in their trajectories, represented as traumatic first encounters with sex difference, failed interpellation into "properly" gendered categories, explicitly transphobic violence, and so on.

While a dissociative poetic is arguably locatable in the writing of transmasculine authors as different in aesthetic, generic, and historical location as Elliott DeLine, Leslie Feinberg, Samuel Ace, Mario Martino, Akwaeke Emezi, Lou Sullivan, Pauli Murray, Jordy Rosenberg, Red Jordan Arobatue, Ely Shipley, and others, it's especially notable in the work of trans/disabled writer Eli Clare. Over the decades, Clare has offered some of the most earnest public accounting of and complex grappling with the entanglements of transmasculine identity formation, trauma, and dissociation, an accounting that has in part been made possible by the form of Clare's prose. Described by Susannah Mintz as a text structured by "formal discontinuity," Eli Clare's 1999 *Exile and Pride* leans on the strategies of narrative fragmentation, halting repetition, accumulation of intensely sensory images, and systematic citation and refusal of tidy stories in order to offer a queer/trans/crip account of the way "bodies are never singular"—never self-same or isolatable from collective histories.[22]

In particular, and in an effort to foreground rather than smooth over discontinuity, Clare's writing often returns to his animating questions, regarding them first one way and then another, making the varied attempts at answering visible as part of the answer itself. One such animating question is precisely about the relationship between Clare's queerness and transmasculine identity and the terrors of surviving childhood sexual and physical abuse. As he guides us through his thinking, he turns the question over like a stone, first considering the simplest dialectic: on the one hand, the trans-antagonistic and homophobic line of thought asserting that queer sexuality and trans gender are caused by abuse and, on another, the fact that "most feminist and queer activists reject these linkages" outright.[23] Although he acknowledges the "good reason" undergirding the activists' stance, Clare refuses their refusal because of the way it neatens "messy reality."[24] Eventually, he settles on a messy story, one in which shattering violence is both a "form of social control," a mechanism by which structures of domination (race, class, gender, ability, etc.) are embodied and so reproduced, and also a mechanism that fails and in so doing can allow other possibilities, other embodied knowledges, to be felt more palpably.[25] Gendered violence, in this analysis, might make gender move in at least two directions.

I must confess that this is *my* animating question, the one I am turning over like a stone: how should I understand the relationship between feminized forms of harm and trans[masculine] expressive culture? That is, it has been difficult, it seems, to publish a transgender narrative without at least one scene of sexual or other intimate, gendered violence.[26] In the fiction of nontrans writers like Kim Fu, Felicia Luna Lemus, Rose Tremain, and Jeffrey Eugenides—in which trans protagonists often function as figures for the postmodern/postcolonial/globalized world and its discontents—these scenes of violation often seem to figure the violence of the transition from the old world to the new, of the unmooring of national identity, and of fantasies of assimilation.[27] Or occasionally, it seems that some nontrans authors simply imagine that trans lives are wretched, and rape is used to signify that wretchedness. However, in literature by trans people, such scenes are also in no short supply.

Undoubtedly, the prevalence of sexual violence in trans lit is related to the fact of structural vulnerability.[28] However, I suspect that its aesthetic function is related to the centrality of sexual violence to some academic and mainstream forms of feminist thinking about the production and regulation of gender. In particular, feminist attention to both the fact of rape and its retrospective figuring in the courtroom, literature, and media provided the crucial insight that "rape and rapability are central to the very construction of gender identity."[29] This formulation, in turn, makes sexual violence legible as a trope in trans narratives, which are often precisely about negotiating constructions of gender identity. Admittedly, however, this feminist legacy is complicated by the way in which it has, often unintentionally, knotted together being raped and being f into a kind of constitutive injury and has made other configurations of power and violation unthinkable. Or at least this is the argument of scholars like Wendy Brown and, more recently, Janet Halley.[30] Indeed, the problem of how to theorize sexual violence as central to the operations of gender without writing women's sexual subordination into the law, how to recognize the structuring power of sexual violence without reducing women's subjectivity to injury, has formed the ground for a longstanding impasse/anxiety within white feminist thought. While Halley's response is to, at least momentarily, split from feminism for the side of queer, others have responded by insisting on the need to critically rethink feminist antirape discourse's own terms. For example, Sorcha Gunne and Zoë Brigley Thompson, the editors of *Feminism, Literature, and Rape Narratives* (2011), frame their anthology as both building on and diverging from Lynn Higgins and Brenda R. Silver's foundational *Rape and Representation* (1991). Whereas the earlier anthology critiqued representations of gender and female sexuality in canonical Western literature by making sexual violence visible, the essays collected in *Feminism, Literature, and Rape Narrative* look to twentieth- and twenty-first-century writing by women that subverts, rather than reinforces, dominant rape narratives. By "foreground[ing] narratives about rape that challenge assumptions," this anthology models an antirape feminism that aims to "establish new spaces for the subjectivity of the women who either have been raped or have been threatened with rape," rather than, as Halley charges, imagining that feminism necessarily sets up an opposition between injury and agency.[31]

This chapter, then, is firmly within a strand of critical feminist scholarship on representations of sexual violence. And yet, ultimately, because of the way such analyses tend to reify two and only two discrete sexed classes (an image of the world that simply does not and cannot hold in trans life), they tend to begin with an assumption about what sexual violence—in fact and in figuring—*does*: produce and reproduce heteropatriarchal gender, "(social) man against . . . (social) woman."[32] Conversely, thinking with the archive of dissociative transmasculinity might require taking seriously the myriad ways in which sexual violence as a gendering discourse *fails* to reliably reproduce "man" and "woman."

How this generative failure happens, Clare admits, "is not simple."[33] But, certainly, dissociation is one name for the means by which Clare survived the brutality of the given and the formal strategies he persistently employs to understand and deconstruct it and insist it might be—and already is—otherwise. Put another way, what Mintz calls Clare's post-structuralist sensibility—his "formal discontinuity," his texts' refusal of a "unified 'I'" in favor of "rupture [and] a proliferation of perspectives"—could just as easily be described as a dissociative sensibility. Indeed, when Clare returns to the question raised by the impacts of childhood abuse on his bodymind in *Brilliant Imperfection: Grappling with Cure*, it arrives as a moment of meta commentary on writing: "I had mastered the fine art of dissociation, surviving unbearable childhood violence only by splitting body-mind from self. . . . Body-mind shattered, piece split from piece, broken. Self leapt into trees, squeezed into rocks, went free fall into the Milky Way. It was the only way survive. Don't be fooled: it wasn't beautiful, even as I spin pretty images."[34] Here, Clare's description of dissociation as an "art" seems at once tongue-in-cheek and sincere. After all, the "pretty images" he spins from it describe the formal qualities of Clare's writing and thinking—visceral identification with the environment, a "never singular" first person, the occupation of contradictory positions simultaneously. And Clare's rejoinder, "Don't be fooled: it wasn't beautiful, even as I spin pretty images," seems to acknowledge this element of his craft, even as he insists that if this is an art, it is a terrible one, one that he has indeed "mastered" and is demonstrating in the present tense.

In the interplay between *Brilliant Imperfection* and *Exile and Pride*, Clare's account of dissociation returns us to the vexed nexus of trans/mad, calling for ways of thinking with trans maladjustment. At this nexus, dissociation is the name for an embodied capacity for survival; an outcome of a brokenness that both cannot be cured and can make one subject to the full force of the violence of the ideology of cure; a source of life-threatening distress; a barrier to intimacy and a visceral knowledge of interdependence; something that might be difficult to reconcile with certain protocols of disability pride; a writerly technique; a phenomenological experience of being multiple and beside oneself; a way of being both "not a girl" and a girl "in no uncertain terms."[35] Through this multiplication, Clare helps us see dissociation as integral to his cripistemology, even as it also installs a crisis at the heart of transmasculinity. That is, what Clare's dissociative poetics offers is not a redemptive vision of whole, unfractured transmasculinity. Rather, it offers a way of knowing that is inextricably tethered to unbearable social and historical conditions and so is a particular way of bearing them. But also, as Clare's writing discloses, dissociation is not necessarily a livable position in the long term, though at the same time it must be.

Transmasculinity Goes to School

One of the unbearable conditions of trans[masculine] life has certainly been the hostility, flattening, and "indiscriminate erasure" that pervades discourses that claim to interpret it, discourses emanating from the academy, the clinic, the state, and the culture industry.[36] Related to the way that Clare puts a dissociative poetic to work in order to refuse to allow his bodymind and life to be interpreted by ableism, heteronormativity, and ideologies of cure, Elliott DeLine—who has written publicly about his life with dissociative identity disorder—likewise employs dissociation as a writerly defense against constraining, diminishing forms of interpretation.[37] At the same time, dissociation in DeLine's work must also be understood as the outcome of gendered and gendering violation.

As an author, DeLine's trajectory has in many ways mimicked the dynamics of pre-tipping-point trans literary production; DeLine self-published his debut young adult novel *Refuse* in 2011, has put out three books since, and seems to be read nearly exclusively but widely by other trans people, especially young transmasculine people. That is, DeLine's career has proceeded both quickly and unevenly and has been conducted largely outside of the press economy. Most generously, DeLine's novels are hyper-self-reflexive engagements with the question of what it means to write trans literature in a social context where trans stories are already overdetermined; to sell the display of oneself as trans in a context where transness is a "curio"; and to tell messy trans stories—about neurodivergence, sex, trauma, and the ways we fail each other—in a context where one's access to care might depend on telling neat ones.[38] Most basically, however, *Refuse* is a thinly veiled work of autofiction about an annoying, depressive trans guy named Dean and the way his life unfolds on a college campus, in his parent's suburban house, in relation to shifting economies of trans masc desirability, in the numbing bureaucracy of identity documents and prescriptions, at trans support groups, and through the iconography of alternative white masculinities. As such, it offers an account of transmasculinity as lived by a white, mad, bookish, college-educated, New York–adjacent millennial in the first decade of the twenty-first century. Whatever else it might be, then, *Refuse* is necessarily a campus novel, one in which the protagonist is schooled in the transmasculinity of the early 2000s queer/feminist academy. Transmasculinity in this context was often figured as desirable and potentially radical (or otherwise hopelessly conservative and antifeminist), but its felt experience could not circulate with the same academic capital-generating force. For this reason, *Refuse*'s dissociative structure—both its obvious, overwrought function as a defense and its origins in a scene of sexualized abjection that the novel cannot disclose—is inextricable from the conflicted terrain of queer/feminist studies.

* * *

There are many ways to tell the story of what Lynne Huffer calls the "queer feminist split"—as a story about intergenerational conflict, as a story whose logics depend on overlooking black and women of color feminisms, as a story that is no story at all.[39] But I understand the story of the split, which is more often than not located within texts rather than between them, as primarily a story about the conflicting and conflicted force of our attachments. This is why something like the queer/feminist split reasserted itself with force in relation to #MeToo and the enforcement of Title IX in the vast comment section of the queer/feminist academic internet. In one such post, Greggor Mattson succinctly diagnosed the mood as wavering between "feminist glee at powerful rapists getting their due" and "queer concern that another front in the sex wars has opened," concern, that is, about the institutional regulation of sex.[40]

Perhaps a paradigmatic exposure of the divergent trajectories of "feminist glee" and "queer concern" (and vice versa) periodically emerges around a moment in one of queer theory's hearts, Michel Foucault's *History of Sexuality*, volume 1. There, Foucault draws on a case in which a "somewhat simple-minded" adult farmhand named Charles Jouy paid a few pennies and "obtained a few caresses" from Sophie Adam, "a little girl" who, in this telling, remains without a name. What seems to interest Foucault in this case (at least in this iteration) is that "these inconsequential bucolic pleasures" became "the object not only of a collective intolerance but of a judicial action, a medical intervention, a careful clinical examination, and an entire theoretical elaboration."[41] That is, Jouy obtained a few, inconsequential caresses and then became the object of knowledge of an emergent psychiatric discourse that translated these actions into a constitutive, pathological fact about Jouy. Foucault, therefore, uses this case as a "window into the transition to the system of sexuality and the concomitant emergence of a new apparatus of power-knowledge," so it must be understood that the then emergent discourse of sexuality in which we understand Jouy as pervert is also what produces the little girl as victim.[42] However, it has also seemed clear to many feminists that Foucault's inclination in *The History of Sexuality* to understand this scene as one of inconsequential bucolic pleasures—of "timeless gestures" rather than, say, of a historically produced, gendered division of "the worst sort[s] of labor"—demonstrates that his attachments to the (male) pervert leads Foucault to overlook (female) harm.[43] Or put much more forcefully by Monique Plaza: "Really, Michel Foucault? . . . From the place of potential rapist to which your status as a man 'subjects' you, you can only hide the networks of oppressive power that women are subject to."[44] That is, undergirding this persistent queer/feminist unease, overtly or otherwise, is "the case of women, for whom the dangers and discomforts of sex . . . have been all too readily apparent."[45]

It's no surprise, then, that in the 1990s and early 2000s, the figure of the trans man was recruited into and marked by terms of this debate. That is, at first glance, the academic paper trail of 1990s discourse about transmasculinity reveals what seems to be a conversation driven by an impulse to taxonomy: What *was* a trans man, exactly? What was his relation to that more familiar figure of female masculinity, the butch? Was their difference historical? Technological? Political? Economic? And, ultimately, what difference did that difference make? While work that attended to these questions was written in response to intense intracommunity conflicts, in retrospect it seems that the impulse to pin down the FTM, in academic writing in particular, was also related to the way that he seemed to both serve as evidence for and threaten the terms of the feminist/queer split. After all, he both insisted on the importance of sex difference and, simultaneously, that this difference might not be readily apparent.

* * *

"From its inception," Huffer argues, "queer theory has embraced the performative rupture of constrictive (hetero)normative narratives, including those narratives that would bind the queer subject in any static or definitive way."[46] Indeed, in a useful 1994 mapping, Biddy Martin charts the ways in which the then-emergent protocols of queer theory relied on a performative separation from feminism (and the female) as the confining ground against which *queer* could move. In particular, Martin suggests that in trying to secure their institutional position as practitioners of a new or "vanguard" discipline, queer theorists mobilized figures of gender-crossing and cross-identification in order to produce *queer* as "figural, performative, playful, and fun" in opposition to "their own projections of fixity, constraint, or subjection . . . onto feminism or the female body."[47] "In the process," Martin worries, "the female body becomes its own trap and the operations of misogyny disappear from view."[48] Martin's critique certainly rhymes with trans critiques of queer theory, which also focus on the queer theory's preference for figural crossings and discourse analysis at the expense of the material of trans lives, the force of the interior, the "drag" of the body, and the operations of transphobia.[49] At the same time, Martin's use of a trans metaphor to describe the misogynist damage that *queer* does indexes a certain trouble with transmasculinity that haunts her essay.

Although this trouble threads through Martin's argument, it is most obvious at the moment when the existence of the "female-to-male transsexual" comes fully into view.[50] Here, Martin objects to Gayle Rubin's cartography of butch masculinity and particularly to Rubin's stressing the proximity of butch to FTM. According to Rubin, some butches are gender dysphoric, and some aren't; many are erotically oriented to more feminine partners, whereas others aren't; "[m]any butches have partially male gender identities," while "others border on being, and some are, female-to-male transsexuals (FTMs), although many lesbians *and* FTMs find the area of overlap between butchness and transsexualism disturbing."[51] Indeed, what Martin finds disturbing about the area of overlap is that it seems to make "gender dysphoria or gender dysfunction too central to butchness, [which] constructs butchness in negativity, curiously makes anatomy the ground of identity, . . . [and] suggests that femmes, by contrast to butches, are at least implicitly gender conformist."[52] But by insisting on the distance between butch and FTM, Martin makes the trans man into the "real" holding place of gender trouble. Trans men, then, are *by definition* mired in negativity, attach too much meaning to anatomy, and cast femininity and the female body as a decidedly unresistant and unqueer "swamp."[53]

In pointing this out, I do not mean to take away from the force of Martin's critique. Rather, I mean to suggest that Martin's essay clarifies something about the peculiar status of transmasculinity in much 1990s queer and queer-feminist thinking. On the one hand, as Martin argues, *figures of* transmasculine cross-identification were central to, for example, Eve Kosofsky Sedgwick's analytic separation of gender and sexuality and, therefore, to the domains of feminist and queer critique. But in a real way, the queerness of cross-identification in Martin's schema more or less depends on it remaining figural, on the cross-identifying lesbian not transitioning to become James Dean.[54] On the other hand, because Martin herself understands these cross-identifications as forms of "escape from gender," trans men can only appear in her analysis as literalizing the excesses of her vision of queer theory, including its projections of conformity onto female femininity, its neglect of the body's function as "a drag on signification," and its forgetting of "the all-too-obvious and thus invisible difference that it makes to be a woman."[55] In both the queer theory she critiques and her queer-feminist rejoinder, trans men actually have no place.

Of course, what happens in the "territories of queer gender" is in fact nothing like freedom from gender.[56] Rather, as a variety of 1990s and early 2000s dispatches attest, inhabiting that territory was and is an experience shot through with fracturing dislocation and vulnerability to gendered and gendering abuse, even as there was not a language for making that vulnerability known that did not require forms of self-splitting and self-erasure. Indeed, C. Jacob Hale narrated his attempts to be known in and by feminist theoretical contexts as encounters with "indiscriminate erasure."[57] Other transsexual writers of the time, most notably Jay Prosser, responded to this sense of the placelessness of trans men within queer and feminist thought—even as transmasculine people and something we should certainly call transness were central to both—by insisting on the absolute difference of *trans*. For Prosser, only by insisting on this difference could "*the* transsexual man's story–his particular narrative of becoming" be rendered in its specificity as a story that is precisely about crossing *through* the "uninhabitable space" of queer gender in order to resolve painful divisions of consciousness and be delivered "home."[58] Hale, on the other hand, asks after what can be known from a "subject position . . . constituted by dislocatedness" and fracture.[59] Without rehearsing the full nature of the disagreement between Prosser and Hale, I mean only to point out that both scholars depict trans[masculine] subjectivity as fundamentally dissociative, fractured, split. But whereas for Prosser what *trans* discloses is the unlivability of "double consciousness," for Hale it is only and precisely the capacity to hold and bear "plural self-images," some of which might be utterly unrecognizable, that will enable transmasculine people to remain bound to feminist worlds, despite the way those images are used.[60]

* * *

At this juncture I would like to ask a question. Didn't the function of transmasculinity in these exchanges arise from the uncomfortable proximity of (implicitly nontrans) lesbian and FTM, from the suspicion that the trans man's very existence is a version of f's displacement? This suspicion animates Hale's attempt to construct a feminist vocabulary for transmasculinity that does not understand FTMs as "gender traitors" and is enacted explicitly in the exchange between Rubin and Martin.[61] Rubin argues that the trans man should be kept inside the lesbian fold, whereas Martin ejects him in order to claim the butch as a woman because what appeared to be a description of "the wild profusion of existing things" from one perspective, from another looked like a displacement or denigration of f by m under the sign of *queer*.[62] But the same suspicion certainly haunts the feminist academic present. An example is Huffer's 2013 *Are the Lips a Grave?* whose very title foregrounds the queer/feminist split as a problem related to sex difference, which "identfie[s] . . . a masculinist universalism at work in the deployment of the seemingly inclusive category of 'queer'" and mentions *trans* only once, in the notes, where Huffer aligns *The Transgender Studies Reader* with *queer*.[63] And so, if the answer to my question is yes, then the follow-up question is: But mightn't trans masculinities have just as much to do with gay male genders as with lesbian ones? In fact, hasn't this been latent in the discourse surrounding the butch/FTM border all along, in Rubin's *catamite*, in Lou Sullivan's excavation of Jack Garland, even in the Brandon Teena archive?[64]

From the vantage point of the present, the pairing of the trans man and the nontrans gay man should seem utterly unsurprising. Indeed, before the plot proper of *Boys Don't Cry* begins to unfold, we are presented with a scene in which Brandon's cousin, who we'll come to know later as Lonny, participates in the making of Brandon's masculinity. Lonny, whose vocal inflection marks him as queer even before he appears on screen, cuts Brandon's hair and instructs him on the proper performance of boyhood. His admonishments—stuff the crotch with one sock instead of two, cut the hair short but not too short, don't wear that ridiculous cowboy hat—are all about paring down excess: masculinity, in this scene, is a performance but one that rests on the relative invisibility of its props.[65] Notably, whenever the two are in the same shot in this opening scene, Lonny appears behind Brandon; gay male masculinity appears not only as what fashions transmasculinity but stands behind it as a kind of prerequisite or ground. In part, the film suggests, this is because both inhabit, knowingly, the contingency of m: looking at Brandon, cigarette dangling precariously from his lip, Lonny jokes, approvingly, "If you was a guy, I might even wanna fuck you," to which Brandon replies, "You mean if *you* was a guy, you might even wanna fuck me."

This mirrored relationship is captured in a moment in the scene in which the camera is positioned such that Lonny's body is outside the shot, but we can see Brandon's back and his reflection as he looks into the mirror and Lonny's reflection standing behind him, looking on as Brandon smooths his hair and postures in the frame. After this scene, Lonny more or less vanishes

FIGURE 3.1. Mirrored masculinity (*Boys Don't Cry*, Twentieth Century Fox, 1999).

FIGURE 3.2. Lonny as Brandon's vanishing ground (*Boys Don't Cry*, Twentieth Century Fox, 1999).

from the story, so this shot is metonymic of their relationship: the gay man, like a reflection, enables the expression of transmasculinity but is only visible when our attention is trained in the right direction. The cultural recurrence of this scene in which a nontrans gay man inaugurates and props up a transmasculine gender/narrative suggests that there is something to this relation that unease about the proximity of the butch and FTM has caused critics to overlook. In turn, doesn't this pairing suggest that formulations that take for granted the butch/FTM border—that take for granted that Brandon and therefore the transmasculine "subject [is] dependent on the recognition of a woman"—might be missing something about transmasculinity?[66] That is, whatever else it might be, *Boys Don't Cry* remains useful to think with, at least for me, insofar as it formalizes and renders cinematic a set of habits of thought and argumentation that left their mark on this paper trail of 1990s queer and feminist theorizing: worries about the ontological status of the trans man, an animating concern about the gendering work of sexual violence, the active erasure of race as meaningful in order to make these conversations cohere, and gay male gender as transmasculinity's vanishing ground.

Following this frequently gestured toward but—in the academic literature—relatively unexplored pairing of the trans man and nontrans gay man offers ways of thinking about dissociative transmasculinity in terms other than those offered by the impasse between *feminist* and *queer*, animated as it often was by intracommunity conflicts surrounding *butch* and *FTM*. In particular, it allows me to dwell with the reality that traumas of sex *are* integral to much transmasculine literature and thought, but it also allows me to insist that this need not lead to readings that understand transmasculinity as fundamentally a "[defense] against the vulnerabilities and degradations associated with femininity."[67] By way of conclusion, I would like to think with one such pairing by reading Elliott DeLine through an essay by Ernesto Martínez. While no one trans appears in Martínez's essay, I insist that it is trans, insofar as it requires something trans from us. Specifically, it requires a willingness to suspend what we think we know about hardened divisions in the social, a suspension of belief that is the prerequisite for trans movements and trans thought.

Finally, in selecting what to read alongside DeLine here, I gravitated toward Martínez's essay because of the way this pairing implicitly troubles the whitened, binary, and tacitly white supremacist logic that structures incessant conversations about which people and bodies do or do not belong to gendered categories and spaces.[68] This logic, which was literalized in the nuisance ordinances discussed in chapter 1, undergirds the TERF wars that were the subject of chapter 2, and lingers on in the rhetoric of the butch/FTM "border wars." In what follows, I read DeLine through Martínez, but it is equally possible to read the two against—or, more nearly, alongside—one another as racially differentiated accounts of living with the damage of the "modern/colonial gender system."[69]

"I Know Very Well How I Got My Name"

In an autotheoretical essay interested in developing frameworks for understanding "queer Latino forms of embodied consciousness that do not fit conventional expectations of 'liberatory' activity in response to oppression," Martínez meditates on his own seeming unresponsiveness, his unwillingness to fight back, in the face of violence.[70] The essay opens with a scene in which an older cousin fondles young Ernesto and then proceeds to pin him to the bed, choke him, and grind against him. This scene is just one of the essay's many examples of heteropatriarchal violence committed against the body of the child Martínez was, but it is the most fully elaborated, the one which colors each subsequent encounter. Rather than viewing his inaction as a lack of agency, as "someone whose gender and sexuality came into formation through violence," Martínez returns to the scene of his childhood in order to reflect on the things such a gendered position allowed him to learn.[71] Namely, such violent masculinity was "a time- and space-contingent fiction, a public-sphere expression of heteronormative impenetrability revealed to be astoundingly porous behind closed doors," but also there was a cost to that knowledge (submitting oneself to violation).[72]

Specifically, Martínez suggests that to have been a boy in such a position produced alternatives to the queer masculinity that would identify with Foucault's institutionalized pervert and not also the little girl he "almost, partly, or more or less raped."[73] Indeed, by responding with inaction and not with violence in kind, Martínez understands himself to have been refusing or postponing his own entrance into such constructions of masculinity. In turn, this trans gendering leads him toward, and not away from, the world of women who responded to his inaction by bringing him "into their fold, not only helping me postpone the coercive demands of heteropatriarchal masculinity but also offering me new spaces within which I could practice my gender differently. . . . Among women, I was not free from violence . . . but among women, nonetheless, I felt the glimmer of new possibilities."[74] Unlike Leo Bersani, then, whose queer knowledge of the "suicidal ecstasy" of sexualized powerlessness inaugurates the antisocial thesis in queer theory, Martínez's similar knowledge is leveraged toward understanding how selves are made and how relationality can be sustained.[75]

For Martínez, inaction was facilitated by a kind of retreat—what he calls inwardness—into an expanded interior life, a retreat that allowed him to inhabit a gap between capital-M masculinity and "differently" or something else. While Martínez defines this retreat inward as the "opposite of what psychologists mean by maladaptive dissociation," as it involves a retreat into reality and not away from it, it's also clear that inwardness *is* a kind of dissociation, a psychic product of violence and also a way of surviving it, a breach or split introduced into psychic life by trauma.[76] In writing the essay, that is, Martínez inhabits the breach intentionally in order to understand what it has made possible. This method of narrating from the breach is part of what makes Elliott DeLine's *Refuse* a noteworthy piece of trans cultural production.

In contrast to Prosser's argument that the function of trans life writing is to "join [the] split" that inaugurates the trans plot, DeLine uses the autofiction form to further multiply himself through splitting.[77] Formally, the novel is fractured between a first-person narrator (Dean) and a protagonist (also Dean) who is talked about in the third person. This fracturing has many effects, one of which is that the narrator repeatedly interrupts our ability as readers to sympathize with Dean the protagonist and to interpret the novel. For example, early on Dean the narrator asserts: "I imagine . . . this text won't make it into classroom settings. By the end I will have picked over this story to death. There will be nothing left for you hungry vultures to say in your Contemporary Queer Literature Seminars that I haven't made plain in English."[78] Like this one, Dean the narrator's asides are nearly always snarky and declare that they are intended to keep us at an emotional and interpretive distance; because Dean is narrating from the future of the diegetic frame, we are alerted to the fact that this protagonist will turn out not to be worth our sympathy and that the novel has been thoroughly theorized before we arrived.

Thus, DeLine's fractured narration enacts a series of, well, refusals. The novel refuses to cohere as a text just as the novel's narrator-protagonist refuses to cohere as a self. Dean the narrator—who recognizes and overperforms his self-involvement; who insults his readers, himself, and trans discourse in general—is almost entirely unsympathetic. DeLine's performed disinterest in producing a sympathetic character enacts a refusal of the tradition of trans autobiography whose function has been precisely to produce sympathy, to convince the reader that the trans person in question "really is" a woman or man, or at least a human being worthy of love and dignity, "just like" the reader. Early on Dean the narrator rejects this possibility outright by declaring, "unlike my kindred memoirists, there's nothing I will beg you to believe. You see, I know I'm not a real man. I inject their hormones into my body, I assume their secondary sex characteristics, I play dress up, prowl about and live in their world, but I am not one of them. Nor am I otherwise."[79] But this also has the effect of refusing trans-antagonistic narratives that insist that trans people are either incredibly deceptive or have been deceived into believing the fiction of gender, because Dean can't be a dupe of gender if he already knows that he is one. Finally, we begin and end the novel in the narrator's present tense, in which Dean has failed to build a world for himself and has consequently moved back in with his parents, where he seems to do nothing but drink coffee and "lounge around the same suburban house, striking bored, artistic poses," the novel itself being one of these bored, artistic poses.[80] This narrative trajectory enacts a refusal to grow up, a refusal to be integrated into the normative narrative in which one must grow up, get married, and have kids, a narrative that underlies the search for "real gender" that has, in the past, largely driven the transsexual plot.[81]

As a genre that seems fundamentally characterized by the desire for integration, first and foremost of self and body but also of the self into society and consequently the state, trans autobiography is often described in terms of its normative desires, its collusion with capitalism, imperialism, nationalism, and heteropatriarchal gender. Dean's plot, however, performs a failure (willed or otherwise) of integration at each of these levels. While Dean's character certainly develops over the course of the novel, this development is not what we might call maturation or aimed at integration. For instance, in the very last scene of the novel, Colin—Dean's friend/love interest who hasn't contacted him in months—turns up on Dean's doorstep begging him to join his relatively successful band. Colin tries to entice Dean with money, the promise of urban life, and the chance to "be somebody" as opposed to being stuck "nowhere" with a bachelor's degree in literature. Ultimately, Dean's development is reflected in his ability to recognize that continuing to chase this particular image of a successful life isn't worth it, but by rejecting it he's left to turn around and head "back inside" to a life he also finds alienating and unsustaining.[82]

That is, making Dean such a bad (i.e., incoherent, nonproductive, antisocial) subject allows DeLine to stage a millennial performance of the antisocial thesis in queer theory by making Dean precisely resemble the subject it valorizes. For that reason, *Refuse* is full of the traces of the academic queer "books on Theories" that it mocks.[83] In particular, it is, for me, difficult to read the novel without hearing distorted echoes of Halberstam's *In A Queer Time and Place*. Both texts frame queerness "as an outcome of strange temporalities, imaginative life schedules and eccentric economic practices" and develop the queer time/space of extended adolescence to figure the way in which queer lives resist institutionalized narratives about the normative life cycle.[84] Halberstam argues, in particular, for the necessity of queer subcultural spaces, since they "produce alternative temporalities" that allow their participants to believe in alternative futures.[85] Likewise, DeLine closes the main text of *Refuse* with a strange scene in which his unemployed twenty-something protagonist almost kills himself but instead listens to the wrong song and finds "[him]self giggling and unable to stop." Rather than foreclosing his own future, Dean enters into the unexpected time and space of a particular song by the Smiths and suddenly realizes that he "was still a child, with all potentials intact. I could be both, I could be neither, I could be nothing," and it's almost as if a queer theoretical, postmodern exuberance has suddenly entered into the narrative to save the day.[86]

Dean, that is, occupies the theoretically overburdened territories of queer gender and much of the project of *Refuse* is charting how it feels—in DeLine's time and place—to do so. However, while both DeLine and Halberstam ultimately offer a politics or ethics of refusal, the feelings that each understands to attend such a life are utterly divergent. Halberstam develops his map of the territory in relation to the AIDS crisis and the exclusion of trans/queer people from institutions of family, inheritance, and labor. While this vision of queer time emerged from institutionalized precarity and shortened life span, Halberstam focuses on how lives lived in queer time are not simply about making do but rather are about exploring and willfully taking up the alternatives that open up "once one leaves the temporal frames of bourgeois reproduction and family, longevity, risk/safety, and inheritance" that underlie the logic of accumulation.[87] Consequently, even as Halberstam acknowledges the risks that attend occupying queer territories—life, livelihood, security—his text is tinged with intimacy, the thrill of performance, the camp humor of Austin Powers, and hope in the antinormative otherwise, a hope that relies on queer subcultural spaces being eccentric to the logic of late capitalism.

DeLine, on the other hand, is writing in a context in which nearly all the queer subcultural forms Halberstam invests hope in have been fairly neatly incorporated into the market, marked within the novel by the mainstream success of Colin's "alternative" band due to his ability to fashion his trans identity into a commodity. Because of this seemingly limitless capacity of late capitalist incorporation, DeLine's novel suggests, the queer space Halberstam charts is increasingly narrow. He insists that while *queer*'s refusal and dogmatic antinormativity might describe what it is like to live in the territories of queer gender, in the absence of workplace protections and decent affordable health care, among other things, and in the face of the increasingly world-organizing force of homonormativity and homonationalism—the contemporary condition of LBG and increasingly T inclusion that colludes with the production of racialized/gendered/classed precarity locally and globally—this is probably not a viable, livable life. Indeed, every character in the novel who takes on the mandate of antinormativity is ultimately and utterly ejected from their social worlds, even ostensibly queer ones, and vanishes from the narrative. For example, Dean bonds with a gloomy trans woman named Teddy when he reluctantly attends a meeting of a trans support group. Because of her inability to cohere into a stably gendered self, the group, though ostensibly meant for her, views Teddy as a disturbance, not a member, and she eventually kills herself—she's socially dead and then just dead. In this context, to refuse, according to DeLine, is to become refuse and to feel like trash.

While DeLine's overt, defensive engagement with his literary and theoretical predecessors enables *Refuse*, it also makes for a very frustrating read. By enacting this series of refusals, DeLine—just like Dean, his proxy—creates a space that is very much like Martínez's "inwardness," "a practice of . . . recognition of oneself to oneself" that might look like doing nothing but is actually a retreat into one's inner life, a means of inhabiting, and reflecting on, while also refusing to occupy "social contexts bent on causing harm."[88] Dean, by reducing his world to his bedroom in his parents' house—and DeLine, by systematically refusing external narratives and theories—expands his inner life, becoming preoccupied with his feelings and thoroughly theorizing them, which is precisely what the novel does. Like Martínez's account of himself as a child who seemed not to respond in the face of violence meant to interpret him, *Refuse* and its protagonist simultaneously solicit and preempt outside interpretation. In light of this, moments in the text that DeLine leaves untheorized take on particular significance, not only because these are rare moments that give the reader space to make their own interpretations but also because they mark the limits of available frames of reference.

One such moment, about a third of the way in, stands out as particularly important. In this scene, Dean, feeling especially wretched, runs along the side of the road and pauses to examine a dead blackbird. From where he is standing, he can also see into the lit windows of domestic spaces, "where there are trophy rooms and kitchenettes and household appliances galore," but he feels estranged from these scenes of hetero-/homonormative life and wonders how it is he came to inhabit this queer territory that has left him feeling "more akin to the bird."[89] For a moment Dean muses:

> On nights like this I can't help but . . . wonder what combination of events brought me to this present. If I could, would I go back and undo the damage, blow out the consecutive candles that lead me down this dark path? Or was it written in the stars, and by this I mean programmed in my mutated genes? Or, dare I say it; was it someone else's influence? Well, was it? If I could go back in time and change that, would I? Could I? No piercing penetration, no stifled terror, no wondering "this is it?" There would be no whiskey or pills in my stomach that night, and so my tongue and lips would be able to form the shapes they required, my pubescent female larynx would be able to utter the vital sound. "No," I would say, "No, no, no, no, no, no, no." I would not be discarded. This is a cop-out. This isn't relevant. I never want to talk about this again.[90]

If, so far, *Refuse* has referred both to the queer refusal of coherence and the social/affective state that follows from it, then this moment introduces and enacts a different kind of refusal. While Dean wonders, retrospectively, about the effects of his inability to literally refuse, to say "no" during an experience of unwanted penetration, the scene also enacts a moment of narrative refusal, a refusal to theorize the relationship between past and present, between experience and identity, between stereotype and self. And while the effect of this refusal is effectively to close off this moment from the rest of the text, it isn't trashed but merely displaced. Indeed, this scene of sexual violence that *Refuse* refuses becomes the core of DeLine's next book.

This next book, *I Know Very Well How I Got My Name*, is something of a prequel to *Refuse*, though it's formally a very different text. It's narrated in the first-person present tense and is a straightforward, linear account of Dean's childhood and adolescence, the story of his unfolding gendered self-awareness, literally the story of how he got his name. However, this title is also mirrored in the scene that *Refuse* refuses, a scene in which Dean is raped by an on-again, off-again friend/love interest named Amy. Within the trajectory of the otherwise linear coming-of-age narrative, this particular scene is quite strange. Narratively, this is the first chapter in which the genre of lesbian coming-of-age plot begins to fray. It begins with Dean—who is not yet out to himself or to others as trans—preparing for a sleepover at Amy's house (where his mom will drop him off, one of the perks of queer adolescence), excited because he anticipates losing his virginity that night. Everything in the story so far leads the reader to expect that they know how this will go: the shy, strange adolescent has gay sex and finally finds her/himself anchored to a world and identity to which s/he belongs. But while DeLine sets up this plot for his readers, and Dean expects his story to unfold according to its logic, something goes terribly wrong.

Slipping in and out of consciousness, Dean surfaces "as a sharp pain shoots through my lower abdomen. Her finger's where I tried to put a tampon once, but it hurt and I gave up and forgot about it after that. It feels similar—that stabbing pain, below my belly." Finding himself unable to speak, Dean wonders: "Is this sex? There must be something wrong with me because this is awful."[91] The event that we anticipate will suture Dean to some coherent sense of sexual identity winds up propelling him even farther away from it though the sensation of pain that registers Dean's visceral failure to be f. If this were not clear enough, afterward Amy affectionately tells Dean that he is "definitely a transgender," giving him a language that had previously been unavailable to him. What's more, Amy names him, declaring, "I'm going to call you Dean."[92] The double meaning of the title is instructive, since it makes both the transgender trajectory *and* the story of an abusive relationship the core of the novella. More than that, it links them, making them (perhaps) indistinguishable. Formally, too, this scene marks the origin of *Refuse* insofar as it is the place in which the straightforwardness of first-person narration breaks down. Precisely by narrating in the first person the experience of moving through discrete states of consciousness, of being present but unable to control one's body/voice and consequently becoming an object to oneself, DeLine sets the conditions by which we retrospectively might understand the fractured narration of *Refuse* in which the "I" and "he," the subject and object of narration, are ostensibly the same. One way of reading this, then, is that the dissociative structure of *Refuse* is produced by this doubled story of how Dean got his name.

To be clear, neither DeLine nor Martínez consents to popular and psychiatric narratives in which homo- or transsexuality are unproblematically "caused by" sexual violation. However, in both texts, such violence is both fracturing and also the vehicle by which shy, strange, queer children come to know more fully the range of gendered and sexual possibilities, ushering their narratives into previously unavailable spaces, and introducing a breach (Martínez's inwardness and DeLine's formally fractured *Refuse*) from within which the gendered world can be more adequately apprehended.[93] Importantly, this is not immediately reconcilable with most articulations of sexual violence's gendering work. For example, while not interested in the feminist/queer split per se, Pamela E. Barnett's *Dangerous Desire: Literature of Sexual Freedom and Sexual Violence since the Sixties* sheds light on and historicizes its terms. Barnett argues that in American literature invested in social change since the 1960s, freedom is figured as transgressive sexuality and liminal identity, and rape has functioned "as a narrative strategy for defensively containing or tragically undermining the liberatory impulses that characterize the social movements each texts explores."[94] For Barnett, rape functions as a gendering (and racializing) discourse that secures the "ossified social structures of mid-twentieth-century America, [and] also the psychological coherence of various raced and gendered subjects" that discourses of freedom linked to black, gay, and women's liberation movements necessarily threaten.[95]

The odd thing about Barnett's book is that her approach to rape as "a discourse and disciplinary technology which instantiates the "social man" and the "social woman" ultimately requires that her study performs the same kind of work as do the texts she analyzes.[96] While Barnett's Foucauldian model is avowedly an attempt to move away from a frame in which "woman" is defined as essentially and naturally prone to injury, "woman" in this formulation is still utterly determined by her violation: "It follows, from [her] argument, that even when a male is raped, he is raped as a woman, as it were" because "the rape victim or survivor is routinely discursively feminized whether he is a man . . . whether she is androgynous and resistant to traditional femininity . . . or whether she is a lesbian."[97] Even while being motivated by an attachment to the politics of liberation figured by the liminal, the androgynous, the trans, Barnett's insistence on reading a "discursively feminized" male, for example, as a woman and not something else strangely works to evacuate the territory of queer gender. Not only does the rape narrative aim to reassert "ossified" binary identity but this way of reading also seems to insist that it is always successful in doing so.

Consequently, *Boys Don't Cry* appears in Barnett's notes as an example of post-1960s representation "in which rape is a mechanism for gendering otherwise liminal subjects."[98] However, it strikes me that it is only possible to read *Boys Don't Cry* in this manner if one has decided in advance how it is that gendering violence works in representation, that raped = woman. Of course, this is actually the intent of the rape both in the narrative of *Boys Don't Cry* and in the real-life events on which it is based. And, of course, in the film's visual and narrative logic, rape *does* function as the dividing line between the men and the women—everyone but Lana is repelled by

Brandon's transsness at first, but his having been raped draws all the women in the film into his sympathetic sphere. Finally, of course, the strange post-rape sex scene in which Brandon lets himself be touched "like" he touches Lana for the first time indicates that the film would like us to believe that the rape's effect was to make Brandon legible—to Lana, to himself—as a lesbian. However, no representation of the Brandon Teena story has done as much to secure Brandon *as* Brandon, as precisely not a woman.

While the question of some feminists' complicity with reifying the link between "woman" and "injury" has been, for others, a productive one, I'm much more interested in how this kind of analysis of rape forcefully reinscribes "ossified" categories of gender in the moment when it forcefully articulates their harms. This rearticulation of m/f, m > f in order to account for its harms doesn't seem inevitable; after all, just as *Boys Don't Cry* seems to have divergent intents and effects with regards to gendering its protagonist, the fundamentally fracturing nature of trauma seems to ensure that the intents and effects of gendering violence will never predictably map onto each other. That ossified gender, even where it is most violently enforced, is not inevitable is the lesson of DeLine's and Martínez's narration from the breach. In particular, with Clare, they make a space from which to think about how sexual violence as a gendering discourse can, and does, fail. Or more specifically, these narratives take sexual violence, which both in fact and in figuring is inextricable from conventional understandings of the relationship between sex, sexuality, and gender and produce gender failure rather than reproducing its binary form. Trans gender, they suggest, might be properly understood not as fantasies of uninhibited crossing but rather as one trace of the glitches in mechanisms of social reproduction.

But finally, and of course, the impulse to naturalize m/f in the context of sexual violence is so strange precisely because many forms of feminism have long understood producing gender failure as their aim. While Halberstam identifies gender failure as the aim of what he terms "shadow feminisms" driven by "negativity, rejection, and transformation" rather than "positivity, reform, and accommodation," it also certainly drives feminisms overtly organized around things like healing and harm reduction.[99] Feminists invested in battered women's shelters and rape crisis centers, for example, not only because they offered respites from violence but also because they served as consciousness-raising centers; these were spaces in which women learned to apprehend gendered webs of power in order to alter them or extricate themselves from them, to *become feminists*. As Patrick Califia suggested three decades ago, feminism itself can be understood as an expression of gender dysphoria or, in my terms, a trace of the failure of gender to be reliably reproduced.[100] Put another way, the shelter—like Martínez's time in the fold of women—was produced in response to shattering experiences of gendering violence, but in being inhabited, it produced something other than heteropatriarchal gender. As Martínez notes, this knowledge of contingency gained through violation might not be—and certainly does not feel—worth it for the individual, but it is, perhaps, a more apt description of what is going on.

4

We's Company

[Transsexuals] see their true self . . . as residing inside, hidden from view, and separated from the world. —**LESLIE LOTHSTEIN, *FEMALE-TO-MALE TRANSSEXUALISM* (1983)**

I'm all alone inside
a riddle. —**ELY SHIPLEY, "PLAYING DEAD," *SOME ANIMAL* (2018)**

In spring 1960, Lobzang Jivaka—formerly known as Michael Dillon, an Englishman who was technically next in line to be the Baronet of Lismullen—was on his way to Rizong, a monastery in Ladakh, perched high in the Himalayas. For three months, Jivaka lived and worked as a novice in the monastery, and although he was perpetually hungry, unable to speak the language of those around him, and occupying a social position meant for boys many years his junior, these were among the best times of his life. At Rizong, "something had loosened inside him; some channel to joy had opened up."[1] In fact, he'd felt this way before, notably in a place less susceptible to his Orientalist projections. Between 1946 and 1949, Dillon spent much of his life in a very different kind of heterotopia: Rooksdown House, a unit of Park Prewitt Hospital in Basingstoke, England, overseen by pioneering plastic surgeon Sir Harold Gillies.

Rooksdown was established as a military plastic surgery unit during World War II. During the war, Gillies and his team tended primarily to wounded soldiers and civilians, reconstructing singed eyelids and faces injured by shrapnel. However, from World War I until his retirement in the early 1950s, Gillies also performed many of what we would now consider to be mundane cosmetic and reconstructive surgeries, as well as surgeries to "correct" ambiguous genitalia.[2] As a result, at any given moment, Rooksdown housed people with a wide array of nonnormative morphologies, forming what Jivaka/Dillon's biographer Pagan Kennedy calls "a small society of the mutilated and the maimed."[3] There, as a patient among patients, Dillon, who was ordinarily "stunted . . . turned witty, expansive, even popular."[4] Indeed, he describes emceeing the Rooksdown Christmas party as the experience of "making [his] debut into the social world."[5]

Aside from these moments of interpersonal loosening and expansiveness, Dillon's life was marked by periods of intense withdrawal, sequestering, and retreat. While his withdrawal often took the form of self-imposed solitude, it also included a series of retreats into smaller and more bounded social institutions; over the course of his life, Dillon moved from the university, to Rooksdown, to a fifty-bed hospital he tried to remake in Rooksdown's image, to a series of ships, to a monastery in India run by a fellow Englishman, and finally to Rizong. And while Jivaka/Dillon's movement between these worlds doubtlessly resulted from his lifelong "Search for Truth," his choice to insert himself into ever smaller and more secluded scenes of collective life might be best accounted for by Dillon's status as what many consider to be the first female-to-male transsexual to transition both hormonally and surgically.[6] For this reason, he spent much of his life alternatingly "sequestered" or in flight, going to great lengths to avoid exposure.[7]

Although what follows is not about the historical person Michael Dillon/Lobzang Jivaka per se, it is interested in Dillon—and specifically Michael Dillon as a figure improvising a life between names, onto-epistemologies, regimes of sex, and social locations—as an avatar for the form of trans maladjustment explored here: the trans recluse, trans trouble with all things social.[8] By *the social* I mean nothing less than the organization of the world that both enables and constrains the lives we can and do live, what kinds of subjects it is possible to think and, therefore, be. At the same time, I also mean *sociality*, the tendency toward (and quality of) everyday interactions with other people. These two meanings of *social* are mutually reinforcing: those constructed as trouble to the organization of society often find that they have trouble navigating the dominant world of other people, trouble produced by inaccessible architectures, persistent misreading, lack of regard, epistemological and physical violence, and so on, all the things that led Dillon to "renounc[e] the world" and drove Ralph Ellison's invisible narrator underground.[9] That is, "if one's appearance in a situation or social world is contingent on misrecognition and encounters with macro- and microaggressions," then one might reasonably respond by enacting various kinds of withdrawal in order "to limit or avoid altogether . . . such situations."[10] In turn, being withdrawn from the world comes to be seen as a characteristic of such subjects, something in them and not (also) in the world. We've seen this already in the characterization of transsexuals as a class of "isolated, withdrawn, schizoid individuals," which Sandy Stone highlights as an example of how psychiatric discourse about trans people has told a flattened story; each of these terms links trans identity to a retreat from the external, social world.[11] Indeed, as M. Remi Yergeau has elucidated, the playbook for forms of curative violence regularly enacted on trans, gender-nonconforming, and autistic youth were developed alongside one another and rationalized by the construction of both groups of kids as fundamentally asocial, in need of socialization for their own good.[12]

At the same time, and contradictorily, *trans* is routinely figured as an extreme susceptibility to an external, ideological construction of gender, crystalized in Bernice Hausman's infamous characterization of trans people as "dupes of gender" and extended into the present by social contagion models of trans identity.[13] This particular trans-antagonistic formulation structures many contemporary conflicts around trans speech because it creates an impossible double bind that prevents trans people from ever appearing as authorities of their own experiences and perceptions of the world. Either the trans person misrecognizes their inner life as social reality or misrecognizes scripted social norms as their inner life; either way, transness is by definition a maladjusted relation to "the world."[14]

Admittedly, however, many forms of trans thought *have* long been marked by a certain measure of trouble with the social, and this trouble, in turn, gets *trans* in trouble. It is forever having to ward off charges of naive individualism, gender essentialism, or a lack of understanding of gender's location and function in "the social map of power."[15] Indeed, here, I begin by briefly outlining the major strategies early work in trans studies used to affirm trans speech, ultimately arguing that each of these models *does* begin from forms of withdrawal. But given the durability of withdrawal as a prevalent condition of trans life and thought, I question the assumption that something like asociality—namely, a turning away from the human (and the Human) world in favor of other forms of relationality—is what *trans* should and will overcome.[16] Therefore, in what follows, I conduct an experiment in reading with trans asociality, examining (and enacting) the function of solitary acts of reading in trans projects of world- and self-making, and the formal pressure *trans*'s trouble with sociality has exerted on trans writing. Placing Dillon's alongside more contemporary trans writing reveals, I suggest, an alternative, and enduring, lyric model of the (trans) self.

Affirming Trans Speech

At the core of the dynamics of the trans-antagonistic double bind outlined above is what Talia Bettcher terms "reality enforcement," in which trans speech is denied—whether by violence or substitution—or can never be heard as true.[17] Or as Laverne Cox has put it: "At the heart of the fight for trans justice is . . . that trans folks are often told we don't exist."[18] Consequently, trans scholars, artists, and activists have had to work to produce trans people as subjects of knowledge, which required developing strategies for affirming trans speech, for denying the denial. While I will briefly (certainly not exhaustively) address the three main such strategies as they were deployed in early trans studies—the wrong-body model, the gender-freedom model, and the queer trans model—it's worth pointing out that trans studies has from the beginning been marked, both implicitly and explicitly, by internal conflict between what I will refer to as transsexual theory—sometimes grounded in the wrong-body model, sometimes not—and queer trans theory. At the heart of this conflict, which inflects but is not contained by my mapping below, is not necessarily, as it might seem, different models of *trans* but rather different models of and justifications for *studies*. Whereas queer trans scholarship has tended to value trans people and culture insofar as they can be idealized as potent sites of counterhegemonic political and theoretical possibility, transsexual theory has tended to focus on the always already politically compromised mundane of trans life.

Briefly, the wrong-body model supposes that transness involves a misalignment between gender identity and gendered body, often articulated as being or feeling trapped in the wrong body. This is the most familiar account of trans subjectivity; it emerged in the context of sexology and has long been taken up by (and against) trans people attempting to give an account of themselves, especially in scenes of negotiating medical authority.[19] In *Second Skins*, Jay Prosser provides one of the most compelling accounts of the wrong-body model, derived from his readings of transsexual autobiographies. Rather than, or in addition to, demonstrating that this model is a historical effect of the medicalization of gender nonconformity as transsexuality, Prosser takes it literally, arguing that "because the [transsexual] subject speaks of the imaginary body as more real or more sensible . . . this phenomenon illustrates the material reality of the bodily ego rather than the phantasmatic status of the sexed body: the material reality of the imaginary."[20] In other words, the "correct" body was always already there as a phantom, and transition is merely a way of returning the skin to its own image. Thus, his "contention is that transsexuals continue to deploy the image of wrong embodiment because being trapped in the wrong body is simply what transsexuality feels like."[21] This tendency to take feeling/sensation literally or as something simple and abstractable marks much of transsexual theory. For example, much like Prosser, biologist and cultural critic Julia Serano provides the evidence of feeling in order to argue for the existence of "subconscious sex" that is "most certainly not the result of socialization or social gender constructs."[22] "After twenty years of exploration and experimentation," Serano recounts, "I eventually reached the conclusion that my female subconscious sex had nothing to do with gender roles, femininity, or sexual expression—it was about the personal relationship I had with my own body."[23]

By positing an innate body image, rather than gender identity, accounts like Prosser's and Serano's avoid one of the more potentially troubling tendencies of the wrong-body model. Indeed, this model's appeal to the felt innateness of gender underlies much of the iterative tensions among trans, feminist, and queer discourses.[24] However, even these accounts that focus on feelings about body morphology, rather than the social meanings of morphology, disavow that "our bodies"—including how we interpret them, how we feel about them—"are always shaped by the social world in which we are inescapably situated."[25] After all, the account that Serano gives of first recognizing her subconscious sex—standing in front of the mirror as an eleven-year-old, with lacy white curtains wrapped around her body "like a dress"—seems to have just as much, if not more, to do with social roles.[26] It's not clear, that is, that there can be a felt sense of the body that precedes what the body means. This is not to say that the felt sense of bodily or social dysphoria and its absence don't exert real, undeniable, palpable pressure on the lives of trans people; rather, trans thought that begins from the idea that these are evidence of innate sex/gender begins from a theory of embodiment that is profoundly withdrawn from the social.

Whereas the wrong-body model came to life in the clinic, the gender freedom model was developed as an explicitly transgender politics that aimed to encompass a wide array of people with nonnormative gender expressions: drag queens, butches, transvestites, transsexuals, and so on. *Trans*, here, is not a problem of innate misalignment; instead, it is what reveals the expectation that bodily configuration/gender expression/gender identity (i.e., male/masculine/man) will line up in an inevitable or predictable way to be a problem. As a political strategy for affirming trans speech, the gender freedom model argues that all people ought to be free to determine their genders and that all gender expressions ought to be affirmed.

As many have pointed out, this position withdraws from the social in two ways: first, by positing a subject who is somehow superagential in the formation of their gender, unaffected by social norms, possibilities, and prohibitions; and second, by making less than salient that gender is as much a hierarchical set of relations with others as it is a style or attribute of an individual.[27] Leslie Feinberg, for example, articulating a vision of gender freedom as the basis of trans liberation, argues: "No one's lipstick or flattop is hurting us. No one's gender expression is any more 'liberated' than anyone else's. . . . Each person has the right to express their gender in any way that feels most comfortable to them."[28] While Feinberg's desire to affirm all expressions of gender is understandable, and I belabor this point in chapter 2, it bears repeating that such strategies for affirming trans speech tend to ignore that, as they are also expressions of social power, some expressions of gender *are* indeed "hurting us." Or as Cressida Heyes puts it, "The expression of one gender may limit the possible meanings or opportunities available to others."[29]

Finally, although it's often mistaken for the gender freedom model, the queer trans model merely begins with the same premise. It, too, affirms trans speech on political grounds, and it, too, understands *trans* expansively and as revealing the binary sex/gender system to be a problem. However, whereas the gender freedom model affirms trans speech on the basis that all gender expression ought to be affirmed, the queer trans model affirms trans speech *because* it denaturalizes the logic of the binary sex/gender system. Outlining such a position, Bobby Noble, for example, calls for trans speech to deploy "contradiction and incoherence."[30] As a strategy for self-representation, incoherence, in Noble's account, allows trans to appear in its most "provocative form" by refusing "the medical and psychological categorical imperatives through which [trans] has always been forced to confess."[31]

Perhaps unsurprisingly, the main critique of queer trans theory has come from within trans studies itself; the primary concern is that its normative antinormativity actually, and like the wrong-body model, extends "expert" abstractions of trans life as developed in and by sexology and psychoanalysis. Emma Heaney, for example, traces the allegorization of transfeminine life—"the assumption that trans women's very existence *means something* outside itself, something about the gender of a putatively cis general subject"—from sexology and psychoanalysis, to the modernist novel, and ultimately into 1990s queer theory.[32] While Heaney focuses on transfemininity's itinerary through these expert discourses, transmasculinity has likewise been put to figural use. Indeed, the trans allegory pervaded queer trans theory, albeit in a nominally trans-affirmative way, insofar as *trans* was recruited as a figure of gender's instability, a provocation for imagining otherwise. But as Viviane Namaste argued decades ago, such moves necessarily depict trans life as being always about "challenging the sex/gender system," never about "the banality of buying some bread, of making photocopies, of getting your shoe fixed."[33] These provocative depictions, in turn, work against the ability to conceive of and take seriously "the everyday rhythms of the trans mundane," which are inevitably textured by forms of sociality that make living out gendered incoherence and "categorical indeterminacy" difficult, impossible, and even deadly.[34] Put differently, trans critiques of queer trans theory suggest that this model, too, begins from a turn away from the ways in which trans bodies, lives, and narratives are inescapably embedded in the worlds of other people. While this turning away allows queer trans theory to do some things exceptionally well, its dominance arguably extended expert unwillingness to be responsive to trans life as it is lived.

Appealing to María Lugones's model of the social—in which it is made up of multiple, interconnected worlds of sense that "stand in relations of power to other worlds"—Talia Bettcher has, over the years, developed a robust alternative starting place for trans theory and thought.[35] Of importance is that, following Lugones, she understands trans subcultures as worlds of sense in "resistant relation" to dominant worlds, "where part of what is under contestation are alternative gender practices (including the semantics of gender terms)":

> Indeed, in some trans subcultures, trans women can be taken as paradigmatic women rather than as women who are only marginally so. . . . This contestation is not merely verbal, since it tracks a contrast in underlying gender practices: there can be situations in which a trans woman lives a rich and vibrant life as a woman, has friends as a woman, is loved as a woman, inhabits a social milieu in which she is a woman. . . . and perhaps experiences sexual violence as a woman while simultaneously being viewed as a man who lives as a woman in dominant culture. In that culture, for example, if she were incarcerated, she would be housed in jail as a man, with other men; her entire life as a woman could be obliterated.[36]

Unlike the aforementioned models, which begin with dominant understandings, taking for granted trans worlds of sense removes the requirement for trans theory and politics to justify trans self-identity claims—either by an appeal to innate gender/sex or to political efficacy—because it is only within the dominant sense that these claims require justification. Affirmation of trans speech no longer becomes a continuous project of trans theory; rather, such affirmation must be taken for granted as trans theory's minimum ground.

While I agree with Bettcher that this account provides a more compelling starting place, it's clear that her thinking, too, begins with withdrawal, this time into trans social worlds: this is both where Bettcher has done her thinking and where her account begins.[37] However, I'm not sure how far Bettcher's account goes toward addressing the problem that sets *trans* off in search of a model to begin with. That is, while all minoritized lives are marked by similar conflicts within the social, both cause and effect of their marginality, *trans* does seem to have special trouble insofar as it is, in this time and place, *defined by* a discrepancy between gender attribution and gender identity. The problem, then, that sets trans plots in motion is that, as things stand, the conditions for recognition by others occur largely in the realm of the visible and usually require technologies in addition to language to alter. Thus, because attributed gender is largely what counts, how one is counted, what is ordinarily taken as invariant and true, trans sociality is, from the beginning and by definition, fraught.

In more concrete terms, even before Michael Dillon was "the first man-made man," navigating the world of other people was vexing and vexed. In his memoir, Dillon recounts what he terms a "shattering experience" of walking with a male acquaintance during his late adolescence, an experience whose dynamics are comparable to Bettcher's hypothetical trans woman whose life as a woman can be obliterated by (mis)recognition:

> We came up the cliff from the sea and somewhere there was a gate which he opened and stood aside to let me pass through first. Suddenly I was struck with an awful thought, for no one had done this for me before. "He thinks I'm a woman." It was a horrible moment and I felt stunned. I had never thought of myself as such despite being technically a girl. I finished the walk in silence, the silence of despair, and he never knew what he had done to upset me. But life could never be the same again. People thought I was a woman. But I wasn't. I was just me. How could one live like that? With no one to ask, I brooded long on this at nights in bed.[38]

In this scene, too, there is a conflict over how gender ought to be interpreted, a conflict that might best be understood as between a dominant sense and a trans one. And here, too, the dominant sense has the power to stun, to silence, to cause Dillon to lapse into despair. The difference is that there is "no one" Dillon can turn to for affirmation of his sense, no world outside of himself in which Dillon has ever been recognized as anything other than a woman or a girl, a difference conditioned by Dillon's life at the edge of the historical emergence of transsexuality and his aristocratic distance from extant working-class queer/trans social worlds. While Bettcher's withdrawal into trans worlds undoubtedly provides a more capacious place from which to interpret life and how to live in the "trans WTF"—how it is possible to both live as a paradigmatic woman/man/nonbinary person and be always at risk of having that life obliterated—*trans*'s asociality, its tendency toward withdrawal in the first place, seems rooted in the persistent, prior, and perhaps constitutive scene of misrecognition, of inhabiting the "not (yet)" in the perception of others.[39]

Given this, as well as the thick overlap between trans and autistic histories and presents, I am compelled by Yergeau's ambivalent, neuroqueer theorization of asociality as both a clinical construction that has authorized violence against autistic people and also an "autistic commonplace."[40] Of particular interest here is the way that Yergeau insists on asociality as a form of critique that is related but not identical to the antisocial turns of queer thought: "While antisocial rhetorics are typically conceived as those rhetorics that pervert and disrupt normative structures—that is, negating the already social—asocial rhetorics are rhetorics that complicate what we've come to understand as social. That is, they pose an affront not just to social bodies, but to the idea that sociality holds value unto itself. Asocial rhetorics bristle against the compulsoriness of interaction, of human engagement, on compliance with the neurotypical."[41] But while Yergeau's articulation of asociality bristles against compulsory human engagement, it is still, they stress, irreducibly relational, often in ways that extend "notions of communion and relationality beyond the human."[42] For example, Yergeau offers a common style of autistic play—preferring to line up dolls into "a database of doll bodies" rather than making them interact—as a scene of asociality that might help us "begin to resee irreducible relationality" as not equivalent to sociality as human engagement, but "as that which is forged with and between things, fields, spaces, air particles, moments, motion."[43] Alongside this scene, I would like to place a common trans style of reading—a style defined by perseveration, intensive cataloging, and (over)identification with necessarily nonhuman things like characters and storylines—as likewise a form of relational asociality that characterizes and enables some trans thought. I do so not to collapse trans and autistic styles, nor to weigh in on the widely hypothesized link between these two forms of minoritized difference. Rather, and simply, Yergeau's neuroqueer articulation offers one compelling way of thinking with trans asociality, which likewise emerges as both violent clinical and otherwise trans-antagonistic constructions and also familiar commonplaces in and about trans life.

One of the hallmarks of trans asociality, certainly, has been a tendency of trans thinkers to foreground what Audre Lorde calls the erotic—which, for her, is an interior well of knowledge that makes itself known as "an internal sense of satisfaction" and is explicitly separable from "external directives"—or what Kevin Quashie calls the sovereignty of the interior.[44] "Despite its name," Quashie insists, "the interior is not unconnected to the world of things (the public or political or social world), nor is it an exact antonym for exterior. Instead, the interior shifts in regard to life's stimuli but it is neither resistant to nor overdetermined by the vagaries of the outer world. The interior has its own ineffable integrity and it is a stay against the social world."[45] Although trans thinkers have called this "intra-subjectivity alone" or a sense of self that is had and manifested "alone," it clearly isn't, not exactly.[46] To draw this out, to think through *trans* in the lingering "not (yet)" as both relational and withdrawn—both bristling against and requiring [human] engagement—in what follows I will turn to (and enact) an arguably outdated commonplace of trans life and literature: the solitary prototranssexual brooding in their bedroom, reading and reading and reading and reading whatever they can find. However, my speculations about trans scenes of reading might apply equally well to another scene that is, as of this writing, at the center of a moral panic: the child alone with their computer, becoming trans.

Book People

Just as transsexuality actualizes itself first through narration . . . it also realizes itself through the practice of reading. Perceiving the world beyond oneself anew is vital to the preservation of psychic and somatic security, as is maintaining a sense of self regardless of how one is interpellated. —Alexander Eastwood, "How, Then, Might the Transsexual Read?" (2014)

The more I read, the closer I got to approaching the line that divides women from men, until I finally crossed over it. —Henry Rubin, "Trans Studies: Between a Metaphysics of Presence and Absence" (1999)

Frantz Fanon's famous account of the phenomenology of blackening begins with becoming an object of the white gaze. In his evocative allegory, a child on a train cries "Look! A Negro!" and Fanon's "I" finds itself "fixed . . . [as] a new type of man, a new species. A Negro, in fact!"[47] Further, because blackness is epidermalized, read on the skin, the Negro is "overdetermined from the outside"; he is read as black and, finding his own blackness "dense and undeniable," becomes it.[48] In contrast, *trans* names a species of man that, by official definition, contests the interpretative primacy of the visible in order to contest overdetermination from the outside. That is, while all social categories entail forms of misrecognition, *trans* is perhaps uniquely a social category defined by misrecognition. Dillon's scene at the gate, therefore, provides its own allegory, one that is nearly identical to Fanon's scene on the train, minus the ending. Again, there is a boy whose gaze interpellates an "I" into a particular category. Again, there is the dense undeniability of the body that has been made into categorical proof—Dillon cannot help but know that he is "technically a girl." Again, there is the disorientation that follows finding that one is not just a self but also an object for the other, and the necessary reorientation. But whereas in Fanon's allegory there can be no outside to interpellation—his Negro can fashion blackness into a resistant identity, or can resist the meanings attributed to blackness, but cannot resist that he *is* black—in Dillon's, this scene of interpellation as woman seems only to strengthen his conviction that he is not one. Dillon insists on "a subjectivity that seems to extend beyond interpellation," that can, in fact, flee from interpellation into a location withdrawn from the world of other people.[49] But without the possibility of recognition, how does one become trans?

Often the answer is: *by reading*. This shouldn't be a difficult thing to say, given the utter banality of the claim that encounters with literature and other media participate in shaping all of our senses of self. And yet it has long been the case that trans people's styles of interpreting and disseminating media are used as evidence of our duplicity, naivete, or pathology. For example, Bernice Hausman's readings of transsexual autobiographies in her 1995 *Changing Sex* foreshadow the interpretative playbook of contemporary proponents of social contagion models of trans identity. Briefly, Hausman portrays the autobiographies as formally withdrawn, characterized by a style of "closed narration" that prohibits the "critical reader" from dissenting from a trans author's interpretation of their experience of sex/gender.[50] In particular, she laments the way that the formal and argumentative moves of the autobiographies "force" her as a reader to interpret the mundane vagaries of human experience—bad sex, clumsy babysitting, a weird feeling at a gate—as unambiguous evidence of the author's gender identity.[51] Of course, the closed-offness that Hausman notes is, quite plainly, a strategy for negotiating the misrecognition that characterizes the trans experience of being read, a formal outcome of what trans literary critic Alexander Eastwood might affirmatively term a trans refusal of the "presum[ption that] the reader possesses an epistemologically superior position to the text."[52] "Obsessively aim[ing] at arousing a precise response" from within the shell of a "closed text" is often precisely what enables trans self-authorship in otherwise negating contexts.[53]

Though she acknowledges its self-protective function, Hausman reads the "interpretative foreclosure[s]" she encounters in her objects as nefarious, largely because of the style of interpretation—uncritical identification—that these texts, in turn, seem to solicit from their readers:[54] "For the reader interested in verifying his or her own gender confusions, these narratives provide ample opportunity for identification and mirroring. For a critical reader, on the other hand, the reading process can be confining, especially as the author makes blanket statements concerning gender, and sexuality. The purpose of the narratives is to force the reader to comply with the author's experience, to begin to interpret his or her own life along the same trajectory. To resist this interpretive insistence in the face of these monolithic narratives is exhausting."[55] In short, the asociality Hausman attributes to transsexual autobiographies—their tendency toward monologuing, their bristling against nontrans engagement—leads her to imply that they function as a form of text-based conversion therapy: it is "exhausting," she claims, to "resist" trans autobiographies' attempts to "force the reader to comply with the author's experience, to begin to interpret his or her own life along the same trajectory."[56] In turn, one can only resist by reading symptomatically and deconstructively rather than with and for identification, that is, only if one resists reading, in Hausman's schema, like a transsexual.

Certainly, Hausman's palpable anxiety about the circulation of transsexual autobiographies and their attendant style of reading as identification can and ought be understood as the outcome of an ideological opposition to the proliferation of trans life. At the same time, and plainly, it is a commonplace within trans worlds that reading in a trans way might, in fact, make you trans.[57] From at least 1928—the concurrent publication of Virginia Woolf's *Orlando* and Radclyffe Hall's *The Well of Loneliness*—emergence into ways of life we would now call trans has been represented by its subjects and by others as involving an explicit routing of identity through books (and other forms of media). In particular, as in my epigraphs, reading is often figured as a mode of asocial relation that supplies the self-making and self-sustaining functions that we ordinarily attribute to embodied human others, in place of those others.

Indeed, *The Well of Loneliness*, which follows the life of a female invert named Stephen Gordon, as well as the vast body of criticism that has arisen around the novel, is a prime example of the tendency to represent cross-gender identity and trans modes of interpretation as having to do with a too-close relationship with books, characterized by (over)identificatory reading. From the outset, Stephen's father is described as "too much of a student" and, certain his wife is pregnant with a son, names his unborn child after Saint Stephen, a character who "gripped his imagination" in his readings of the Bible "for its fine literature."[58] Further, quite early in the story, *The Well*'s young protagonist falls in love with a housemaid named Collins, and the "urgent necessity to love," in turn, alters Stephen's own relationship to books.[59] Whereas "at one time she had very much liked being read to, especially from books that were all about heroes . . . now such stories so stirred her ambition that she longed intensely to live them. She, Stephen, now longed to be William Tell, or Nelson."[60] In turn, Stephen attempts to bring the world of the story into her world by persistently dressing up as Nelson. Much of Stephen's ritual of becoming Nelson takes place in her room, alone with her own gaze. Alone, Stephen searches for "garments once used for charades" and dons them "with much swagger and noise, much strutting and posing, and much staring in the mirror."[61] That the garments were *once* used for charades but are no longer suggests that for Stephen there is something fundamentally different about dressing up as Nelson, something in the ritual that is other than play. In the guise of Nelson, Stephen declares, "I must be a boy 'cause I feel exactly like one."[62] Through this early identification with a character in a book, and using, as Heather Love puts it, "the powerful agents of costume, bodily performance, and erotic fantasy, Stephen effectively transforms herself into a cocky young man," a transformation that ultimately cannot survive its encounter with the social order.[63]

Stephen's identification with/as Nelson is often read symptomatically, as a psychic response to the repression of same-sex desire rather than as cross-gender expression in and of itself. Likewise, Hall's marked identification with the inverts who populate sexological writing has been read with much suspicion. Sexology does, in fact, govern the logic of *The Well*, from Hall's decision to plot Stephen's life so that it precisely mimics case studies found in Havelock Ellis's *Sexual Inversion*; to the moment in the story when Stephen discovers a battered, annotated copy of Richard von Krafft-Ebing's *Psychopathia Sexualis* in her father's study and, after a night of reading many such books, comes to understand that she is one of the "thousands of miserable, unwanted people . . . flawed in the making"; to Hall's recruiting Ellis to write a prefatory note to her novel, "so that it could be seen to perform his theory of inversion."[64] Especially in the context of 1970s and 1980s lesbian feminist criticism, and with a few notable exceptions, this obvious influence of sexology in *The Well* has made it something of an infamous novel. Prior to a trans recuperation in the late 1990s, at best, Hall's attachment to the invert—symptomatized by Stephen's masculinity and desire to be a man—has been read as a strategy for making female sexuality legible at a historical moment when female sexual desire was thought to be a contradiction in terms.[65] At worst, it has been interpreted as a total relinquishing of authority, a bolstering of sexological discourse about same-sex desire at the expense of admitting the "lesbian imagination" into representation.[66] More than anything, at least for my purposes, what is revealed by the critical attention to sexology's influence in *The Well* is an anxiety about the ability of texts to overdetermine the gendered lives of their "uncritical" readers.[67] Critics have long suspected that Hall's reading of sexology—a scene of reading that is reproduced in Stephen's encounter with the books locked away in her dead father's library—left her so thoroughly infected with the discourse of sexology that it managed to substitute Hall's true voice with its own, "a mimicry that enforced her own absence from the scene of . . . literary representation."[68]

For better and for worse, sexology in *The Well* and, later, *The Well* itself operate as what Cáel Keegan, following Sara Ahmed, terms "trans media objects," objects that "cultivate trans consciousness by offering an aesthetic space in which the subject might feel a way forward through the closed phenomenological horizon of binary gender."[69] Although Jay Prosser and others have described the importance of scenes of reading transsexual autobiographies in transsexual autobiographies as being related to their function to initiate the trans subject at hand into a sense of categorical belonging, this "recycling of the transsexual narrative from life to text to life (from body to narrative to body again)" doesn't account for the way trans projects of self-making seem to require such expansive bibliographies, why one (or two or three or four) trans text is never enough to assure oneself of one's nonsingular existence.[70] Nor can it capture the range of objects that might be, in Keegan's sense, trans. Keegan, for example, offers a 1990s milk advertisement and Jonathan Glazer's 2013 film *Under the Skin* as objects that "sustained" his own "trans becoming."[71] To this list of trans media objects we might add *Sula*, *Little Shop of Horrors*, *The Animorphs*, the *Star Trek* franchise, *Frozen 2*, David Bowie, Lou Reed, *The Sound of Music*, Tiresias, Spiderman, *The Member of the Wedding*, on and on and on. Indeed, and looking back to chapter 3, Elliott DeLine sardonically suggests that his protagonist/proxy Dean's mode of relating with fiction generally supplies the psychic mechanism underlying his transsexuality: "Convinced that make-believe was a serious business and [his] desires trumped reality," Dean's story begins as a series of identifications with fictional characters. "I wasn't 'Laura,' after all; I wasn't the child they were seeing—not if I didn't want to be. I was Peter Pan, the Big Bad Wolf, even a talking sea lion on occasion—but I was certainly not a little girl."[72]

These ways of relating to texts and media objects—taking on the identity of a fictional character in order to get around constraints placed on the self, amassing a bibliography to facilitate one's own existence—suggest an answer to the question with which we started: How, in the absence of recognition by human others, is Dillon able to maintain "a sense of self regardless of how [he] is interpellated"?[73] Kennedy, it seems, is onto something when she notices a correspondence between Dillon's growing certainty that he was not a woman and the beginning of his compulsive reading life.[74] Reading, in addition to being that which allows for the organization of feeling into narrative, seems, in fact, to already be a form of relationality, a source of meaningfully significant others. Or as C. Riley Snorton has put it, "sometimes, one's social audience can," and must, "be imaginary," or not exactly composed of people at all.[75]

Of course, the scene of reading has been regularly understood as a scene of relationality. While "reader-response criticism" collects together a range of critical practices and frameworks, what the work it names shares is a focus on readers' interactions with texts and the assumption that meaning is made in this encounter.[76] Although influential critic Wolfgang Iser took great pains to emphasize the difference between "reading and all forms of social interaction," his own emphasis on "interaction"—and later the foregrounding of terms like "relationship" and "intimacy" in the work of feminist theorists of reading—metaphorize reading as a meeting between two (or more) subjectivities.[77] This is especially true of phenomenologically inflected work; for example, Georges Poulet understood books to be "subjectified objects" and reading, therefore, to be a "strange invasion," the experience of sharing one's own consciousness with another.[78]

In *The Social Imperative: Race, Close Reading, and Contemporary Literary Criticism*, Paula Moya recruits the tools of social psychology in order to build on this tradition and especially on work that emerged after the heyday of reader-response criticism that sought to particularize "the reader," reembedding relationships between readers and texts in their sociohistorical contexts. In particular, she offers the concept of schema to literary critics as a way of accounting for why and how particular texts have particular effects on particular readers. As she defines it, schema "refers to the active organization of past experiences (physical and emotional) and past reactions (sensory-motor and cognitive-affective) through which a person apprehends and interacts with incoming stimuli."[79] Schemas, therefore, develop in relation to our lived experiences and influence where we direct our attention and how we interpret. Importantly, Moya notes that the concept of schemas helps us to understand how literature works by directing our attention to both the schemas that readers "bring with them to the scene of reading" and to "the way schemas are embedded into a work of literature."[80] And because she is concerned with how reading literature might be involved in shaping and changing the world, Moya is especially interested in what happens in encounters between the two, encounters she compares, significantly, to potential "friendship."[81]

The concept of schema, implicitly, underlies many attempts within reader-oriented criticism to account for particular social groups' habits of reading and interpretation and goes a long way toward explaining why scenes of reading have consistently played a pivotal role in trans narratives. Media, whether in the form of explicitly trans narratives or not, provide schemas for organizing inchoate feelings of unease; reading makes sense of experience, fleshes it out. However, whereas Moya demonstrates that multicultural literature might similarly flesh out a reader's world—"pull[ing her] in and giv[ing her] a kind of access to a way of conceptualizing the world that she might otherwise never be exposed to"—trans scenes of reading also imply another, counterintuitive kind of relationality.[82] Not only does reading provide self-organizing schemas and schemas that might help one more substantively recognize others, but aesthetic objects seem to stand in for embodied human others who might recognize the self. In particular, this function of reading explains the compulsiveness of trans bibliographies, why trans projects of self-making are so often *extensive* research projects: continuous reading is a way of continually confirming and populating a world for oneself in books in the absence of the possibility of recognition outside of them.[83]

Michael Dillon's *Self*

In 1946, William Heinemann Medical Books published an odd little book titled *Self: A Study in Endocrinology and Ethics* by Michael Dillon. Though the book is disguised as a treatise on medical ethics, at the core of *Self* is a "hidden manifesto . . . plead[ing] on behalf of transsexuals."[84] "Surely," Dillon writes, "where the mind cannot be made to fit the body, the body should be made to fit, approximately, at any rate to the mind," allowing for the "achievement of a tolerably happy life."[85] Consequently, *Self* has been read repeatedly as an early articulation of the medicalized wrong-body model of transsexuality. Henry Rubin and Bernice Hausman, for example, have each focused on Dillon's attempts in *Self* to distinguish homosexuality from transsexuality in order to develop a "logic of treatment" that would enable people like Dillon to intervene on their bodies.[86] Although this interpretation is certainly a true one, attending to the poetics of *Self*, rather than only its polemic, reveals that there are other potentials in the text that Hausman and Rubin alike can't account for. Further, while the standard account of *Self* explains Dillon's eagerness to publish the book, it can't account for his eagerness to publish *in his own name*, which is remarkable considering his longstanding anxiety about publicity.[87] Written during a time in his life when Dillon was particularly starved for significant other–recognition, when he was read male among strangers but the majority of his coworkers and acquaintances actively refused to see him as male, *Self* cannot be read only as an attempt to construct himself as a patient. Rather, as a public record of Dillon's own self-making research project, it was also an attempt to construct for himself a world of others by whom he might be recognized.

Self begins with two chapters that, indeed, "drone on and on, lecturing about hormones."[88] But whereas Kennedy interprets these chapters as a cover for the real book, Dillon's overview of the endocrine system was crucial to the plea at the book's center, insofar as endocrinology provided Dillon with a schema for organizing his life experience. By recounting experiments and disease states in which disruptions of the endocrine system altered sex-linked characteristics and behaviors, Dillon constructed a story about homosexuality and gender inversion that both explained his own sense of himself and made it a matter of nature rather than morality. Further, by using endocrinology to thus link biology to personality, Dillon was able to logically substantiate his plea—a plea not only for social tolerance but also for gender transition through hormones and surgery to be made legal and subsidized by the government. In short, Dillon needed the schema that endocrinology provided in order to posit the body, not the personality, as the site of intervention.

This work of building, for himself and for his readers, a schema through which to interpret the kind of person he was continues in his chapter on homosexuality. After he finishes droning on about hormones, Dillon develops a system of classification that allows him to differentiate between forms of homosexuality and ultimately, between homosexuals and "homosexuals," which we would today understand as a distinction between gay and trans people; Dillon's own move to place this word in scare quotes indicates that he is not sure the two belong beneath the same term.[89] Although this chapter does what Rubin and Hausman say it does—develops a logic of treatment that constructs the "homosexual" as a patient—such an interpretation doesn't quite account for the curious form this chapter takes.

Throughout the rest of the book, Dillon relies exclusively on expert knowledge—the voices of doctors and scientists. This appeal to authority is consistent with his aim of constructing the "homosexual" as a patient and with the way Dillon constructs himself as an author—his authorial voice performs scientific objectivity, is merely relaying the information. To this end, Dillon narrates *Self* using the first-person plural, where *we* either denotes the author plus readers or a general *we*. When appealing to this general *we*, Dillon is careful to mark its boundaries as encompassing the ordinary man, certainly not the homosexuals and "homosexuals," "our fellow-men who are not quite like ourselves."[90] Either way, being *we* allows Dillon to establish proximity to his readers; this in turn creates the distance between himself and his object, allowing him to express sympathy for homosexuals and "homosexuals," to publicly express the pain of the stigmatized other, while minimizing the risk that doing so will lead him to be interpreted as one of those others.

Although Dillon retreats into this *we*, the rhetorical authority he composes momentarily breaks down in his chapter on "homosexuality;" this is the only place in the book where artists, not scientists, are ushered into his account as ideal sources of knowledge. Citing Hall's *The Well of Loneliness*, a lengthy quote from "admitted homosexual" Herman Bang that describes homosexuals as "strangers among strangers and without help," and a fragment of a poem by A. E. Housman that laments being "a stranger, and afraid / In a world" not of the speaker's creation, Dillon imbues the chapter with the very feeling that drove him to write: the profound loneliness of living among other people, without recognition.[91] Significantly, the only *I* that appears in this chapter—one of only a handful in the whole book—appears in Housman's poem. Interrupting Dillon's authorial *we*, the poem asks: "How am I to face the odds / Of man's bedevilment and God's, / I, a stranger, and afraid / In a world I never made?"[92] While it might seem that Housman, Hall, and Bang are merely being invoked as sympathetic examples of "our fellow-men who are not quite like ourselves," knowing that Dillon was himself a member of this lonely company makes this move seem much less like an appeal to the authority of others and much more like a displacement of Dillon's own *I* into these others. That is, not only is the chapter arguing for a world in which homosexuals and "homosexuals" alike might belong but it also collects together, within the book itself, a world of others who reflect, recognize, and in that way, substantiate Dillon's *I*.

For this reason, Dillon's *Self* is analogous to, for example, Leslie Feinberg's romp through time and space to collect disparate nonbinary gender formations under the transgender umbrella in *Transgender Warriors: Making History from Joan of Arc to Dennis Rodman*, or as discussed in chapter 1, Lou Sullivan's compiling the traces of Jack Garland in the archives in order to be less alone. In each, research doubly functions to flesh out the self and to actively produce a para-social world for the self to inhabit. In Dillon's case, this world-building function was also surprisingly literal. Kennedy speculates that Dillon was willing to risk revealing his secret for the chance "that a troubled young man or woman would find the book, read it furtively, and then contact him—thus could he create a community of people like himself."[93] And indeed the book functioned like a kind of smoke signal, eventually sending fellow transsexual Roberta Cowell his way. This meeting between Cowell and Dillon ignited the flame of a one-sided romance, causing Dillon to go to extraordinary lengths—even performing a potentially illegal orchiectomy on Cowell—in order to secure her as his wife.[94] Although this story didn't end happily for Dillon, it does suggest how profoundly he needed to create a feeling of category rather than singularity. Notably, however, Dillon expunged this scene of failed t4t sociality from his memoir and never, it seems, pursued this kind of intimacy again.

"Some Kind of We"

Recall Dillon's scene in which a boy holds open a gate and Dillon, interpreting this gesture to mean that this boy sees him as a woman, is "stunned." Reflecting on this moment, he insists: "Life would never be the same again. People thought I was a woman. But I wasn't."[95] What is strange about the speaker of this story, especially about Dillon's adamant assertion that he was not a woman, is that he recognizes that it is him being hailed by the category; he says both that he was "technically a girl" and definitely not a woman. Rather than there being one willful, fully fleshed out self able to resist interpellation, it seems that Dillon represents himself as being split into (at least) two. A similar self appears in *Self*, in which Dillon mobilizes the pronoun *we*, allowing him to occupy both the position of the ordinary man and his interior "stranger among strangers," his *I*, through displacement. This form of representing subjectivity, which simultaneously captures both the self, formed in relation, and the withdrawn self, but which does not or cannot call them by the same name, is clearly identical to neither the immutable subject of the wrong-body model nor the willful subject of the gender freedom model nor the purely resistant subject of queer trans theory. We might call it a lyric subject, a subject defined—as lyric traditionally has been—by a curious simultaneity of absolute interiority and publicity.[96]

In *Lyric Time: Dickinson and the Limits of Genre*, Sharon Cameron asks how it is that a lyric represents complexity, given that "unlike the novel or narrative, which connects isolated moments of time to create a story multiply peopled and framed by a social context, the lyric voice is solitary and generally speaks out of a single moment in time."[97] Whereas narrative genres tend to produce complexity by distributing ideas and points of view among multiple characters, Cameron is interested in how the lyric represents division "not by the ceding of territory to different characters" but through "a speaker who says 'I' and yet is pluralistic."[98] For Cameron, this plural *I* is produced through the particular way that lyric manages time. She argues that while novelistic and dramatic narratives rely on temporal compression—to fit a life into a day's reading, a day into a few hours of theater—they also rely on the expansion of moments in order to "make room for the luxury of articulated self-reflection."[99] Lyric, on the other hand, seems to take place only in this expanded, interior temporality and so renders time into a "still life": moments, and the changes they index, are "not consecutive but . . . rather heaped or layered."[100] This is why, for example, the simple present in English is used most often in poetry; in the simple present moments do not unfold but are layered on top of each other into a perpetual now.[101] "The least mimetic of all art forms," Cameron concludes, "the lyric . . . will withstand the outrage of any complexity for the sake of being able to present sequence as if it were unity."[102]

While Cameron points to this temporality, this potentially outrageous layering of sequence into unity, as a paradigmatic feature of the lyric as a genre, it's also possible to view it as a form of speech that can, like all forms, travel. For example, much of what Bobby Noble calls *incoherence* I would call *lyric*. Speaking about the "strange grammatical and discursive constructions" engendered by attempts to articulate and narrate trans life, Noble insists that "conventions of grammar, logic, and intelligibility break down under the weight of such paradoxes."[103] One such paradox—"lesbian man" or "guy who is half lesbian"—recurs periodically throughout Noble's *Sons of the Movement* as his own attempt at self-naming.[104] Though perhaps a result of my having come of age in a time that Noble calls post-queer, when formulations like "guy who is half lesbian" feel familiar, it seems to me that Noble's claim that such phrases "break down" conventions of grammar, logic, and intelligibility is overstated or at least imprecise. "Guy who is half lesbian" does, after all, make (a kind of) sense. Noble himself gestures toward the kind of sense it makes when he claims, as if in one breath, that "refracting identity through simile . . . is crucial to [his] sense of self" and that "identifying [him]self through paradox as 'guy who is half lesbian' really comes closest to bringing a number of historical moments together into *something like an identity*."[105] Catachresis, simile, collapse of discrete moments into something like a whole; all the stuff of which lyric speech is made. My point is not that trans subjectivity is structured by the paradoxes that compose the lyric; after all, lyric poetry's capacity to treat "strangeness . . . as natural," and thus withstand rather than break down under the weight of complexity is precisely what has earned its designation as the subjective genre par excellence.[106] Rather, my point is that the capacity of lyric speech to sustain temporal and categorical paradox has been continuously used by trans writers to represent the persistent form of trans subjectivity that emerges in Dillon's scene of (mis)recognition. And like Dillon, contemporary poet Ari Banias develops this as *we*.

"Some Kind of We," as the title of the opening poem declares, is what Banias is after in his 2016 collection *Anybody*. Throughout *Anybody*, Banias develops a theory of *we* that resembles Cameron's articulation of the lyric's plural *I* that exists in and as sequence layered into unity. But contrary to the lyric subject's assumed resolve to remain "unaffected by [society's] bustle and commotion," Banias isn't at all interested in speaking as an *I*, from the illusion of singularity.[107] Rather, in line with many minoritized poets, Banias foregrounds that his speech and the lyric subject it animates are contingent on the bustle and commotion of history, politics, and other people; this contingency is itself the formal and theoretical problem driving *Anybody*. In particular, a singular *we*, rather than a plural *I*, allows Banias to navigate the sticky "question of what it means to be a white dude / after having been a white girl," a question about the relationality of gender that the wrong-body model, the gender freedom model, *and* the queer trans model might encourage him to evade or disavow.[108] Thus, unlike Dillon's, Banias's *we* is a withdrawn self, a self in relation to others, *and* an attempt to name a form of ethical engagement. *We* perpetually slides between this particular and general, between the speaker's "feeling confessing itself to itself, in moments of solitude," and a widened theory of relation.[109]

GRANDCHILD

She says so the aunt and uncle and cousins all look
in unison ooooh their approval
What a beautiful girl while we hunch
on the veranda in jeans and baggy t-shirt not

what she means by beauty hardly
a girl our hair barber-cut
five years our chest inside two sports bras flattened
further by the fabric bandage we pin close

around our torso adamant
inside of awkward gesture-awkward awkward
to speak dodging pronouns to visit to sleep
on the lace-draped living room couch

so visible to all avoiding
awkward trips to the sea with cousins
who act like nothing's changed only sitting
beside *yiayia* when she says

our name and pats the cushion deliberately
draws our hand into her shaking ones and puts
on us the same ring that engaged her
to him at sixteen she says

It will be time to start a family soon
looking at our face touching the bristle of our hair
saying Beautiful you are
the only one who has my name[110]

In this poem, Banias both dramatizes *we* by means of narrative and formalizes it by means of a lack of punctuation and heavy use of enjambment, so that distinct clauses, ideas, perspectives, and voices slide into one breathless speech. Also, this is the only poem in the collection in which the speaker persistently and explicitly refers to themself using the first-person plural, a self seemingly multiplied by the discrepancy between how they view themself and how they are viewed by members of their family.

In particular, "Grandchild" begins and ends with a scene of (mis)recognition between the speaker, who is "hardly / a girl" with their barber-cut hair and bound chest, and their grandmother, to whom they are a "beautiful girl." To make matters worse, the logistics of this family gathering—swimming, sleeping on "the lace-draped living room couch"—render this speaker, despite their attempts to "hunch" down into their layers of clothing, "so visible" and so perpetually subject to this (mis)recognition. As in Dillon's scene at the gate, being the subject of (mis)recognition creates a multiplicity, a *we*. And like Dillon's silent walk home with the boy who does not know what he has done, Banias's *we* is profoundly "awkward," creates awkwardness in the grammar of the poem and in the body of the speaker, which hunches and bristles and dodges and avoids but cannot. But Banias's *we* also opens to a tender moment at the end of the poem, in which the grandmother passes on her engagement ring to the speaker who is bound to her, if not exactly by gender, by name.

In this and other poems, Banias gives form to what Jane Ward calls *gender labor*, "the affective and bodily efforts invested in *giving gender* to others, or actively suspending self-focus in the service of helping others achieve the varied forms of gender recognition they long for."[111] While Ward's study of femme/FTM relationships emphasizes the feminized labor of care that femmes often perform to consolidate butch or FTM masculinity—a relationship that mirrors the disavowal and displacement of girlhood that has structured much transmasculine self-narration—in this poem, *he* is suspended in order to allow the grandmother this moment of matrilineal transmission. *We* as awkward and tender, as sign of personal crisis and site of intimate exchange.

In "I Promised Her My Hands Wouldn't Get Any Larger," a poem that opens Oliver Baez Bendorf's 2015 *The Spectral Wilderness*, we are likewise presented with a speaker who is multiply singular, this time in the form of tracings of his hands hung on the walls of his house, an accumulation of ghosts of his pre-exogenous-testosterone body that "look back" at him, exert their own agency. In his 2008 collection *Boy with Flowers*, Ely Shipley's speaker—resolutely a boy, though one "flaring with thorns" and linked perpetually to the marked-feminine signifier "flowers"—is continuously "sliding / backward" into memory, real and dreamed. Likewise, in his introduction to a reprinted edition of two collections published under Linda Smukler, his pretransition name, Samuel Ace speaks as a divided *we*, staging a conversation across category and time between Sam and Sam conjuring Linda's voice.[112]

In this way, the transmasculine lyric affords a way of managing the problem that haunts this project: the strained relation between transmasculinity and the figure of the girl. In chapter 2, this relation, structured as it so often is by disavowal, becomes a problem for imagining transfeminisms. In chapter 3, this relation seems to appear most clearly as and through sexual violence. In lyric, however, in part because of its outrageous "folded" temporality, we find a transmasculinity that can accommodate the girl as also itself.[113] Importantly, then, while *we* allows Banias to represent the personal experience of being simultaneously a beautiful girl and hardly one at all, it also can never be only about the interior. Or as he insists in an earlier poem, "What's personal is being here with all of you."[114]

* * *

Since the turn of the twenty-first century, there has been a remarkable proliferation of visibly trans poets and poetries. More important than the body of work of any individual poet, however, has been the work of collecting together these voices into a fractured, multiple, but still-collective body of work, something called *trans poetry*. This collecting has happened through the founding of journals like *Vetch* and *THEM*; the creation of special issues in the *Offing*, *Cream City Review*, and elsewhere; the rise and fall of presses like Topside and Transgress; and the purposeful work of indie presses to expand their trans offerings. In particular, the work of making a legible body of trans poetry is exemplified (and was in many ways enabled) by *Troubling the Line: Trans and Genderqueer Poetry and Poetics*, published in 2013, the first published anthology of writing by trans/genderqueer poets.

As a project, *Troubling the Line* is driven by many of the same impulses that drove Dillon to pen *Self*, replicating the story in which the trans subject locates, in books, a schema that organizes inchoate feelings of difference into a self and then publishes a book in order to compose a community in which that self might be recognized. T. C. Tolbert's introduction to the anthology says as much: "It would not be an exaggeration to say that my grandfather's greatest fears were realized as a result of me reading poetry. I held onto both of these texts [*This Bridge Called My Back: Writings by Radical Women of Color* and Maureen Seaton's poem "Fiddleheads"] as I made my way into a divorce, a coming out, and a family backlash. I identify as genderqueer and a big part of that for me is how much I embraced (and still embrace) the woman I was becoming as a result of those texts."[115] In this version of the story, an encounter with particular texts enabled Tolbert's transition from married Pentecostal woman to genderqueer poet. At the same time, the anthology is itself a textual project whose aims are, in part, to alleviate the loneliness of that subject position.

Still, the existence of the anthology also indexes a remarkable shift in the conditions of possibility of trans life. Accordingly, Dillon's loneliness is no longer the defining feeling of trans subjectivity: trans others with whom to identify, in the form of physical and online communities, narratives, celebrities, and so on, abound. However, *trans* is still structured by a trouble with recognition, by the split between self- and other-perception that sets the trans plot in motion. Consequently, whereas the bibliographic form of trans thought—exemplified by Dillon's *Self* and Leslie Feinberg's *Transgender Warriors*, among many others—responded by composing para-social worlds populated by not-exactly-human others who might nonetheless provide the function of other-recognition, new forms of trans literature have arisen that continue to address the problem of (mis)recognition but do not function in precisely the same way. In particular, the lyric *we* is one tool trans writers have used to return the world of other people to the scene of trans thought, as it is a form capable of managing both withdrawal into the interior and encounters with embodied others, of contesting—while also preserving—the constitutive asociality of *trans*.

AFTERWARD/ELEGY

An elegiac politics—a stance that admits to the inevitability of these deaths given the . . . landscape—helps make this contradiction (okay, but not okay) not only legible, but livable and dieable.
—LOCHLANN JAIN, *MALIGNANT: HOW CANCER BECOMES US* (2013)

In June 2014, the cover of *Time* magazine declared that we had arrived at "the transgender tipping point."[1] In September 2015, as if to confirm *trans*'s arrival on the scene of inclusion, *Law and Order: SVU* aired an episode called "Transgender Bridge," the first in the sixteen years of the series in which transness was not, however sympathetically, linked to criminality. Embarrassingly, I think about this episode a lot. In it, a confrontation between a group of black cis boys and a white trans girl results in the trans girl's death and a black boy's imprisonment. The episode seems, on the face of it, to have antiracist and anti-transphobic desires; both the black boy and the trans girl are essentially good kids thrown into a world where their trajectories have been unjustly predetermined. The trans girl will inevitably die young—by her own hand, by someone else's—the black boy will inevitably go to jail, die young. We are supposed to notice that this is not the fault of either individual, or any individual. Rather, it is the fault of "historical and social conditions that produce an unjust distribution of death toward" trans, indigenous, racialized, queer, and feminized people.[2]

These years—2014, 2015—were revealing in more ways than one. On the one hand, these were years in which *trans* seemed to again suddenly manifest in the popular imagination, as the marked absence of mainstream representations of trans lives gave way to an abundance. That is, these were years in which a range of trans bodies, lives, and narratives became widely legible, affirmable, and consumable within late capitalism in the United States. However, concurrent with the rise in trans visibility and discourses of trans affirmability, was the ongoing erosion of the conditions of livability for many trans people. As of this writing, six years later, state legislatures across the country are working through a pandemic to actively curtail the freedom of trans people—trans youth and women in particular—by attempting to write binary sex/gender into the law, effectively barring trans people from health care, sport, and other facets of public life.[3]

But back in September 2015, this dismal proposition surfaced in my life in a more immediate way when yet another young trans woman of color died. This time it was someone who I knew peripherally from my time adjacent to trans/queer life in Oakland, California. Let's call her B. What was and is most distinct to me about this event was the temporality of my encounter with the news of its occurrence, an encounter defined both by ongoingness and anticipation. Out of the blue, my friend N. texted me, asking if I was with other people, and then when I said that I was not, they delayed giving me the news until I was, I suppose, in a space capable of holding grief. I let this scene play out for days, even though I already knew that B. had died, that this was the news I was not yet ready to know.

Even before N.'s text, this death was unavoidable, the news of it circulating, as these things did, on Facebook. Also circulating then on Facebook: a recurring claim that trans people or trans women or trans women of color or black trans women live, on average, thirty-seven, thirty-five, thirty-two, twenty-three years.[4] These numbers are not true, but they circulate *as if* they are true. For many, they resonate, feel like an adequate description. Before *trans* described me, it was a term I associated most with Trans Day of Remembrance (TDOR), an annual day of mourning for trans people lost to "anti-trans violence." Many, many activists and scholars have critiqued the deracialized logic of TDOR, which both conceals more than it reveals about the structural forces that curtail trans life and circulates "the trans woman of color," in particular, as always a dead and victimized figure, actively stripping her of her life, her worlds.[5] That is, TDOR's focus on "anti-trans violence" obscures the varied ways that trans people are worn down, live on, make do, fail to. While more hopeful days of trans visibility and trans resilience have arisen to address the limits of TDOR, to offer vocabularies for trans life, I'm particularly interested in how, in its grim adherence a victim-perpetrator model, TDOR offers little by way of a vocabulary for death by suicide, overdose, and so on, all of the most ordinary outcomes of being "worn out by the work of surviving."[6] I'm interested in this, here, at the end of this book on trans[masculine] maladjustment in part because suicidality is endemic to trans life and its representation. But also, and in conjunction with the harsh hypervisibility of transfeminine death, at least one study that circulated widely on the transgender internet has suggested that suicidality is something to which transmasculine adolescents are especially prone.[7]

There are many ways to regard the overdetermined link between *trans* and death in general and death by suicide in particular. Caught most firmly within the medicolegal frame, Elias Vitulli argues, trans prisoners are required to perform extreme distress—through self-injury and attempts at suicide—in order to be considered eligible for gender-affirming care, to be regarded as who they are.[8] In this frame, the codification of trans as unbearable feeling is violently self-reinforcing. And following C. Riley Snorton and Jin Haritaworn, among others, we might be wary of the way that the living—parents, activists, nonprofits, artists, academics—extract value from the trans, and particularly black transfeminine, dead.[9] Still, it also is true that I in part came to understand *trans* as something it was possible for me to be when my high school's tiny gay-straight alliance erected cardboard tombstones in the hallway to mark those predominantly South American trans women who had been lost. Trans life became an intimate possibility in reference to strangers' deaths.

* * *

B. did not, exactly, kill herself, but on the day that N. told me she had died, I stumbled across an article about another young trans person of color, let's call him L., who had. On that day, I began keeping a list, simply a collection of names and online articles about those who had in one way or another taken their own lives since the list began. Others found their way onto the list because their earlier deaths haunt the stories told about later ones. The rule was that I couldn't go looking for these stories, I only included ones that came to me. This rule was self-protective, yes, but it was also an attempt to be beholden to the way news travels in the age of social media, to get a feel for being awash in information.

I must admit that suicide marks the limit of my own ability to think with trans maladjustment, which accounts for the form of this afterword, its failure to be, properly, an argument. There is a part of me that interprets many trans youths' public suicide notes and subsequent memorializations as reworkings of the trap that binds together trans identity and short life span, a way of using death, tinged with inevitably, as a speech act against the conditions in which so many were born to die. That is, they died "early" in the present in order to insist on a future in which they would not have to. And yet. There is also the part of me that makes the list, that writes the book, that attempts in the way of elegy "not merely to recognize the dead but also to bring them back to life."[10] And then there is the part of me that has "become increasingly suspicious of the idea that *death itself* is unjust. Often, what is unjust is everything that preceded the end. What is unjust is the terms of living."[11] And finally, I am certain that reading suicide as a "reworking" is profoundly irresponsible because it suggests to and of trans youth that they wield more "affective agency" in death—"in death's position"—than they ever could in life, displacing agency to the moment in which it has already failed the individual at hand.[12]

* * *

In *The Transgender Child: A Handbook for Families and Professionals*, which has been described as a "compassionate and caring," "long overdue and extremely well-executed" guide to gender nonconforming children, we are told that: "When a child transitions . . . parents and siblings alike . . . may feel a sense of grief at the idea that they are 'losing' their son or daughter, brother or sister. Even though the child is alive and well, changing gender can elicit strong feelings of loss. In fact, most parents compare it to the death of their child. Their child becomes, in a sense, a new child."[13]

Often, when talking about the self- and world-making work of loss, scholars begin with Sigmund Freud's opposition between mourning and melancholia. While mourning, in this rendering, is relatively simple, melancholia has appeared to queer, feminist, and critical race scholars to be a mechanism that might account for—or at least compellingly describe—the psychic life of race, gender, sexuality, and so on, especially insofar as it can account for the simultaneity of cultural investments in and repudiations of difference.[14] That is, because the object of melancholia is sticky—sticks around—it's easier to understand this structure of loss as productive. Still, mourning seems to have more to say to this scenario, in which gender transition elicits in loved ones feelings of loss.

In mourning, Freud writes, "Reality-testing has shown that the loved object no longer exists, and it proceeds to demand that all libido shall be withdrawn from its attachments to that object . . . [but] people never willingly abandon a libidinal position, not even, indeed, when a substitute is already beckoning to them."[15] So, as both the lost love and the substitute, what choice do trans children have but to look on, to bear it? Put another way: in her suicide note, L. H. moves jarringly between tenses until it is as if she is writing from the future of her own death. *I was alive. I was a real person*. What becomes of the object after it has survived its own loss?

* * *

In many public accounts of the lives that preceded these deaths, we are given an image of someone who was loved, affirmed, and legible. L., for example, described himself as someone who was *motivated and empowered* who found *strength in identity*. At the same time, no one seems (publicly) surprised that he is gone, as if trans life is inevitably yoked to unlivability, even or especially in this time and place. This project's interest in maladjustment, then, is an interest in this sometimes-deadly misfit produced between contemporary discourses of trans affirmability and what it feels like to inhabit them. I hope, though, that it's been clear that I'm not trying to offer feeling bad as a good, as an ethic or a state to aim for. Rather, it seems to me that the move to excise maladjustment from transgender discourse has participated in exacerbating this situation in which the inevitable failure of affirmation, love, and legibility to fulfill their promises have made it increasingly difficult for individuals to bear their bad feelings, the residue of their own maladjustment to the narrow terms of the given. That is, I am not convinced it's possible right now, no matter how much we would like it to be, to separate the experience of inhabiting the territory of queer gender from feelings of dysphoria; the lingering sense of strangeness that attends having grown sideways; the anxiety of identity management; the particular mix of anger, diminishment, fear, and envy that attends being constantly misgendered; the palpable cruelty of some of our optimistic attachments to endocrinology and plastic surgery; and so on. While unlinking the concept of trans from terms like *sick*, *maladjusted*, *mad*, and so on is ostensibly meant to open up the space for politics, trans discourse that disavows bad feeling is insufficient to the task of learning how to live with, through, and despite it.

In "affirmative" discourse, that is, *trans* becomes a protectable form of life only insofar as it can overcome, or be rehabilitated from, maladjustment, which, I have been arguing is one of its defining features. This, as Cáel Keegan puts it, is "an innovation in the history of transgender representation: a body that journeys from negative to redemptive affect, from psychosis to mental health, from self-hatred to a celebration of liberal individuality, from a position of political mourning to one of requited 'national love.'"[16] Almost tautologically, then, the affirmable trans subject is the affirmed subject, the one who has moved from bad feeling, self-occlusion, incongruity, and so on, into cheery forms of social life. In the same moment in which gender dysphoria replaces gender identity disorder in the DSM, in which transness becomes officially codified as unbearable feeling, the good trans subject is that one who can *get over it*. Either this or the trans subject has died precisely because they could not get over it and so can be recruited into this story anyway, a cautionary tale of value only after they are gone. Of course, this can't be a surprise, because, as Grace Hong puts it, the present is characterized by "an epistemological structure of disavowal, a means of claiming that racial and gendered violences are things of the past" that operates "by *affirming* certain modes of racialized, gendered, and sexualized life . . . *so as to* disavow its exacerbated production of premature death."[17]

* * *

In the preface to *Black on Both Sides*, C. Riley Snorton, too, finds ongoing trans youth suicide in the shadow of "the tipping point" unavoidable as he grapples with the 2015 death of Blake Brockington, a black trans teenager who had first made the news by being elected homecoming king at his North Carolina high school in 2014. Brockington was positioned by the media as evidence of the folding of trans people into "the people." However, Brockington did not survive the attention garnered by his being made evidence. In his own words, it was only after he circulated as evidence of trans inclusion that he "saw" by way of the vitriol of strangers, "how narrow minded the world really is."[18]

Pointing us to this conundrum, the seeming impossibility of a black/trans life at the very moment when—and because of the very mechanisms by which—it is heralded as newly possible, Snorton turns our attention to time: he asks not *what happened* but what is the time "when" he "might be." *When he might be*. In this phrasing, it is not exactly that Brockington died too early. Rather, or also, he lived in the wrong time, one in which he could not yet be. But there is another resonance to *when he might be* that insists that there is, in fact, against all odds, a when of black and trans life. That insists not only on the *not yet* but also on the *sometime* that strains in and against the present. That quests after the answer to this question of when and what the conditions of this sometime "in which Brockington would be understood according to his own self-definition" might be.[19]

* * *

Let me put it this way: "If haunting," as Avery Gordon writes, "describes how that which appears to be not there is often a seething presence, acting on and often meddling with taken-for-granted realities" then every trans story proceeds according to the logic of ghosts.[20] In turn, the ghostly, as a recalcitrant trope of trans expressive culture, registers two things at once, both the active/passive production of [black] trans death and *trans*'s own persistent meddling, its insistence—sometimes playful, sometimes deadly serious—that gender, embodiment, selfhood, and so on are all very strange, much stranger than we ordinarily take them to be.

In fact, strangeness—as survival strategy, as subjective experience, as creative form—is what *trans* knows best. Feeling strange. Being regarded by others as strange, perpetually out of place. Considering oneself a stranger, one who looks back, "a monstrous fetter."[21] In Jennifer Finney Boylan's words:

"I knew very little for certain . . . but I did know this much: that in order to survive, I'd have to become something like a ghost myself . . . and so I haunted that young body of mine . . . as a hopeful, wraithlike presence otherwise invisible to the naked eye."[22] The ghostly, that is, both sutures trans to death and, in so doing, allows for the insistence that what is, is not all there is; it asks us to live in suspension—even if only temporarily—to suspend what we think we know about hardened divisions in the social, a suspension of belief that is the prerequisite for trans movements and trans thought.

In relation to their experiences of gender transition and seroconversion during the height of the AIDS epidemic, respectively, Chase Joynt and Mike Hoolboom call the condition of having survived one's own loss living "in the second life."[23] Speaking about the reordering of time by cancer diagnosis, Lochlann Jain calls it "living in prognosis."[24] Christina Crosby, in her memoir about being undone by a disabling accident, calls it "living . . . beyond reason" or simply "living on."[25] Often we find ourselves in this condition not because of any identifiable change in embodiment but rather a new perception of how our embodiment is registered, as in W. E. B. Du Bois's description of, as a child, being refused by a classmate and "with a certain suddenness" finding himself "shut out from [the white] world"—which he had, until this moment, taken to be his own—cast behind a "vast veil."[26] Don't get me wrong: these forms of living are not identical. How one finds oneself in the second life matters, profoundly. But what these situations have in common is that they can prompt a reconsideration of what it means to live a life, a good life. They force us, too, to withdraw our attachments from ourselves, from "the fairytales that sustain the first life"—of wholeness, of seamless integration, of "happiness . . . as the point of life, the aim of life," arrived at by taking only certain paths.[27]

"But now that we've survived the death of our former selves," Hoolboom asks of Joynt toward the beginning of their joint epistolary experiment, "how do we keep a new kind of hope alive when part of the cost of passage, part of the necessary toll-taking, was that we had to leave all the old hopes at the door? I guess I'm really asking: can you help me?"[28] In the end, in delayed response, Joynt concludes, "What I hear in your writing is a longing, not for death, but for the release from disappointment. Perhaps that is what our second life keeps proving over and over again: that we can endure disappointment by changing our descriptions."[29] Here and now, *trans*, I have been arguing, is at its best when lived and thought in the second life, which often feels terrible—"I do feel like I died"—and is "not so terrible. How would I describe it? . . . I'm here but in a different way."[30] So many don't survive it, being forced to withdraw their attachments; my point, then, in lumping together these blackened, queer, sick, wounded articulations of living is that they collectively provide resources for survival, resources that are unavailable to a discourse/life structured by the (trans) narrative that describes bad feelings as always and only a trap, opposed to joyful movement. Or to return to where I began—with Carson McCullers's *The Member of the Wedding*—these are resources that are made available in the "sad and ugly," "silent and crazy and sad" kitchen, when we sit together there.[31] Sitting together, it turns out, also requires changing our descriptions, and thinking with maladjustment is an exercise in feeling through what that might mean.

NOTES

PREFACE/ACKNOWLEDGMENTS

1 Stryker, "Institutionalizing Trans* Studies."
2 Keegan, "Getting Disciplined," 388; Bettcher, "What Is Trans Philosophy?," 651.
3 Adair, Awkward-Rich, and Marvin, "Before Trans Studies."
4 Erica L. Green, Katie Benner, and Robert Pear, "'Transgender' Could Be Defined Out of Existence Under Trump Administration," *New York Times*, October 21, 2018; Ahmed, *The Promise of Happiness*, 14. For an incisive read of the emergence of transition tech companies, see Geffen and Howard, "Quantifying Transition."

INTRODUCTION

1 Levasseur, "Gender Incongruence."
2 Kunzel, "The Flourishing of Transgender Studies," 268.
3 Stryker, "(De)subjugated Knowledges," 1–2.
4 Stryker, "(De)subjugated Knowledges," 2.
5 Gibson, Glazier, and Olson, "Evaluation of Anxiety," 4. See also Durwood et al., "Mental Health and Self-Worth."
6 Pyne, "Autistic Disruptions, Trans Temporalities," 346, 346–47.
7 Ahmed, *The Promise of Happiness*, 54. See also Metzl, "Why 'Against Health'?"
8 Nash, *Black Feminism Reimagined*, 12.
9 "Transvestite and Transsexual Liberation," *Gay Dealer*, October 1970, 9, Gale Archives of Sexuality and Gender, accessed October 23, 2019, https://link-gale-com.silk.library.umass.edu/apps/doc/TZIRKR632512870/AHSI?u=mlin_w_umassamh&sid=bookmark-AHSI&xid=aa7955c2.
10 Puar, "Disability," 77–78.
11 Puar, "Disability," 78.
12 "Transvestite and Transsexual Liberation," *Gay Dealer*.
13 Lewis, "'We Are Certain.'"
14 "Transvestite and Transsexual Liberation," *Gay Dealer*; my emphasis.
15 Baril, "Transness as Debility," 61.
16 Lewis, "'I Am 64,'" 24.
17 *Oxford English Dictionary Online*, s.v. "maladjustment, n.," accessed December 30, 2021, https://www.oed.com.silk.library.umass.edu/view/Entry/112724?redirectedFrom=maladjustment.
18 *Oxford English Dictionary Online*, s.v. "maladjustment, n."
19 Rekers, "Atypical Gender Development," 559n2, 561.

20 Rekers, "Atypical Gender Development," 569; Rekers and Lovaas, "Behavioral Treatment," 174.

21 Rekers and Lovaas, "Behavioral Treatment," 174; Rekers et al., "Child Gender Disturbances," 4.

22 Toward such a genealogy, see Harrington, *Mind Fixers*, especially chap. 3; de la Cour, "From 'Moron' to 'Maladjusted.'"

23 Garland-Thomson, "Misfits," 594.

24 Language excluding "socially maladjusted" children from those guaranteed an education has carried over from the 1975 Education for All Handicapped Children Act (Public Law 94-142) into the present Individuals with Disabilities Education Improvement Act, passed in 2004.

25 I owe this condensed formulation to Bruce, *How to Go Mad without Losing Your Mind*, 6–9.

26 Stryker, "My Words to Victor Frankenstein," 237.

27 Malatino, "Future Fatigue," 642, 644.

28 Ngai, *Ugly Feelings*, 1

29 Mitchell and Snyder, *Narrative Prosthesis*, 3.

30 Crawford, "Transgender without Organs," 132.

31 Prosser, *Second Skins*, 69.

32 Hemmings, *Why Stories Matter*; Love, *Feeling Backward*, 4; Nash, *Black Feminism Reimagined*; Amin, *Disturbing Attachments*; Wiegman, *Object Lessons*, 20.

33 Wiegman, *Object Lessons*, 3.

34 Wiegman, *Object Lessons*, 4

35 Wiegman, *Object Lessons*, 7.

36 Hausman, *Changing Sex*, 140.

37 Long Chu and Drager, "After Trans Studies," 105, 106.

38 Long Chu and Drager, "After Trans Studies," 107.

39 Long Chu and Drager, "After Trans Studies," 108, 107.

40 Adair, Awkward-Rich, and Marvin, "Before Trans Studies."

41 Stryker, "My Words to Victor Frankenstein," 224.

42 Stryker, "Portrait of a Transfag," 79.

43 Chen, "Brain Fog"; Aho, Ben-Moshe, and Hilton, "Mad Futures."

44 Price, *Mad at School*, 26.

45 Hale, "Tracing a Ghostly Memory in My Throat," 104.

46 One of the most striking examples of this dismissal can be found by comparing the first and second volumes of the *Transgender Studies Reader*. Published just seven years apart, volume 1 opens with a section on "Sex, Gender, and Science," which critically engages with the work of psychologists and others in the medical sciences, whereas this possible branch of trans studies is all but invisible in volume 2.

47 Cited in Stone, "The *Empire* Strikes Back," 153.

48 Stone, "The *Empire* Strikes Back," 153.

49 Withers, *Disability Politics and Theory*, 112.

50 A nonexhaustive list of such work includes Gill-Peterson, *Histories of the Transgender Child*; Keegan, *Lana and Lilly Wachowski*; Beauchamp, *Going Stealth*; Hayward, "More Lessons from a Starfish"; Spade, *Normal Life*; Snorton, *Black on*

Both Sides; Steinbock, *Shimmering Images*; Heaney, *The New Woman*; and Aizura, *Mobile Subjects*.

51 See, for example, Spade, "Resisting Medicine, Re/modeling Gender"; and Prosser, *Second Skins*.

52 Gould, *Moving Politics*, 34.

53 Gould, *Moving Politics*, 3.

54 Gould, *Moving Politics*, 36.

55 Spade, "Resisting Medicine, Re/modeling Gender," 21n20; my emphasis.

56 Carter, "Embracing Transition," 130; Vaccaro, "Felt Matters," 92–93; Steinbock, "Groping Theory," 111, 116.

57 Gorton, "Transgender as Mental Illness," 644.

58 McCullers, *Member of the Wedding* (2004), 3–4.

59 McCullers, *Member of the Wedding* (2004), 23.

60 McCullers, *Member of the Wedding* (2004), 23

61 McCullers, *Member of the Wedding* (2004), 42.

62 McCullers, *Member of the Wedding* (2004), 159.

63 White, "Loss of Self," 127.

64 Halberstam, *Female Masculinity*, 9.

65 Halberstam, *Female Masculinity*, 9

66 Halberstam, *Female Masculinity*, 8.

67 Halberstam, *Female Masculinity*, 190.

68 Halberstam, *Female Masculinity*, 8.

69 Halberstam, *Female Masculinity*, 19.

70 McCullers, *Member of the Wedding* (2004), 3.

71 Halberstam, *Female Masculinity*, 8. On (queer) collectivity/utopianism in McCullers, see Miller, "Utopian Function of Affect"; Adams, *Sideshow U.S.A.*; Hoang, *A View from the Bottom*.

72 McCullers, *Member of the Wedding* (2004), 43.

73 McCullers, *Member of the Wedding* (2004), 38, 80, 32, 75, 81.

74 McCullers, *Member of the Wedding* (2004), 96.

75 McCullers, *Member of the Wedding* (2004), 3.

76 McCullers, *Member of the Wedding* (2004), 3.

77 McCullers, *Member of the Wedding* (2004), 95.

78 McCullers, *Member of the Wedding* (2004), 42.

79 Carr, *The Lonely Hunter*.

80 Carr, *The Lonely Hunter*, 2.

81 McDowell, *Carson McCullers*, 15. On McCullers's gender and sexuality as central to the content of her fiction see, for example, Gleeson-White, *Strange Bodies*.

82 McCullers, *Member of the Wedding* (2004), 118–20.

83 McCullers, *Member of the Wedding: A Play* (1951), 1.

84 Martínez-San Miguel and Tobias, "Introduction: Thinking beyond Hetero/Homo Normativities," 15n1.

85 Stryker, *Transgender History*, 3.

86 Snorton, *Black on Both Sides*, 143. On this point, see also Aizura, *Mobile Subjects*.

87 McCullers, *Member of the Wedding* (2004), 81.

88 Snorton, *Black on Both Sides*, 12.

89 McCullers, *Member of the Wedding* (2004), 81.

90 Muñoz, *Disidentifications*, 8.

91 Muñoz, *Disidentifications*, 11.

92 Combahee River Collective, "Combahee River Collective Statement," 269.

93 Combahee River Collective, "Combahee River Collective Statement," 272, 271, 269.

94 Malatino, "Future Fatigue," 639.

95 Muñoz, *Disidentifications*, 108.

96 For critical reflections on the use of violence in trans discourse see Valentine, *Imagining Transgender*, chap. 6; and Lamble, "Retelling Racialized Violence."

97 In *The Report of the 2015 U.S. Transgender Survey*, 51 percent of transgender men and 58 percent of nonbinary female-assigned people reported having been sexually assaulted in their lifetime (James et al., *Report of the 2015 U.S. Transgender Survey*, 205).

98 Sears, *Arresting Dress*, 10.

99 Butler, "Gender Is Burning," 131.

1. DISABLED HISTORIES OF *TRANS*

An earlier version of this chapter appeared as "'She of the Pants and No Voice': Jack Bee Garland's Disability Drag," TSQ: *Transgender Studies Quarterly* 7, no. 1 (2020): 20–36.

1 Renaissance Education Association, "Who's Disabled? . . . I'm Okay but You're Not," *Renaissance News* 3, no. 11 (1989), 3, Digital Transgender Archive, https://www.digitaltransgenderarchive.net/files/b8515n36q

2 Renaissance Education Association, "Who's Disabled?"

3 For an account of the vexed relationship between gender nonconformity and disability law, see Colker, *The Disability Pendulum*, 22–68.

4 Renaissance Education Association, "Who's Disabled?"

5 Halberstam, *In a Queer Time*, 18.

6 Mitchell and Snyder, *Narrative Prosthesis*, 3. See also Baynton, "Disability and the Justification."

7 Mitchell and Snyder, *Narrative Prosthesis*, 2.

8 Withers, *Disability Politics and Theory*, 112.

9 Kunzel, "The Rise of Gay Rights," 459–75.

10 Sears, *Arresting Dress*, 10.

11 Chambers-Letson, *After the Party*, 25.

12 Following Carrie Sandahl's sense of "cripping" as performance that "spins mainstream representations or practices to reveal able-bodied assumptions and exclusionary effects," I use *crip* to emphasize disability performance as critique (Sandahl, "Queering the Crip," 37).

13 Renaissance Education Association, "Who's Disabled?"

14 Dinshaw, *Getting Medieval*; Love, *Feeling Backward*; Freeman, *Time Binds*; Amin, *Disturbing Attachments*.

15 Eskridge, *Gaylaw*, 27.

16 Eskridge, *Gaylaw*, 338–41.

17 This set of city laws, more often named "the unsightly beggar ordinance," came to be known as "the ugly laws" within disability studies and activism. While "the ugly law" strips the original ordinance of its classed implications, the term has had a significant life in disability scholarship, activism, and art as a concrete sign of the violent excising of visible disability and disabled people from the public sphere. For a thorough, compelling account of the "effectively imaginary" work of the ordinance in the nineteenth- and twentieth-century United States, as well as in disability studies, see Schweik, *The Ugly Laws.*

18 The Municipal Code of Chicago: Comprising the Laws of Illinois Relating to the City of Chicago, and the Ordinances of the City Council, 1881, law no. 1612, 377. Cited in Schweik, *The Ugly Laws*, 1–2, 293.

19 Samuels, *Fantasies of Identification*, 11, 2.

20 Sears, *Arresting Dress*, 69.

21 Rita Fitzpatrick, "Parity in Pants Stirs Up Feminine Ire," *Chicago Daily Tribune*, January 9, 1943.

22 Fitzpatrick, "Parity in Pants."

23 D'Emilio, "Who Wears the Pants?"

24 D'Emilio, "Who Wears the Pants?"

25 Sears, *Arresting Dress*, 69.

26 Sears, *Arresting Dress*, 14.

27 D'Emilio, "Who Wears the Pants?"; "Slacks Don't Make the Woman: Male Impersonator, Decision," *Milwaukee Journal*, January 16, 1943.

28 "Slacks Don't Make the Woman," *Milwaukee Journal.*

29 "Slacks Don't Make the Woman," *Milwaukee Journal.*

30 Sears, *Arresting Dress*, 74–75. See also Lobdell, *"Strange Sort of Being."*

31 Schweik, *The Ugly Laws*, 65.

32 Sears, "Electric Brilliancy," 561.

33 "Queerest Career Ended at Last," *San Jose Mercury News*, July 4, 1907.

34 "Queerest Career Ended at Last," *San Jose Mercury News.* A description of Matson's being compelled by the jailer's "loosening the vest of Matson" can be found in "Posed as Her Brother: Romantic Story of a Prisoner in a California Jail," *Evening Journal*, March 13, 1895.

35 "Matson, the Woman, Gets Drunk," *Fresno Weekly Republican*, February 8, 1895.

36 "Queerest Career Ended at Last," *San Jose Mercury News.*

37 Dennett, *Weird and Wonderful*, 7.

38 Coined by Rosemarie Garland-Thomson, "the term normate usefully designates the social figure through which people can represent themselves as definitive human beings" (*Extraordinary Bodies*, 8).

39 "She's a Freak: Miss Matsen, the Male Impersonator, in a Dime Museum," *Jersey Journal*, March 13, 1895.

40 "She's a Freak," *Jersey Journal.*

41 Adams, *Sideshow U.S.A.*, 4.

42 "Louisa Matson's Double Sued," *San Francisco Call*, February 15, 1895.

43 Sears, *Arresting Dress*, 110–11.
44 Garland-Thomson, *Extraordinary Bodies*, 62–63.
45 Adams, *Sideshow U.S.A.*, 167.
46 Spillers, "Mama's Baby, Papa's Maybe," 67.
47 For more on Benga, see Newkirk, *Spectacle*.
48 Stryker, "My Words," 250.
49 Sears, *Arresting Dress*, 93.
50 Sears, *Arresting Dress*, 95.
51 Schuller, *The Biopolitics of Feeling*, 59.
52 Gill-Peterson, *Histories of the Transgender Child*, 80.
53 Lothstein, *Female-to-Male Transsexualism*, 45–46.
54 Stallings, *Funk the Erotic*, 205.
55 Fitzpatrick, "Parity in Pants."
56 Fears of "deception"—in particular, fears that nondisabled people were passing as disabled in order to unfairly benefit from public aid/sympathy—also animated the regulation of disability. See Samuels's *Fantasies of Identification*; and Schweik's *The Ugly Laws* for more on "the disability con" as justification for regulating/surveilling public spaces, as well a strategy for navigating these constraints, and its effects in nineteenth- and twentieth-century US discourse.
57 Renaissance, "Who's Disabled?"
58 Mendoza, *Metroimperial Intimacies*, 206.
59 Mendoza, *Metroimperial Intimacies*, 208–9; Boyd, "Bodies in Motion," 420–43.
60 It's worth noting that it was reported in at least one story that Jackie Bross's dad was Cherokee. While this was often unmentioned in the news about them, the apparent fixedness of their masculinity was undoubtedly racialized—a dark contrast to Theodora Fitzpatrick's blonde femininity.
61 Sullivan, *From Female to Male*, 1.
62 Victoria A. Brownworth, "Is S/He or Isn't S/He: The Biography of an American Crossdresser," review of *From Female to Male*, by Louis Sullivan, *Lambda Rising Book Report* 2, no. 4 (1990), 19, 35, in box 4, folder 143, 91–97, Louis Graydon Sullivan Papers, the Gay and Lesbian Historical Society of Northern California, San Francisco.
63 Kate Bornstein, "What Makes a Man a Man?," review of *From Female to Male*, by Louis Sullivan, *Bay Area Reporter*, May 24, 1990, 42, in box 4, folder 143, 91–97, Louis Graydon Sullivan Papers, the Gay and Lesbian Historical Society of Northern California, San Francisco.
64 William A. Henkin, "Walks like a Man, Talks like a Man. . . . ," review of *From Female to Male*, by Louis Sullivan, in box 4, folder 143, 91–97, Louis Graydon Sullivan Papers, the Gay and Lesbian Historical Society of Northern California, San Francisco.
65 Halberstam, *Female Masculinity*, 22–28.
66 Munt, "The Butch Body," 102.
67 Munt, "The Butch Body," 103.
68 Sullivan, *From Female to Male*, 132.

69 Sullivan, *From Female to Male*, 17.
70 Sullivan, *From Female to Male*, 25.
71 Schuller, *The Biopolitics of Feeling*.
72 Kafer, *Feminist, Queer, Crip*, 27.
73 Sullivan, *From Female to Male*, 24.
74 Sears, *Arresting Dress*, 74–75.
75 Siebers, *Disability Theory*, 116.
76 Crip time as drag, or crip time accessed through disability drag, is certainly different from Elizabeth Freeman's theory of "temporal drag" as a way that "the pull of the past on the present" comes to be embodied (*Time Binds*, 62). However, the concepts are linked insofar as both highlight forms of slowness—delay, halting sociality, being "interested in the tail end of things, willing to be bathed in the fading light of whatever has been declared useless" (xiii)—as methods of criticism, engagement, and living.
77 Louis Sullivan, letter to Judy Van Maasdam, May 21, 1987, in box 2, folder 45, 91–97, Louis Graydon Sullivan Papers, the Gay and Lesbian Historical Society of Northern California, San Francisco.
78 Sullivan, *We Both Laughed*, 399.
79 "Story of a Modern Rosalind: Strange Adventures of a Girl Who Roams in Male Attire," *San Francisco Call*, August 27, 1897.
80 Mendoza, *Metroimperial Intimacies*, 209.
81 "Death Ends Charities: 'Jack Bee' Was a Woman," *San Francisco Chronicle*, September 21, 1936.
82 Kafer, *Feminist, Queer, Crip*, 157.
83 Kafer, *Feminist, Queer, Crip*, 156.
84 West, *Transforming Citizenships*, 64.
85 GLAD, "Blatt v. Cabela's Retail Inc."
86 Hiegel, "Sexual Exclusions."
87 Americans with Disabilities Act, Sec. 12211.
88 Levi and Klein, "Pursuing Protection," 74.
89 Barry, "Disabilityqueer," 33.
90 Barry, "Disabilityqueer," 14.
91 Barry, "Disabilityqueer," 24.
92 Sec. 12208 of the ADA reads: "For the purposes of this chapter, the term 'disabled' or 'disability' shall not apply to an individual solely because that individual is a transvestite."
93 Lewis, "'I Am 64,'" 14.
94 Mendoza, *Metroimperial Intimacies*, 205.
95 Lewis, "'I Am 64,'" 24.
96 Lewis, "'I Am 64,'" 27.
97 Stryker, "My Words," 224.
98 Keegan, *Lana and Lilly Wachowski*, 2–3.
99 Snorton, *Black on Both Sides*, 175.
100 Lewis, "'I Am 64,'" 22, 14.

1 Scholinski, "After-Wards."
2 Scholinski, *72 Hour Hold*.
3 Scholinski, *Last Time*, 153.
4 Scholinski, quoted in Ophelian, *Diagnosing Difference*.
5 Miyatsu, "'Hundreds of People,'" 52.
6 Ophelian, *Diagnosing Difference*.
7 Some notable texts that go otherwise unmentioned in this book include Mog and Lock Swarr, "Threads of Commonality"; Fink, *Forget Burial*; Wilkerson, "Normate Sex"; and cárdenas, "Sick."
8 Clare, "Body Shame, Body Pride," 262.
9 Kim, *Curative Violence*; Clare, "Body Shame, Body Pride," 262.
10 Clare, "Body Shame, Body Pride," 265.
11 Clare, "Body Shame, Body Pride," 265.
12 Clare, *Brilliant Imperfection*, 142.
13 Love, *Feeling Backward*; Ophelian, *Diagnosing Difference*.
14 Amin, *Disturbing Attachments*, 10.
15 Scholinski, *The Last Time*, 196.
16 Butler, "The Body You Want," 84.
17 The text of Raymond's NCHCT paper largely rehashes arguments from *The Transsexual Empire*. Both this paper and the resulting NCHCT 1981 report that was used to assess whether trans surgeries ought be covered under Medicare are accessible in Harvard's Schlesinger Library. Raymond, HEW commissioned paper and report on social and ethical aspects of transsexual surgery, 1980–1981, MC 968, carton 2, Papers of Janice G. Raymond, Schlesinger Library on the History of Women in America, Radcliffe Institute for Advanced Study, Harvard University, Cambridge, Massachusetts.
18 Raymond, *The Transsexual Empire*, 178.

2. TRANS, FEMINISM; OR, READING LIKE A DEPRESSED TRANSSEXUAL

An earlier version of this chapter appeared as "Trans, Feminism: Or, Reading like a Depressed Transsexual," *Signs: Journal of Women in Culture and Society* 42, no. 4 (2017): 819–41.

1 Ruth Padawer, "When Women Become Men at Wellesley," *New York Times Magazine*, October 15, 2014.
2 Wiegman, *Object Lessons*, 3.
3 Wiegman, *Object Lessons*, 3.
4 Rubin, "Reading like a (Transsexual) Man," 305. Although I focus specifically on discussions of transmasculinities in feminist contexts, this conversation is simultaneously a part of and a distorted echo of a wider conversation about the place of men in feminism.
5 Janet Halley offers a helpful shorthand for what she deems a minimalist description of a feminist project. First, she makes a distinction between something

f (women, female, and/or femininity) and something m (men, male, and/or masculinity); Halley's shorthand for this is m/f. Next, Halley posits "some kind of subordination . . . in which f is the disadvantaged or subordinated element," or m > f. Halley, *Split Decisions*, 18. Finally, a feminist project opposes this subordination, or carries a brief for f. In many ways, this essay is a meditation on the persistence of m/f as a way of dividing up the world, particularly in contexts where it is taken for granted that m/f does not do justice as a description of it.

6 Rubin, "Reading like a (Transsexual) Man," 309.

7 Rubin, "Reading like a (Transsexual) Man," 309.

8 Rubin, "Reading like a (Transsexual) Man,"309–10.

9 Hale, "Tracing a Ghostly Memory in My Throat," 101.

10 Hale, "Tracing a Ghostly Memory in My Throat," 111.

11 Freud, "Mourning and Melancholia," 249

12 Freud, "Mourning and Melancholia," 246.

13 Hale, "Tracing a Ghostly Memory in My Throat," 121. See also Lugones, "Playfulness, 'World'-Traveling, and Loving Perception," 24.

14 Hale, "Tracing a Ghostly Memory in My Throat," 115.

15 Hale, "Suggested Rules."

16 Salamon, *Assuming a Body*, 122. See also Hansbury, "The Middle Men."

17 If this seems abstract or absurd, one need only think of how the popular television show *The L Word* handled its trans character, Max. While Max lived and dated within the lesbian world of the main characters, the writers presented him as utterly out-of-place, having legitimate claim neither to this world nor to the world of normative manhood. That is, his proximity to both of these worlds undid his claims of belonging to either. It isn't until the show introduces a gay male love interest for Max—a queer homosocial world—that Max becomes legible as a stable, transmasculine subject. See Chaiken, Abbot, and Greenberg, *The L Word*, seasons 3–6, 2006–9.

18 Salamon, *Assuming a Body*, 122.

19 Salamon, *Assuming a Body*, 120.

20 Sedgwick, *Touching Feeling*.

21 Siebers, *Disability Theory*, 59–64.

22 Siebers, *Disability Theory*, 64.

23 Wendell, "Unhealthy Disabled."

24 Price, "The Bodymind Problem," 274. See also Mollow, "'When *Black* Women Start'"; Kafer, "Un/safe Disclosures"; Chen, "Brain Fog"; Baril, "Transness as Debility"; and Johnson, "Bad Romance."

25 Davis, *The End of Normal*, 66–67.

26 Davis, *The End of Normal*, 67.

27 Price, quoted in Johnson and McRuer, "Proliferating Cripistemologies," 162.

28 Cvetkovich, *Depression*, 14

29 Scheman, "Queering the Center," 132.

30 Solomon, *The Noonday Demon*, 81; Kenyon, "Having It Out with Melancholy," 24.

31 Donaldson, "The Corpus of the Madwoman."

32 Cvetkovich, *Depression*, 20.
33 Cvetkovich, *Depression*, 7.
34 The NCD in question has since been removed from the Medicare National Coverage Determinations Manual. For commentary on Raymond's contribution to the coverage decision, see Williams, "Fact Checking Janice Raymond," as well as US Department of Health and Human Services, Departmental Appeals Board, "Supplemental Declaration."
35 Riddell, "Divided Sisterhood," 158.
36 For a fuller version of the story, see Stryker, *Transgender History*.
37 Stone, "The *Empire* Strikes Back," 164.
38 Stryker, "Transgender Studies," 212.
39 Stone, "The *Empire* Strikes Back," 154.
40 Hausman, *Changing Sex*, 140.
41 Goldberg, "What Is a Woman?"
42 See, for example, Truitt, "Why the *New Yorker*'s Radical Feminism and Transgenderism Piece Was One-Sided"; and Serano, "Op-Ed: An Open Letter to the *New Yorker*."
43 Goldberg and Talbot, "On Transgender Activists and Radical Feminists."
44 Goldberg, "What Is a Woman?"
45 Goldberg and Talbot, "On Transgender Activists and Radical Feminists."
46 Here are Margaret Talbot's words on the subject: "Now, I mean, it is true that a female-to-male trans person who has not had a hysterectomy and has chosen to stop taking testosterone and is having unprotected sex, so a lot of categories there, a lot of ifs, could get pregnant unintentionally and seek an abortion. That's a very, very, I would venture to say, small group. And so I think when you're addressing reproductive rights it is fair to say that you are essentially addressing women. And I think it's a little problematic to get so careful about the language that you are kind of denying reality" (Goldberg and Talbot, "On Transgender Activists and Radical Feminists").
47 Serano, "Op-Ed: An Open Letter to the *New Yorker*."
48 Jeffreys, *Gender Hurts*, 1.
49 Jeffreys, *Gender Hurts*, 5.
50 Goldberg, "What Is a Woman?"
51 Hemmings, *Why Stories Matter*, 219.
52 Noble, "Trans. Panic," 48.
53 Halberstam, *Female Masculinity*, 2.
54 Halberstam, *Female Masculinity*, 1, 2.
55 Halberstam, *Female Masculinity*, 19.
56 Halberstam, *Female Masculinity*, 6.
57 Edelman, *No Future*, 3.
58 Halberstam, *In a Queer Time and Place*, 1.
59 Halberstam, *In a Queer Time and Place*, 153.
60 Halberstam, *In a Queer Time and Place*, 153.
61 Noble, *Sons of the Movement*, 47.

62 To be fair to Noble, he recognizes this deferral as potentially problematic and ends his book with a discussion of queer femme, in which femme does for femininity what he understands boy/trans to do for masculinity.

63 Halberstam, *Female Masculinity*, 268–69.

64 Enke, introduction to *Transfeminist Perpsectives*, 2; my emphasis.

65 Koyama, "The Transfeminist Manifesto," 245.

66 Koyama, "The Transfeminist Manifesto," 258.

67 Koyama, "The Transfeminist Manifesto," 258, 259.

68 Hogan, *Peter Pan*.

69 Barrie, *Peter Pan*, 138.

70 Kissel, "'But When at Last She Really Came, I Shot Her,'" 32.

71 Berlant, *Desire/Love*, 6–7.

72 Hedwig, the protagonist of John Cameron Mitchell's rock musical and 2001 film *Hedwig and the Angry Inch*, is a debatably transgender rock singer, aching to feel unified, whole. "Origin of Love"—the song that organizes the pathos of the show and that I encourage you to hear playing in the background of my argument—rewrites Aristophanes's speech on love in Plato's *Symposium*, which famously provides a mythic story of the origin of human nature. In this account, we were once round, powerful, two-faced creatures but, cut down to our current size by threatened (and threatening) gods, have been left to perpetually and painfully seek our former unity. As Hedwig croons, "That's the pain, cuts a straight line down through the heart; we call it love."

73 Berlant, *Cruel Optimism*, 23.

74 Berlant, *Desire/Love*, 106.

75 Enke, introduction to *Transfeminist Perpsectives*, 3.

76 Underlying this formulation—that depressives are more likely to sit in the painful/jagged realities of love that the fantasy of the love plot smooths over—is the widely circulating "depressive realism" hypothesis, which posits that depressed people judge reality more accurately than nondepressed people, likely because of a willingness to accept contingency. While "depressive realism" is attributed to psychologists Lauren Alloy and Lyn Abramson (Alloy and Abramson, "Judgment of Contingency"; Alloy et al., "Depressive Realism"), it resonates with Freud's thoughts on the melancholic's "keener eye for the truth" in "Mourning and Melancholia," 246.

3. SOME DISSOCIATIVE TRANS MASC POETICS

1 Pierce, *Boys Don't Cry*.

2 Gage, "The Inconvenient Truth."

3 Lothstein, *Female-to-Male Transsexualism*, 253.

4 Stoller "Etiological Factors," 62.

5 Jeffreys, *Gender Hurts*, 111; Shrier, *Irreversible Damage*, 1–7.

6 Donna Minkowitz, "Love Hurts," *Village Voice*, April 19, 1994.

7 Kissel, "'But When at Last She Really Came, I Shot Her,'" 32.

8 Spade, *Normal Life*, 19.

9 Berlant, "She's Having an Episode," 25.
10 Van der Hart and Dorahy, "History of the Concept of Dissociation."
11 Van der Hart, Nijenhuis, and Steele, *The Haunted Self.*
12 Winnicott, "Dreaming, Fantasying, and Living," 43.
13 Halberstam, *In a Queer Time and Place*, 78.
14 Bettcher, "Trapped in the Wrong Theory," 392.
15 Halberstam, *In a Queer Time and Place*, 88.
16 Keegan, *Lana and Lilly Wachowski*, 25.
17 Halberstam, *In a Queer Time and Place*, 77,88.
18 Keegan, *Lana and Lilly Wachowski*, 25.
19 Devor, "Transsexualism, Dissociation, and Child Abuse," 66.
20 Devor, "Transsexualism, Dissociation, and Child Abuse," 64.
21 Cvetkovich, *An Archive of Feelings*, 15.
22 Mintz, *Unruly Bodies*, 136; Clare, *Exile and Pride*, 11.
23 Clare, *Exile and Pride*, 145.
24 Clare, *Exile and Pride*, 145.
25 Clare, *Exile and Pride*, 149.
26 Plett, "Rise of the Gender Novel."
27 Fu, *For Today I Am a Boy*; Lemus, *Like Son*; Tremain, *Sacred Country*; Eugenides, *Middlesex*. Cal, the protagonist of Eugenides's *Middlesex* is intersex, but the opening line of the novel ("I was born twice") locates it squarely within the logic of the trans plot.
28 Data about sexual and other forms of intimate violence in trans and other gender nonconforming lives reinforces the point that liberal, cis feminist framings of sexual assault often work to obscure realities of trans and queer life. For example, the AAU's recent survey about sexual violence on college campuses suggested that trans/gender nonconforming college students experience "nonconsensual sexual contact" at a similar, or even slightly higher, rate than their cis female peers; see Cantor et al., "AAU Climate Survey." In fact, nearly half of all respondents to the *2015 U.S. Transgender Survey* reported having been sexually assaulted in their lifetime.
29 Higgins and Silver, introduction to *Rape and Representation*, 3.
30 Brown, *States of Injury*. See Halley's *Split Decisions* for this: "While feminism is committed to affirming and identifying itself with female injury, it may thereby, unintentionally, intensify it. Oddly, representing women as end points of pain, imagining them as lacking the agency to cause harm to others and particularly harm to men, feminists refuse also to see women—even injured ones—as powerful actors" (346).
31 Gunne and Thompson, introduction to *Feminism, Literature, and Rape Narratives*, 4, 3.
32 Plaza, "Our Damages," 28–29.
33 Clare, *Exile and Pride*, 151.
34 Clare, *Brilliant Imperfection*, 119–20.
35 Clare, *Exile and Pride*, 147.
36 Hale, "Tracing a Ghostly Memory in My Throat," 55.

37 DeLine, "Trans People, Trauma, and Dissociative Identities."

38 Marvin, "Transsexuality, the Curio, and the Transgender Tipping Point."

39 Huffer, *Are the Lips a Grave?*, 12

40 Mattson, "Teaching Weinstein, Spacey, Sexual Assault, and New Skirmishes in Old Sex Wars."

41 Foucault, *The History of Sexuality*, 31–32.

42 Ball, "'More or Less Raped,'" 56.

43 Foucault, *The History of Sexuality*, 32, 31.

44 Plaza, "Our Damages," 30. See Ball, "'More or Less Raped'"; Plaza, "Our Damages"; and Cahill, "Foucault, Rape, and the Construction of the Feminine Body." See also Alcoff, "Dangerous Pleasures"; Huffer, *Are the Lips a Grave?*, chap. 3; and Heyes, introduction to "Foucault and Feminism," among others, for considerations (and reconsiderations) of tensions between feminism and Foucault regarding sexual violence and, by extension, a particular kind of feminism and the kind of queer theory enamored of the gesture at the end of volume 1 to the possibility of "different economies of bodies and pleasures" Foucault, *History of Sexuality*, 159. See Tremain's "Educating Jouy" for a critical disability studies reading of this debate. Tremain points out, crucially, that readings of Jouy as a proto-pedophile persistently miss that Jouy is medicalized not as a pervert but as an "imbecile," a predecessor of today's "cognitively disabled person."

45 Cvetkovich, *An Archive of Feelings*, 63.

46 Huffer, *Are the Lips a Grave?*, 105–6.

47 Martin, "Sexualities without Genders," 104.

48 Martin, "Sexualities without Genders," 104.

49 Martin, "Sexualities without Genders," 110. For some more elaborated readings of the interrelations of early queer and trans studies, see Prosser, *Second Skins*; Rubin, "Trans Studies"; Heaney, *New Woman*; and Namaste, *Invisible Lives*.

50 Martin, "Sexualities without Genders," 117.

51 Rubin, "Of Catamites and Kings," 473.

52 Martin, "Sexualities without Genders," 117.

53 Martin, "Sexualities without Genders," 105.

54 Sedgwick, *Epistemology of the Closet*, 27–39. Grace Lavery has written about the seeming impossibility of transition in Sedgwickian and related queer theory in "Egg Theory's Early Style."

55 Martin, "Sexualities without Genders," 105, 110, 112.

56 Halberstam, "Transgender Butch," 287–88.

57 Hale, "Tracing a Ghostly Memory in My Throat," 55.

58 Prosser, "No Place like Home," 488–89; my emphasis.

59 Hale, "Consuming the Living, Dis(re)membering the Dead," 338.

60 Prosser, "No Place like Home," 496; Hale, "Tracing a Ghostly Memory in My Throat," 56.

61 Hale, "Tracing a Ghostly Memory in My Throat," 57.

62 Foucault, cited in Rubin, "Of Catamites and Kings," 476.

63 Huffer, *Are the Lips a Grave?*, 86.

64 In his assessment of the butch/FTM "border," C. Jacob Hale notes that the construction of Brandon as either stone butch or heterosexual FTM required "eliding those parts of the young Nebraskan's history that include attractions to boys during high school . . . ease with having close gay male friends . . . enjoyment of gay male bars . . . and acceptance of being called one of Grandma's 'faggots'" ("Consuming the Living," 341–42n1).

65 Halberstam, *Female Masculinity*, 4.

66 Halberstam, *In a Queer Time and Place*, 89.

67 Martin, "Sexualities without Genders," 105.

68 On the racial dynamics of such category/space policing in 1990s feminist discourse, see Koyama, "Whose Feminism Is It Anyway?"

69 Lugones, "Toward a Decolonial Feminism."

70 Martínez, "Reflections on Joto Passivity," 237.

71 Martínez, "Reflections on Joto Passivity," 239.

72 Martínez, "Reflections on Joto Passivity," 244.

73 Foucault, *Abnormal*, 292.

74 Martínez, "Reflections on Joto Passivity," 243.

75 Bersani, "Is the Rectum a Grave?," 212.

76 Martínez, "Reflections on Joto Passivity," 242.

77 Prosser, *Second Skins*, 102.

78 DeLine, *Refuse*, 18.

79 DeLine, *Refuse*, 14.

80 DeLine, *Refuse*, 14.

81 See Prosser's *Second Skins* for an extended discussion of transsexual autobiography as a literature structured by the desire for gendered realness.

82 DeLine, *Refuse*, 344–46.

83 DeLine, *Refuse*, 35.

84 Halberstam, *In a Queer Time and Place*, 1.

85 Halberstam, *In a Queer Time and Place*, 2.

86 DeLine, *Refuse*, 330.

87 Halberstam, *In a Queer Time and Place*, 6.

88 Martínez, "Reflections on Joto Passivity," 242.

89 DeLine, *Refuse*, 107–8.

90 DeLine, *Refuse*, 108.

91 DeLine, *I Know Very Well How I Got My Name*, 80.

92 DeLine, *I Know Very Well How I Got My Name*, 82.

93 If it has not yet been clear, my thinking about the doubling of childhood violence and possibility in these texts owes a debt to Katheryn Bond Stockton's portrait of (queer) children grown sideways, especially her question: "Given that children and teens have not found it safe by and large to express their same-sex longings to peers . . . to what extent has man/boy love, at least for a century, in some contexts, functioned as a substitute lateral relation for men and boys?" (*The Queer Child*, 62).

94 Barnett, *Dangerous Desires*, xv.

95 Barnett, *Dangerous Desires*, xv.
96 Barnett, *Dangerous Desires*, xx.
97 Barnett, *Dangerous Desires*, xx, xxi.
98 Barnett, *Dangerous Desires*, xx.
99 Halberstam, *The Queer Art of Failure*, 4.
100 Califia, *Sex Changes*, 6.

4. WE'S COMPANY

1 Kennedy, *The First Man-Made Man*, 176.
2 Gillies and Millard, *The Principles and Art of Plastic Surgery*; and Pound, *Gillies, Surgeon Extraordinary*.
3 Kennedy, *The First Man-Made Man*, 8.
4 Kennedy, *The First Man-Made Man*, 8.
5 Dillon, *Out of the Ordinary*, 114.
6 Dillon, *Out of the Ordinary*, 29. Dillon's surgical case history is recorded in Gillies and Millard, *Plastic Surgery*, 383–84.
7 Kennedy, *The First Man-Made Man*, 8.
8 Lau, "Between the Times."
9 Dillon, *Out of the Ordinary*, 30.
10 Malatino, "Future Fatigue," 246.
11 Stone, "The *Empire* Strikes Back," 153.
12 Yergeau, *Authoring Autism*, 98–106.
13 Hausman, *Changing Sex*, 140. "As is well known, the accusation of being in ideology only applies to others, never to oneself" (Althusser, "Ideology and Ideological State Apparatuses," 265).
14 Lothstein, *Female-to-Male Transsexualism*, 241.
15 Butler, "Gender Is Burning," 131.
16 While this chapter focuses on trans styles of reading as a form of being in relation with the nonhuman world, trans turnings away from the human world might and do also entail human/nonhuman animal relationalities; staying with the motley and terrible *we* composed of all those forms of life rendered unhuman or contingently human; and "boycotting the humanist (antiblack) project of the ontological (sex centrism)" (Hayward, "Don't Exist," 192).
17 Bettcher, "Trapped in the Wrong Theory," 392. See also Bettcher, "Evil Deceivers and Make-Believers," in which she develops this account of transphobia but terms it *identity enforcement*.
18 Cox, "Bullies Don't Draw."
19 See Meyerowitz, *How Sex Changed*.
20 Prosser, *Second Skins*, 44.
21 Prosser, *Second Skins*, 69.
22 Serano, *Whipping Girl*, 82.
23 Serano, *Whipping Girl*, 84–85.
24 See, for example, Prosser, *Second Skins*, 1–61; Elliot, *Debates in Transgender, Queer, and Feminist Theory*; and Salamon, *Assuming a Body*, especially 69–94.

25 Salamon, *Assuming a Body*, 76.

26 Serano, *Whipping Girl*, 79.

27 For a critique of trans thought that relies on a willful agent, see Salamon, *Assuming a Body*, 69–94. See Valentine, "Sue E. Generous," for a critique not of Salamon but of the tendency to begin from the assumption that transsexuality involves agency/choice while nontranssexuality does not.

28 Feinberg, *Trans Liberation*, 53.

29 Heyes, "Feminist Solidarity after Queer Theory," 1095.

30 Noble, *Sons of the Movement*, 3.

31 Noble, *Sons of the Movement*, 3.

32 Heaney, *New Woman*, 6.

33 Namaste, *Sex Change*, 25.

34 Malatino, *Trans Care*, 5; Noble, *Sons of the Movement*, 29.

35 Lugones, *Pilgrimages/Peregrinajes*, 21.

36 Bettcher, "Trapped in the Wrong Theory," 389.

37 Further, Bettcher conceptualizes *trans* as itself a form of resistant withdrawal. In her framework, because she understands gender presentation as ordinarily taken to be a public representation of our intimate persons (i.e., gender represents genitals), trans people are understood as resisting this coercive system by withdrawing intimate information from public circulation. See Bettcher, "Full-Frontal Morality"; and Bettcher, "Trans Identities and First-Person Authority."

38 Dillon, *Out of the Ordinary*, 73.

39 Bettcher, "What Is Trans Philosophy?," 657; Keegan, *Lana and Lilly Wachowski*, 2.

40 Yergeau, *Authoring Autism*, 87.

41 Yergeau, *Authoring Autism*, 71.

42 Yergeau, *Authoring Autism*, 72.

43 Yergeau, *Authoring Autism*,72.

44 Lorde, "Uses of the Erotic," 54, 57.

45 Quashie, *Sovereignty of Quiet*, 21.

46 Rubin, *Self-Made Men*, 15; Cromwell, *Transmen and FTMs*, 42.

47 Fanon, *Black Skin, White Masks*, 95.

48 Fanon, *Black Skin, White Masks*, 95, 96.

49 Quashie, *Sovereignty of Quiet*, 40.

50 Hausman, *Changing Sex*, 156.

51 Hausman, *Changing Sex*, 156.

52 Eastwood, "How, Then, Might the Transsexual Read?," 593.

53 Eco, *The Role of the Reader*, 8.

54 Hausman, *Changing Sex*, 157.

55 Hausman, *Changing Sex*, 156.

56 Eastwood, "How, Then, Might the Transsexual Read?," 593; Hausman, *Changing Sex*, 156.

57 See Prosser, *Second Skins*, especially chaps. 3 and 4. Gherovici also writes in a sustained way about the role of autobiography in trans self-making; see Gherovici, *Please Select Your Gender*, chap. 10. While Prosser and Gherovici rely on psycho-

analytic models, see Rubin, *Self-Made Men*, chap. 4, for a sociological discussion of the role of print and other media in the consolidation of transmasculine identities. Further, the possibility that nonnormative sex/gender configurations can be acquired through reading is a persistent source of anxiety in both transphobic and anti-transphobic thought. In quite a different tone from Hausman, Judith Butler remarks: "The diagnosis [of gender dysphoria] . . . wants to establish that gender is a relatively permanent phenomenon. It won't do, for instance, to walk into a clinic and say that it was only after you read a book by Kate Bornstein that you realized what you wanted to do, but that it wasn't really conscious for you until that time" ("Undiagnosing Gender," 81).

58 Hall, *The Well of Loneliness* (2005), 6.

59 Hall, *The Well of Loneliness* (2005), 10.

60 Hall, *The Well of Loneliness* (2005), 13.

61 Hall, *The Well of Loneliness* (2005), 13.

62 Hall, *The Well of Loneliness* (2005), 13.

63 Love, *Feeling Backward*, 113.

64 Hall, *The Well of Loneliness* (2005), 186. Parkes, "Lesbianism, History, and Censorship," 441. Most subsequent editions of *The Well of Loneliness* are printed without Ellis's prefatory remarks. Ellis praises the novel for its "notable psychological and sociological significance," insofar as it is "the first English novel which presents" the invert "in a completely faithful and uncompromising form." Hall, *The Well of Loneliness* (1981), with commentary by Havelock Ellis.

65 See Newton, "The Mythic Mannish Lesbian."

66 Parkes, "Lesbianism, History, and Censorship," 441. The literature on *The Well of Loneliness* is enormous. For some trans/butch readings of Stephen's masculinity see Noble, *Masculinities without Men?*, chaps. 1 and 2; Prosser, *Second Skins*, chap. 4; and Halberstam, *Female Masculinity*, chap. 3. For an overview of the history of *The Well of Loneliness*'s critical reception see Doan and Prosser's introduction to *Palatable Poison*.

67 For example, Lillian Faderman and Ann Williams argue that, from reading Hall's novel, the young lesbian "learned that inverted women, the real lesbians, were generally tall, or had boyish qualities in their voices, or had ankles that were too strong to be womanly. Furthermore, like Stephen she has no taste for feminine clothes, feminine occupations . . . In short, the real lesbian was masculine, preferred male attire and male pursuits" ("Radclyffe Hall and the Lesbian Image," 31–32). Learning that real lesbians are masculine, the young lesbian sets out to become real. In effect, Faderman and Williams charge *The Well of Loneliness* with infecting later generations of lesbians with undue masculinity.

68 Parkes, "Lesbianism, History, and Censorship," 441.

69 Keegan, "Revisitation," 27.

70 Prosser, *Second Skins*, 125.

71 Keegan, "Revisitation," 29.

72 Deline, *Refuse*, 13.

73 Eastwood, "How, Then, Might the Transsexual Read?," 596.

74 Kennedy, *First Man-Made Man*, 21–22.
75 Snorton, "'A New Hope,'" 83.
76 Tompkins, "An Introduction to Reader-Response Criticism."
77 Iser, "Interaction between Text and Reader," 22. See also Schweickart, "Reading Ourselves."
78 Poulet, "Criticism and the Experience of Interiority," 43, 44.
79 Moya, *The Social Imperative*, 15.
80 Moya, *The Social Imperative*, 21.
81 Moya, *The Social Imperative*, 53.
82 Moya, *The Social Imperative*, 54.
83 Prosser's *Second Skins* and Halberstam's *Female Masculinity*, two touchstones of white trans[masculine] studies, are both explicitly framed as self-consolidating research projects. Halberstam insists that "this book is an attempt to make my own female masculinity plausible, credible, and real" (*Female Masculinity*, 19). While Prosser states, "Without a doubt, my turning as a critic to write on transsexual narratives represents a displaced autobiographical act . . . but articulating the transitions in these texts is not only an oblique means of articulating mine; it has also been quite profoundly a way of working on mine" (*Second Skins*, 4). But the self-making research project is not only an academic's pursuit. In his diary, Lou Sullivan describes spending much of his time in 1973 "reading every article on transvestism and transsexualism I could get my hands on," a reading practice that both preceded and helped to consolidate his identity as "Lou." See Sullivan, "7-17-73," in *Journals, 1972–74*, typed transcripts, box 1, folder 20, 91–97, Louis Graydon Sullivan Papers, the Gay and Lesbian Historical Society of Northern California, San Francisco. Further, the Obligatory Transsexual Files that Sandy Stone describes in "The *Empire* Strikes Back" as personal collections of trans related newspaper articles, diary entries, and autobiographies are certainly the archival evidence of such self-making research, archives thorough enough that they enabled Stone's foundational essay where university and clinic archives failed her ("The *Empire* Strikes Back," 155).
84 Kennedy, *First Man-Made Man*, 83.
85 Dillon, *Self*, 53.
86 Rubin, *Self-Made Men*, 51. See Hausman, *Changing Sex*, chap. 1. In *How Sex Changed*, Meyerowitz likewise reads it as an early example of literature on transsexuality that appeals to a "vision of immutable psychological sex" to justify physical intervention (112).
87 In fact, Dillon takes time in the book itself to denounce the popular press for "seiz[ing] upon the story" of intersex people who seek out medical and legal intervention to live more easily as one or the other sex, "and annouc[ing] it in large headlines as if it were a miracle, while no regard is paid to the enormous difficulties that beset the patient, which difficulties are only increased by a false account—or, for that matter, by any account being given at all" (*Self*, 63).
88 Kennedy, *First Man-Made Man*, 83.
89 Dillon, *Self*, 54.

90 Dillon, *Self*, 121.
91 Dillon, *Self*, i, 51, 47, 54.
92 Quoted in Dillon, *Self*, 54. This is from "XII" in Housman's *Last Poems*.
93 Kennedy, *First Man-Made Man*, 84.
94 Until the late 1960s, doctors in the United States and England worried—and occasionally refused to perform surgeries on the grounds—that the removal of unwanted but otherwise healthy testicles/penile tissue constituted "mayhem," in violation of "mayhem statutes, based on English common law that outlawed the maiming of men who might serve as soldiers." Meyerowitz, *How Sex Changed*, 120–21.
95 Kennedy, *First Man-Made Man*, 22.
96 Think here of John Stuart Mill's classic definition of poetry as "soliloquy . . . overheard," in "Thoughts on Poetry," 96. Or Barbara Hardy's sense that lyric is something that gives "undiluted attention to feeling and feeling alone" but manages to transfer "this from privacy to publicity," in *The Advantage of Lyric*, 2.
97 Cameron, *Lyric Time*, 23.
98 Cameron, *Lyric Time*, 210.
99 Cameron, *Lyric Time*, 240.
100 Cameron, *Lyric Time*, 241.
101 Culler, *Theory of the Lyric*, 283–95.
102 Cameron, *Lyric Time*, 241.
103 Noble, *Sons of the Movement*, 21.
104 Noble, *Sons of the Movement*, 84.
105 Noble, *Sons of the Movement*, 80.
106 Culler, *Theory of the Lyric*, 33.
107 Adorno, "On Lyric Poetry and Society," 37.
108 Banias, "Handshake," 46.
109 Mill, "Thoughts on Poetry," 95.
110 Banias, "Grandchild," 16.
111 Ward, "Gender Labor," 237.
112 Bendorf, "I Promised Her My Hands Wouldn't Get Any Larger," 3; Shipley, "Boy with Flowers," 9; Shipley, "In the Film," 21; Ace, *Meet Me There*.
113 Carter, "Embracing Transition, or Dancing in the Folds of Time."
114 Banias, "At Any Given Moment," 6.
115 Tolbert, "Open, and Always, Opening," 8.

AFTERWARD/ELEGY

1 Steinmetz, "The Transgender Tipping Point."
2 Chambers-Letson, *After the Party*, 4; this paragraph reworks part of an earlier mini-essay, Awkward-Rich, "Feeling Strange."
3 Gill-Peterson, "Anti-Trans Lobby's Real Agenda."
4 Thom, "Someone Tell Me That I'll Live."
5 Lamble, "Retelling Racialized Violence."
6 Berlant, *Cruel Optimism*, 45.

7 Toomey, Syvertsen, and Shramko, "Transgender Adolescent Suicide Behavior," 8.
8 Vitulli, "Racialized Criminality and the Imprisoned Trans Body."
9 Snorton and Haritaworn, "Trans Necropolitics."
10 Diana Fuss, *Dying Modern*, 7.
11 Awkward-Rich, "Craft Capsule."
12 Wanzo, *The Suffering Will Not Be Televised*, 3; Rankine, *Don't Let Me Be Lonely*, 7.
13 St. John, "Interview"; Massey, "A Review," 175; Brill and Pepper, *The Transgender Child*, 47.
14 Cheng, *The Melancholy of Race*; Eng and Kazanjian, *Loss*.
15 Freud, "Mourning and Melancholia," 244.
16 Keegan, "Moving Bodies."
17 Hong, *Death Beyond Disavowal*, 7.
18 Katya Lezin, "Transgender People in Charlotte Struggle to Find Tolerance," *Charlotte Observer*, January 5, 2015.
19 Snorton, *Black on Both Sides*, xiv.
20 Gordon, *Ghostly Matters*, 8.
21 Hall, *The Well of Loneliness (2005)*, 169
22 Boylan, *I'm Looking through You*, 25.
23 Joynt and Hoolboom, *You Only Live Twice*, 26.
24 Jain, *Malignant*, 29.
25 Crosby, *A Body, Undone*, 189, 12.
26 Du Bois, *Souls of Black Folk*, 8.
27 Joynt and Hoolboom, *You Only Live Twice*, 53; Ahmed, *Living a Feminist Life*, 48.
28 Joynt and Hoolboom, *You Only Live Twice*, 53.
29 Joynt and Hoolboom, *You Only Live Twice*, 142.
30 Bendorf, "After I Came Out."
31 McCullers, *The Member of the Wedding* (2004), 6, 22.

BIBLIOGRAPHY

Ace, Samuel. *Meet Me There: Normal Sex and Home in Three Days; Don't Wash.* Brooklyn: Belladonna*, 2019.

Adair, Cassius, Cameron Awkward-Rich, and Amy Marvin. "Before Trans Studies." *TSQ: Transgender Studies Quarterly* 7, no. 3 (2020): 306–20.

Adams, Rachel. *Sideshow U.S.A.: Freaks and the American Cultural Imagination.* Chicago: University of Chicago Press, 2001.

Adorno, Theodor W. "On Lyric Poetry and Society." In *Notes to Literature*, vol. 1, edited by Rolf Tiedemann, translated by Shierry Weber Nicholsen, 37–54. New York: Columbia University Press, 1991.

Ahmed, Sara. *Living a Feminist Life.* Durham, NC: Duke University Press, 2017.

Ahmed, Sara. *The Promise of Happiness.* Durham, NC: Duke University Press, 2010.

Aho, Tanja, Liat Ben-Moshe, and Leon J. Hilton. "Mad Futures: Affect/Theory/Violence." *American Quarterly* 69, no. 2 (2017): 291–302.

Aizura, Aren Z. *Mobile Subjects: Transnational Imaginaries of Gender Reassignment.* Durham, NC: Duke University Press, 2018.

Alcoff, Linda Martín. "Dangerous Pleasures: Foucault and the Politics of Pedophilia." In *Feminist Interpretations of Michel Foucault*, edited by Susan Hekman, 99–135. University Park: Pennsylvania State University Press, 1996.

Alloy, Lauren B., and Lyn Y. Abramson. "Judgment of Contingency in Depressed and Nondepressed Students: Sadder but Wiser?" *Journal of Experimental Psychology* 108, no. 4 (1979): 441–85.

Alloy, Lauren B., Jeanne S. Albrights, Lyn Y. Abramson, and Benjamin M. Dykman. "Depressive Realism and Nondepressive Optimistic Illusions: The Role of the Self." In *Contemporary Psychological Approaches to Depression*, edited by Rick E. Ingram, 71–86. New York: Plenum, 1990.

Althusser, Louis. "Ideology and Ideological State Apparatuses." In *On the Reproduction of Capitalism: Ideology and Ideological State Apparatuses*, translated by G. M. Goshgarian, 232–73. London: Verso, 2014.

Amin, Kadji. *Disturbing Attachments: Genet, Modern Pederasty, and Queer History.* Durham, NC: Duke University Press, 2017.

Awkward-Rich, Cameron. "Craft Capsule: Elegy." *Poets and Writers*, December 23, 2019. https://www.pw.org/content/craft_capsule_elegy.

Awkward-Rich, Cameron. "Feeling Strange." *Evening Will Come: A Monthly Journal of Poetics*, no. 65 (2017). https://thevolta.org/ewc65-eshockley-p13.html.

Ball, Kelly H. "'More or Less Raped': Foucault, Causality, and Feminist Critiques of Sexual Violence." *Philosophia* 3, no. 1 (2013): 52–68.

Banias, Ari. "At Any Given Moment." In *Anybody*, 5–7. New York: Norton, 2016.
Banias, Ari. "Grandchild." In *Anybody*, 16. New York: Norton, 2016.
Banias, Ari. "Handshake." In *Anybody*, 46. New York: Norton, 2016.
Baril, Alexandre. "Transness as Debility: Rethinking Intersections between Trans and Disabled Embodiments." *Feminist Review* 11, no. 1 (2015): 59–74.
Barnett, Pamela E. *Dangerous Desire: Literature of Sexual Freedom and Sexual Violence since the Sixties*. New York: Routledge, 2004.
Barrie, J. M. *Peter Pan*. New York: Barnes and Noble, 2005. First published in 1911 by Scribner as *Peter and Wendy*.
Barry, Kevin M. "Disabilityqueer: Federal Disability Rights Protection for Transgender People." *Yale Human Rights and Development Journal* 16, no. 1 (2013): 1–50.
Baynton, Douglas. "Disability and the Justification of Inequality in American History." In *The New Disability History: American Perspectives*, edited by Paul Longmore and Lauri Umansky, 33–57. New York: NYU Press, 2001.
Beauchamp, Toby. *Going Stealth: Transgender Politics and U.S. Surveillance Practices*. Durham, NC: Duke University Press, 2019.
Bendorf, Oliver. "After I Came Out as a Transgender Man, I Was Asked If It Felt like I Had Died." *Buzzfeed*, January 20, 2014. https://www.buzzfeed.com/oliverbendorf/after-i-came-out-as-a-transgender-man-a-teacher-asked-if-it.
Bendorf, Oliver. "I Promised Her My Hands Wouldn't Get Any Larger." In *The Spectral Wilderness*, 3. Kent, OH: Kent State University Press, 2015.
Berlant, Lauren. *Cruel Optimism*. Durham, NC: Duke University Press, 2011.
Berlant, Lauren. *Desire/Love*. Brooklyn: Punctum, 2012.
Berlant, Lauren. "She's Having an Episode: Patricia Williams and the Writing of Damage Life." *Columbia Journal of Gender and Law* 27, no. 1 (2014): 19–35.
Bersani, Leo. "Is the Rectum a Grave?" *October*, no. 43 (1987): 197–222.
Bettcher, Talia Mae. "Evil Deceivers and Make-Believers: On Transphobic Violence and the Politics of Illusion." *Hypatia: A Journal of Feminist Philosophy* 22, no. 3 (2007): 43–65.
Bettcher, Talia Mae. "Full-Frontal Morality: The Naked Truth about Gender." *Hypatia: A Journal of Feminist Philosophy* 27, no. 2 (2012): 319–37.
Bettcher, Talia Mae. "Trans Identities and First-Person Authority." In *You've Changed: Sex Reassignment and Personal Identity*, edited by Laurie Shrage, 98–120. Oxford: Oxford University Press, 2009.
Bettcher, Talia Mae. "Trapped in the Wrong Theory: Rethinking Trans Oppression and Resistance." *Signs: Journal of Women in Culture and Society* 39, no. 2 (2014): 383–406.
Bettcher, Talia Mae. "What Is Trans Philosophy?" *Hypatia: A Journal of Feminist Philosophy* 34, no. 4 (2019): 644–67.
Boyd, Nan Alamilla. "Bodies in Motion: Lesbian and Transsexual Histories." In *The Transgender Studies Reader*, edited by Susan Stryker and Stephen Whittle, 420–33. New York: Routledge, 2006.
Boylan, Jennifer Finney. *I'm Looking through You: Growing Up Haunted*. New York: Broadway, 2008.

Brill, Stephanie, and Rachel Pepper. *The Transgender Child: A Handbook for Families and Professionals*. San Francisco: Cleis, 2008.

Brown, Wendy. *States of Injury: Power and Freedom in Late Modernity*. Princeton, NJ: Princeton University Press, 1995.

Bruce, La Marr Jurelle. *How to Go Mad without Losing Your Mind: Madness and Black Radical Creativity*. Durham, NC: Duke University Press, 2021.

Butler, Judith. "Gender Is Burning: Questions of Appropriation and Subversion." In *Bodies That Matter: On the Discursive Limits of "Sex,"* 121–40. New York: Routledge, 1993.

Butler, Judith. "Undiagnosing Gender." In *Undoing Gender*, 75–101. New York: Routledge, 2004.

Cahill, Ann J. "Foucault, Rape, and the Construction of the Feminine Body." *Hypatia: A Journal of Feminist Philosophy* 15, no. 1 (2000): 43–62.

Califia, Patrick. *Sex Changes: The Politics of Transgenderism*. San Francisco: Cleis, 1997.

Cameron, Sharon. *Lyric Time: Dickinson and the Limits of Genre*. Baltimore, MD: Johns Hopkins University Press, 1979.

Cantor, David, Bonnie Fisher, Susan Chibnall, Reanne Townsend, Hyunshik Lee, Carol Bruce, and Gail Thomas. "Report on the AAU Climate Survey on Sexual Assault and Sexual Misconduct." Center for Victim Research Repository, October 10, 2017. https://ncvc.dspacedirect.org/handle/20.500.11990/1448.

cárdenas, micha. "Sick." *TSQ: Transgender Studies Quarterly* 1, nos. 1–2 (2014): 181–84.

Carr, Virginia Spencer. *The Lonely Hunter: A Biography of Carson McCullers*. Garden City, NJ: Doubleday, 1975.

Carter, Julian. "Embracing Transition, or Dancing in the Folds of Time." In *The Transgender Studies Reader 2*, edited by Susan Stryker and Aren Z. Aizura, 130–44. New York: Routledge, 2013.

Cassese, James. Introduction to *Gay Men and Childhood Sexual Trauma: Integrating the Shattered Self*, edited by James Cassese, 1–18. New York: Harrington Park, 2000.

Chaiken, Ilene, Michele Abbot, and Kathy Greenberg. *The L Word*, seasons 3–6. New York: Showtime, 2006–2009.

Chambers-Letson, Joshua. *After the Party: A Manifesto for Queer of Color Life*. New York: NYU Press, 2018.

Chen, Mel Y. "Brain Fog: The Race for Cripistemology." *Journal of Literary and Cultural Disability Studies* 8, no. 2 (2014): 171–84.

Cheng, Anne Anlin. *The Melancholy of Race: Psychoanalysis, Assimilation, and Hidden Grief*. Oxford: Oxford University Press, 2001.

Clare, Eli. "Body Shame, Body Pride: Lessons from the Disability Rights Movement." In *The Transgender Studies Reader 2*, edited by Susan Stryker and Aren Z. Aizura, 261–65. New York: Routledge, 2013.

Clare, Eli. *Brilliant Imperfection: Grappling with Cure*. Durham, NC: Duke University Press, 2017.

Clare, Eli. *Exile and Pride: Disability, Queerness, and Liberation*. 1999. Cambridge, MA: South End, 2009.

Colker, Ruth. *The Disability Pendulum: The First Decade of the Americans with Disabilities Act*. New York: NYU Press, 2005.
Combahee River Collective. "The Combahee River Collective Statement." In *Home Girls: A Black Feminist Anthology*, edited by Barbara Smith, 264–74. 1983. Reprint, New Brunswick, NJ: Rutgers University Press, 2000.
Cox, Laverne. "The Bullies Don't Draw a Distinction." *New York Times*, October 15, 2013.
Crawford, Lucas Cassidy. "Transgender without Organs: Mobilizing a Geoaffective Theory of Gender Modification." *Women's Studies Quarterly* 36, nos. 3–4 (2008): 127–43.
Cromwell, Jason. *Transmen and FTMs: Identities, Bodies, Genders, and Sexualities*. Champaign: University of Illinois Press, 1999.
Crosby, Christina. *A Body, Undone: Living On after Great Pain*. New York: NYU Press, 2016.
Culler, Jonathan D. *Theory of the Lyric*. Cambridge, MA: Harvard University Press, 2015.
Cvetkovich, Ann. *An Archive of Feelings: Trauma, Sexuality, and Lesbian Public Cultures*. Durham, NC: Duke University Press, 2003.
Cvetkovich, Ann. *Depression: A Public Feeling*. Durham, NC: Duke University Press, 2012.
Davis, Lennard J. *The End of Normal: Identity in a Biocultural Era*. Ann Arbor: University of Michigan Press, 2014.
de la Cour, Lykke. "From 'Moron' to 'Maladjusted': Eugenics, Psychiatry, and the Regulation of Women, Ontario, 1930s–1960s." PhD diss., University of Toronto, 2013.
DeLine, Elliott. *I Know Very Well How I Got My Name*. Self-published, 2013.
DeLine, Elliott. *Refuse*. Self-published, 2011.
DeLine, Elliott. "Trans People, Trauma, and Dissociative Identities." *The Body Is Not an Apology*, September 12, 2018. https://thebodyisnotanapology.com/magazine/trans-people-trauma-and-dissociative-identities/#comments
D'Emilio, John. "Who Wears the Pants?" *Windy City Times*, September 9, 2009. http://www.windycitymediagroup.com/lgbt/History-Who-wears-the-pants/22829.html.
Dennett, Andrea Stulman. *Weird and Wonderful: The Dime Museum in America*. New York: NYU Press, 1997.
Department of Health and Human Services, Departmental Appeals Board. "Supplemental Declaration of Dr. Randi C. Ettner in Support of Complainant." Complaint *in re* NDC 140.3, March 23, 2013. Accessed April 24, 2017. http://legacy.glad.org/uploads/docs/publications/medicare/affidavit-ettner-02-redacted.pdf.
Devor, Aaron. "Transsexualism, Dissociation, and Child Abuse." *Journal of Psychology and Human Sexuality* 6, no. 3 (1994): 49–72.
Dillon, Michael. *Out of the Ordinary: A Life of Gender and Spiritual Transitions*. Edited by Jacob Lau and Cameron Partridge. New York: Fordham University Press, 2016.
Dillon, Michael. *Self: A Study in Ethics and Endocrinology*. London: William Heinemann Medical Books, 1946.
Dinshaw, Carolyn. *Getting Medieval: Sexualities and Communities, Pre- and Postmodern*. Durham, NC: Duke University Press, 1999.

Doan, Laura, and Jay Prosser. Introduction to *Palatable Poison: Critical Perspectives on "The Well of Loneliness,"* edited by Laura Doan and Jay Prosser, 1–31. New York: Columbia University Press, 2001.
Donaldson, Elizabeth J. "The Corpus of the Madwoman: Toward a Feminist Disability Studies Theory of Embodiment and Mental Illness." NWSA *Journal* 14, no. 3 (2002): 99–119.
Du Bois, W. E. B. *The Souls of Black Folk*. New York: Barnes and Noble, 2003.
Durwood, Lily, Katie A. McLaughlin, and Kristina R. Olson. "Mental Health and Self-Worth in Socially Transitioned Transgender Youth." *Journal of the American Academy of Child and Adolescent Psychiatry* 56, no. 2 (2017): 116–23.
Eastwood, Alexander. "How, Then, Might the Transsexual Read? Notes toward a Trans Literary History." TSQ: *Transgender Studies Quarterly* 1, no. 4 (2014), 590–604.
Eco, Umberto. *The Role of the Reader: Explorations in the Semiotics of Texts*. Bloomington: Indiana University Press, 1979.
Edelman, Lee. *No Future: Queer Theory and the Death Drive*. Durham, NC: Duke University Press, 2004.
Elliot, Patricia. *Debates in Transgender, Queer, and Feminist Theory: Contested Sites*. Burlington, VT: Ashgate, 2010.
Eng, David, and David Kazanjian, eds. *Loss: The Politics of Mourning*. Berkeley: University of California Press, 2003.
Enke, Finn. Introduction to *Transfeminist Perspectives in and beyond Transgender and Gender Studies*, edited by A. Finn Enke, 1–15. Philadelphia: Temple University Press, 2012.
Eskridge, William N. *Gaylaw: Challenging the Apartheid of the Closet*. Cambridge, MA: Harvard University Press, 1999.
Eugenides, Jeffrey. *Middlesex*. New York: Picador, 2002.
Faderman, Lillian, and Ann Williams, "Radclyffe Hall and the Lesbian Image." *Conditions* 1, no. 1 (1977): 31–49.
Fanon, Frantz. *Black Skin, White Masks*. Translated by Richard Philcox. 1952. Reprint, New York: Grove, 2008.
Feinberg, Leslie. *Stone Butch Blues*. 1993. Reprint, New York: Alyson Books, 2003.
Feinberg, Leslie. *Trans Liberation: Beyond Pink or Blue*. Boston: Beacon, 1998.
Fink, Marty. *Forget Burial:* HIV *Kinship, Disability, and Queer/Trans Narratives of Care*. New Brunswick, NJ: Rutgers University Press, 2021.
Foucault, Michel. *Abnormal: Lectures at the Collège de France, 1974–1975*. Edited by Valerio Marchetti and Antonella Salomoni. Translated by Graham Burchell. New York: Picador, 2003.
Foucault, Michel. *The History of Sexuality*. Vol. 1, *An Introduction*. Translated by Robert Hurley. 1978. Reprint, New York: Vintage, 1990.
Freeman, Elizabeth. *Time Binds: Queer Temporalities, Queer Histories*. Durham, NC: Duke University Press, 2010.
Freud, Sigmund. "Mourning and Melancholia." *The Standard Edition of the Complete Psychological Works of Sigmund Freud*. Vol. XIV (1914–1916), *On the History of the Psycho-Analytic Movement, Papers on Metapsychology and Other Works*, edited by James Strachey, 237–58. London: Hogarth, 1953.

Fu, Kim. *For Today I Am a Boy*. New York: Houghton Mifflin Harcourt, 2014.
Fuss, Diana. *Dying Modern: A Meditation on Elegy*. Durham, NC: Duke University Press, 2013.
Gage, Carolyn. "The Inconvenient Truth about Teena Brandon." *Trivia: Voices of Feminism* 10 (2010). http://www.triviavoices.com/the-inconvenient-truth-about-teena-brandon.html.
Garland-Thomson, Rosemarie. *Extraordinary Bodies: Figuring Disability in American Culture and Literature*. New York: Columbia University Press, 1997.
Garland-Thomson, Rosemarie. "Misfits: A Feminist Materialist Disability Concept." *Hypatia: A Journal of Feminist Philosophy* 26, no. 3 (2011): 591–609.
Geffen, Sasha, and Annie Howard. "Quantifying Transition." *Baffler*, March 22, 2021.
Gherovici, Patricia. *Please Select Your Gender: From the Invention of Hysteria to the Democratizing of Transgenderism*. New York: Routledge, 2010.
Gibson, Dominic J., Jessica J. Glazier, and Kristina R. Olson. "Evaluation of Anxiety and Depression in a Community Sample of Transgender Youth." *JAMA Network Open* 4, no. 4 (2021).
Gill-Peterson, Jules. "The Anti-Trans Lobby's Real Agenda." *Jewish Currents*, April 27, 2021. https://jewishcurrents.org/the-anti-trans-lobbys-real-agenda.
Gill-Peterson, Jules. *Histories of the Transgender Child*. Minneapolis: University of Minnesota Press, 2018.
Gillies, H. D., and D. R. Millard. *The Principles and Art of Plastic Surgery*. Vol. 2. Boston: Little, Brown, 1957.
GLAD. "Blatt v. Cabela's Retail Inc." Accessed March 28, 2020. https://www.glad.org/cases/blatt-v-cabelas-retail-inc/.
Gleeson-White, Sarah. *Strange Bodies: Gender and Identity in the Novels of Carson McCullers*. Tuscaloosa: University of Alabama Press, 2003.
Goldberg, Michelle. "What Is a Woman? The Dispute between Radical Feminism and Transgenderism." *New Yorker*, August 4, 2014. https://www.newyorker.com/magazine/2014/08/04/woman-2.
Goldberg, Michelle, and Margaret Talbot. "Michelle Goldberg and Margaret Talbot on Transgender Activists and Radical Feminists." *Out Loud* (podcast), July 30, 2014. https://www.newyorker.com/podcast/out-loud/michelle-goldberg-and-margaret-talbot-on-transgender-activists-and-radical-feminists.
Gordon, Avery. *Ghostly Matters: Haunting and the Sociological Imaginary*. Minneapolis: University of Minnesota Press, 2008.
Gorton, R. Nick. "Transgender as Mental Illness: Nosology, Social Justice, and the Tarnished Golden Mean." In *The Transgender Studies Reader 2*, edited by Susan Stryker and Aren Z. Aizura, 644–52. New York: Routledge, 2013.
Gould, Deborah B. *Moving Politics: Emotion and ACT UP's Fight against AIDS*. Chicago: University of Chicago Press, 2009.
Gunne, Sorcha, and Zoë Brigley Thompson. Introduction to *Feminism, Literature, and Rape Narratives*, edited by Sorcha Gunne and Zoë Brigley Thompson, 1–20. New York: Routledge, 2011.
Halberstam, Jack. *Female Masculinity*. Durham, NC: Duke University Press, 1998.

Halberstam, Jack. *In a Queer Time and Place: Transgender Bodies, Subcultural Lives.* New York: NYU Press, 2005.
Halberstam, Jack. *The Queer Art of Failure*. Durham, NC: Duke University Press, 2011.
Halberstam, Jack. "Transgender Butch: Butch/FTM Border Wars and the Masculine Continuum." *GLQ: A Journal of Gay and Lesbian Studies* 4, no. 2 (1998): 287–310.
Halberstam, Jack, and C. Jacob Hale. "Butch/FTM Border Wars: A Note on Collaboration." *GLQ: A Journal of Gay and Lesbian Studies* 4, no. 2 (1998): 283–85.
Hale, C. Jacob. "Consuming the Living, Dis(re)membering the Dead in the Butch/FTM Borderlands." *GLQ: A Journal of Gay and Lesbian Studies* 4, no. 2 (1998): 311–48.
Hale, C. Jacob. "Suggested Rules for Non-transsexuals Writing about Transsexuals, Transsexuality, Transsexualism, or Trans ____." *Sandy Stone: Would You Like Theory with That?*, January 5, 1997. http://sandystone.com/hale.rules.html.
Hale, C. Jacob. "Tracing a Ghostly Memory in My Throat: Reflections on FTM Feminist Voice and Agency." In *Men Doing Feminism*, edited by Tom Digby, 99–129. New York: Routledge, 1998.
Hall, Radclyffe. *The Well of Loneliness*. 1928. Reprint, Ware, UK: Wordsworth, 2005.
Hall, Radclyffe. *The Well of Loneliness*. Commentary by Havelock Ellis. 1928. Reprint, New York: Avon, 1981.
Halley, Janet. *Split Decisions: How and Why to Take a Break from Feminism*. Princeton, NJ: Princeton University Press, 2006.
Hansbury, Griffin. "The Middle Men: An Introduction to the Transmasculine Identities." *Studies in Gender and Sexuality* 6, no. 3 (2005): 241–64.
Hardy, Barbara. *The Advantage of Lyric: Essays on Feeling in Poetry*. Bloomington: Indiana University Press, 1977.
Harrington, Anne. *Mind Fixers: Psychiatry's Troubled Search for the Biology of Mental Illness*. New York: Norton, 2019.
Hausman, Bernice L. *Changing Sex: Transsexualism, Technology, and the Idea of Gender*. Durham, NC: Duke University Press, 1995.
Hayward, Eva. "Don't Exist." *TSQ: Transgender Studies Quarterly* 4, no. 2 (2017): 191–94.
Hayward, Eva. "More Lessons from a Starfish: Prefixial Flesh and Transspeciated Selves." *Women's Studies Quarterly* 36, nos. 3–4 (2008): 64–85.
Heaney, Emma. *The New Woman: Literary Modernism, Queer Theory, and the Trans Feminine Allegory*. Evanston, IL: Northwestern University Press, 2017.
Hemmings, Clare. *Why Stories Matter: The Political Grammar of Feminist Theory*. Durham, NC: Duke University Press, 2011.
Heyes, Cressida J. "Feminist Solidarity after Queer Theory: The Case of Transgender." *Signs: Journal of Women in Culture and Society* 28, no. 4 (2003): 1093–120.
Heyes, Cressida J. Introduction to "Foucault and Feminism" (special issue). *Foucault Studies* 16 (2013): 3–14.
Hiegel, Adrienne L. "Sexual Exclusions: The Americans with Disabilities Act as a Moral Code." *Columbia Law Review* 94, no. 4 (1994): 1451–94.

Higgins, Lynn A., and Brenda R. Silver. Introduction to *Rape and Representation*, edited by Lynn A. Higgins and Brenda R. Silver, 1–11. New York: Columbia University Press, 2001.
Hoang, Nguyen Tan. *A View from the Bottom: Asian American Masculinity and Sexual Representation*. Durham, NC: Duke University Press, 2014.
Hogan, P. J., dir. *Peter Pan*. Universal City, CA: Universal Studios, 2003.
Hong, Grace Kyungwon. *Death beyond Disavowal: The Impossible Politics of Difference*. Minneapolis: University of Minnesota Press, 2015.
Huffer, Lynne. *Are the Lips a Grave? A Queer Feminist on the Ethics of Sex*. New York: Columbia University Press, 2013.
Iser, Wolfgang. "Interaction between Text and Reader." In *Readers and Reading*, edited by Andrew Bennett, 20–31. London: Longman, 1995.
Jain, Lochlann. *Malignant: How Cancer Becomes Us*. Berkeley: University of California Press, 2013.
James, Sandy E., Jody L. Herman, Susan Rankin, Mara Keisling, Lisa Mottet, and Ma'ayan Anafi. *The Report of the 2015 U.S. Transgender Survey*. Washington, DC: National Center for Transgender Equality, 2016.
Jeffreys, Sheila. *Gender Hurts: A Feminist Analysis of the Politics of Transgenderism*. New York: Routledge, 2014.
Johnson, Merri Lisa. "Bad Romance: A Crip Feminist Critique of Queer Failure." *Hypatia: A Journal of Feminist Philosophy* 30, no. 1 (2015): 251–67.
Johnson, Merri Lisa, and Robert McRuer, eds. "Cripistemologies: Part I." Special issue, *Journal of Literary and Cultural Disability Studies* 8, no. 2 (2014).
Johnson, Merri Lisa, and Robert McRuer, eds. "Proliferating Cripistemologies: A Virtual Roundtable." *Journal of Literary and Cultural Disability Studies* 8, no. 2 (2014): 149–69.
Joynt, Chase, and Mike Hoolboom. *You Only Live Twice: Sex, Death, and Transition*. Toronto: Coach House, 2016.
Kafer, Alison. *Feminist, Queer, Crip*. Bloomington: Indiana University Press, 2013.
Kafer, Alison. "Un/safe Disclosures: Scenes of Disability and Trauma." *Journal of Literary and Cultural Disability Studies* 10, no. 1 (2016): 1–20.
Keegan, Cáel M. "Getting Disciplined: What's Trans* about Queer Studies Now?" *Journal of Homosexuality* 67, no. 3 (2020): 384–97.
Keegan, Cáel M. *Lana and Lilly Wachowski: Sensing Transgender*. Champaign: University of Illinois Press, 2018.
Keegan, Cáel M. "Moving Bodies: Sympathetic Migrations in Transgender Narrativity." *Genders*, no. 57 (2013). http://www.colorado.edu/gendersarchive1998-2013/2013/06/01/moving-bodies-sympathetic-migrations-transgender-narrativity.
Keegan, Cáel M. "Revisitation: A Trans Phenomenology of the Media Image." *MedieKultur: Journal of Media and Communication Research* 61 (2016): 26–41.
Kennedy, Pagan. *The First Man-Made Man: The Story of Two Sex Changes, One Love Affair, and a Twentieth-Century Medical Revolution*. New York: Bloomsbury, 2007.
Kenyon, Jane. "Having It Out with Melancholy." In *Constance: Poems*, 24. Minneapolis: Graywolf, 1993.

Kim, Eunjung. *Curative Violence: Rehabilitating Disability, Gender, and Sexuality in Modern Korea*. Durham, NC: Duke University Press, 2017.

Kissel, Susan S. "'But When at Last She Really Came, I Shot Her': *Peter Pan* and the Drama of Gender." *Children's Literature in Education* 19, no. 1 (1988): 32–41.

Kotz, Liz. "The Body You Want: Liz Kotz Interviews Judith Butler." *Artforum* (November 1992): 82–89.

Koyama, Emi. "The Transfeminist Manifesto." In *Catching a Wave: Reclaiming Feminism for the Twenty-First Century*, edited by Rory Dicker and Alison Piepmeier, 244–59. Boston: Northeastern University Press, 2003.

Koyama, Emi. "Whose Feminism Is It Anyway? The Unspoken Racism of the Trans Inclusion Debate." In *The Transgender Studies Reader*, edited by Susan Stryker and Stephen Whittle, 698–705. New York: Routledge, 2006.

Kunzel, Regina. "The Flourishing of Transgender Studies." *TSQ: Transgender Studies Quarterly* 1, nos. 1–2 (2014): 285–97.

Kunzel, Regina. "The Rise of Gay Rights and the Disavowal of Disability in the United States." In *The Oxford Handbook of Disability History*, edited by Michael Rembis, Catherine Kudlick, and Kim E. Nielsen, 459–75. New York: Oxford University Press, 2018.

Lamble, Sarah. "Retelling Racialized Violence, Remaking White Innocence: The Politics of Interlocking Oppressions in Transgender Day of Remembrance." In *The Transgender Studies Reader 2*, edited by Susan Stryker and Aren Z. Aizura, 30–45. New York: Routledge, 2013.

Lau, Jacob. "Between the Times: Trans-Temporality and Historical Representation." PhD diss., UCLA, 2016.

Lavery, Grace. "Egg Theory's Early Style." *TSQ: Transgender Studies Quarterly* 7, no. 3 (2020): 383–98.

Lemus, Felicia Luna. *Like Son*. New York: Akashic, 2007.

Levasseur, M. Dru. "Gender Incongruence: Update and Discussion on the DSM-5 Revision." Workshop held at Transgender Lives: The Intersections of Health and Law conference, University of Connecticut, Farmington, CT, April 17, 2010.

Levi, Jennifer L., and Bennett H. Klein. "Pursuing Protection for Transgender People through Disability Laws." In *Transgender Rights*, edited by Paisley Currah, Richard M. Juang, and Shannon Price Minter, 74–92. Minneapolis: University of Minnesota Press, 2006.

Lewis, Abram J. "'I Am 64 and Paul McCartney Doesn't Care': The Haunting of the Transgender Archive and the Challenges of Queer History." *Radical History Review*, no. 120 (2014): 13–34.

Lewis, Abram J. "'We Are Certain of Our Own Insanity': Antipsychiatry and the Gay Liberation Movement, 1968–1980." *Journal of the History of Sexuality* 25, no. 1 (2016): 83–113.

Lobdell, Bambi L. *"A Strange Sort of Being": The Transgender Life of Lucy Ann/Joseph Israel Lobdell, 1829–1912*. Jefferson, NC: McFarland, 2012.

Long Chu, Andrea, and Emmett Harsin Drager. "After Trans Studies." *TSQ: Transgender Studies Quarterly* 6, no. 1 (2019): 103–16.

Lorde, Audre. "Uses of the Erotic: The Erotic as Power." *Sister Outsider: Essays and Speeches*, 53–59. Berkeley, CA: Crossing, 1984.

Lothstein, Leslie M. *Female-to-Male Transsexualism: Historical, Clinical, and Theoretical Issues.* New York: Routledge and Kegan Paul, 1983.

Love, Heather. *Feeling Backward: Loss and the Politics of Queer History.* Cambridge, MA: Harvard University Press, 2007.

Lugones, María. *Pilgrimages/Peregrinajes: Theorizing Coalition against Multiple Oppressions.* Lanham, MD: Rowman and Littlefield, 2003.

Lugones, María. "Playfulness, 'World'-Traveling, and Loving Perception." *Hypatia: A Journal of Feminist Philosophy* 2, no. 2 (1987): 3–19.

Lugones, María. "Toward a Decolonial Feminism." *Hypatia: A Journal of Feminist Philosophy* 25, no. 4 (2010): 742–59.

Malatino, Hil. "Future Fatigue: Trans Intimacies and Trans Presents (or How to Survive the Interregnum)." *TSQ: Transgender Studies Quarterly* 6, no. 4 (2019): 635–58.

Malatino, Hil. *Trans Care.* Minneapolis: University of Minnesota Press, 2020.

Martin, Biddy. "Sexualities without Genders and Other Queer Utopias." *Diacritics* 24, nos. 2–3 (1994): 104–21.

Martínez, Ernesto. "*Con quién, dónde, y por qué te dejas?* Reflections on Joto Passivity." *Aztlán: A Journal of Chicano Studies* 39, no. 1 (2014): 237–46.

Martínez-San Miguel, Yolanda, and Sarah Tobias. "Introduction: Thinking beyond Hetero/Homo Normativities." In *Trans Studies: The Challenge to Hetero/Homo Normativities*, edited by Yolanda Martínez-San Miguel and Sarah Tobias, 1–18. New Brunswick, NJ: Rutgers University Press, 2016.

Marvin, Amy. "Transsexuality, the Curio, and the Transgender Tipping Point." In *Curiosity Studies: A New Ecology of Knowledge*, edited by Perry Zurn and Arjun Shankar. Minneapolis: University of Minnesota Press, 2021.

Massey, Renelle. "A Review of *The Transgender Child: A Handbook for Families and Professionals.*" *American Journal of Family Therapy* 39, no. 2 (2011): 175.

Mattson, Greggor. "Teaching Weinstein, Spacey, Sexual Assault, and New Skirmishes in Old Sex Wars." *Who Needs Gay Bars* (blog), November 16, 2017. https://greggormattson.com/2017/11/16/teaching-weinstein-spacey-sexual-assault-and-new-skirmishes-in-old-sex-wars/.

McCullers, Carson. *The Member of the Wedding.* New York: Houghton Mifflin, 1946. Reprint, New York: Mariner Books, 2004. Kindle Edition. Page references are to the 2004 edition.

McCullers, Carson. *The Member of the Wedding: A Play by Carson McCullers.* New York: New Directions, 1951.

McDowell, Margaret B. *Carson McCullers.* Boston: Twayne, 1980.

Mendoza, Victor Román. *Metroimperial Intimacies: Fantasy, Racial-Sexual Governance, and the Philippines in U.S. Imperialism, 1899–1913.* Durham, NC: Duke University Press, 2015.

Metzl, Jonathan M. "Why 'Against Health'?" Introduction to *Against Health: How Health Became the New Morality*, edited by Jonathan M. Metzl and Anna Kirkland, 1–12. New York: NYU Press, 2010.

Meyerowitz, Joanne J. *How Sex Changed: A History of Transsexuality in the United States*. Cambridge, MA: Harvard University Press, 2002.
Mill, John Stuart. "Thoughts on Poetry and Its Varieties, Part 1." *Crayon* 7, no. 4 (1860): 93–97.
Miller, Darren. "The Utopian Function of Affect in Carson McCullers's *The Member of the Wedding* and *The Ballad of the Sad Café*." *Southern Literary Journal* 41, no. 2 (2009): 87–105.
Mintz, Susannah. *Unruly Bodies: Life Writing by Women with Disabilities*. Chapel Hill: University of North Carolina Press, 2007.
Mitchell, David T., and Sharon L. Snyder. *Narrative Prosthesis: Disability and the Dependencies of Discourse*. Ann Arbor: University of Michigan Press, 2000.
Mitchell, John Cameron, dir. *Hedwig and the Angry Inch*. New York: New Line, 2001.
Miyatsu, Rose. "'Hundreds of People like Me': A Search for a Mad Community in *The Bell Jar*." In *Literature of Madness: Disability Studies and Mental Health*, edited by Elizabeth J. Donaldson, 51–69. London: Palgrave Macmillan, 2018.
Mollow, Anna. "'When *Black* Women Start Going on Prozac': Race, Gender, and Mental Illness in Meri Nana-Ama Danquah's *Willow Weep for Me*." *MELUS* 31, no. 3 (2006): 67–99.
Mog, Ashley, and Amanda Lock Swarr. "Threads of Commonality in Transgender and Disability Studies." *Disability Studies Quarterly* 28, no. 4 (2008). http://dsqsds.org/article/view/152/152.
Moya, Paula M. L. *The Social Imperative: Race, Close Reading, and Contemporary Literary Criticism*. Stanford, CA: Stanford University Press, 2016.
Muñoz, José Esteban. *Disidentifications: Queers of Color and the Performance of Politics*. Minneapolis: University of Minnesota Press, 1999.
Muñoz, José Esteban. "Feeling Brown, Feeling Down: Latina Affect, the Performativity of Race, and the Depressive Position." *Signs: Journal of Women in Culture and Society* 31, no. 3 (2006): 675–88.
Munt, Sally. "The Butch Body." In *Contested Bodies*, edited by Ruth Holliday and John Hassard, 95–106. London: Routledge, 2001.
Namaste, Viviane K. *Invisible Lives: The Erasure of Transsexual and Transgendered People*. Chicago: University of Chicago Press, 2000.
Namaste, Viviane K. *Sex Change, Social Change: Reflections on Identity, Institutions, and Imperialism*. Toronto: Women's Press, 2005.
Nash, Jennifer. *Black Feminism Reimagined: After Intersectionality*. Durham, NC: Duke University Press, 2018.
Newkirk, Pamela. *Spectacle: The Astonishing Life of Ota Benga*. New York: HarperCollins, 2015.
Newton, Esther. "The Mythic Mannish Lesbian." *Signs: Journal of Women in Culture and Society* 9, no. 4 (1984): 557–75.
Ngai, Sianne. *Ugly Feelings*. Cambridge, MA: Harvard University Press, 2005.
Noble, Bobby. *Masculinities without Men?: Female Masculinity in Twentieth-Century Fictions*. Vancouver: University of British Columbia Press, 2004.

Noble, Bobby. *Sons of the Movement: FTMs Risking Incoherence on a Post-queer Cultural Landscape*. Toronto: Women's Press, 2006.

Noble, Bobby. "Trans. Panic. Some Thoughts toward a Theory of Feminist Fundamentalism." In *Transfeminist Perspectives in and beyond Transgender and Gender Studies*, edited by A. Finn Enke, 45–59. Philadelphia: Temple University Press, 2012.

Ophelian, Annalise, dir. *Diagnosing Difference*. San Francisco: Floating Ophelia Productions, 2009. DVD.

Parkes, Adam. "Lesbianism, History, and Censorship: *The Well of Loneliness* and the Suppressed Randiness of Virginia Woolf's *Orlando*." *Twentieth-Century Literature* 40, no. 4 (1994): 434–60.

Pierce, Kimberly, dir. *Boys Don't Cry*. Beverly Hills, CA: Twentieth Century Fox, 1999.

Plaza, Monique. "Our Damages and Their Compensation: Rape: The Will Not to Know of Michel Foucault." *Feminist Issues* 1, no. 3 (1981): 25–35.

Plett, Casey. "Rise of the Gender Novel." *Walrus*, March 18, 2015. https://thewalrus.ca/rise-of-the-gender-novel/.

Poulet, Georges. "Criticism and the Experience of Interiority." In *Reader-Response Criticism: From Formalism to Post-structuralism*, edited by Jane P. Tompkins, 41–49. Baltimore, MD: Johns Hopkins University Press, 1980.

Pound, Reginald. *Gillies, Surgeon Extraordinary: A Biography*. London: M. Joseph, 1964.

Price, Margaret. "The Bodymind Problem and the Possibilities of Pain." *Hypatia: A Journal of Feminist Philosophy* 30, no. 1 (2015): 268–84.

Price, Margaret. *Mad at School: Rhetorics of Mental Disability and Academic Life*. Ann Arbor: University of Michigan Press, 2011.

Prosser, Jay. "No Place like Home: The Transgendered Narrative of Leslie Feinberg's *Stone Butch Blues*." *Modern Fiction Studies* 41, nos. 3–4 (1995): 483–514.

Prosser, Jay. *Second Skins: The Body Narratives of Transsexuality*. New York: Columbia University Press, 1998.

Puar, Jasbir K. "Disability." *TSQ: Transgender Studies Quarterly* 1, nos. 1–2 (2014): 77–81.

Pyne, Jake. "Autistic Disruptions, Trans Temporalities: A Narrative 'Trap Door' in Time." *South Atlantic Quarterly* 120, no. 2 (2021): 343–61.

Quashie, Kevin E. *The Sovereignty of Quiet: Beyond Resistance in Black Culture*. New Brunswick, NJ: Rutgers University Press, 2012.

Rankine, Claudia. *Don't Let Me Be Lonely: An American Lyric*. Minneapolis: Graywolf, 2004.

Raymond, Janice G. *The Transsexual Empire: The Making of the She-Male*. 1979. Reprint, New York: Teachers College Press, 1994.

Rekers, George A. "Atypical Gender Development and Psychosocial Adjustment." *Journal of Applied Behavior Analysis* 10, no. 3 (1977): 559–71.

Rekers, George A., and O. Ivar Lovaas. "Behavioral Treatment of Deviant Sex-Role Behaviors in a Male Child." *Journal of Applied Behavior Analysis* 7, no. 2 (1974): 173–90.

Rekers, George A., Peter M. Bentler, Alexander C. Rosen, and O. Ivar Lovaas. "Child Gender Disturbances: A Clinical Rationale for Intervention." *Psychotherapy: Theory, Research and Practice* 14, no. 1 (1977): 2–11.

Riddell, Carol. "Divided Sisterhood: A Critical Review of Janice Raymond's *The Transsexual Empire*." In *The Transgender Studies Reader*, edited by Susan Stryker and Stephen Whittle, 144–58. New York: Routledge, 2006.
Rubin, Gayle. "Of Catamites and Kings: Reflections on Butch, Genders, and Boundaries." In *The Transgender Studies Reader*, edited by Susan Stryker and Stephen Whittle, 471–81. New York: Routledge, 2006.
Rubin, Henry. "Reading like a (Transsexual) Man." In *Men Doing Feminism*, edited by Tom Digby, 305–24. New York: Routledge, 1998.
Rubin, Henry. *Self-Made Men: Identity and Embodiment among Transsexual Men*. Nashville: Vanderbilt University Press, 2003.
Rubin, Henry. "Trans Studies: Between a Metaphysics of Presence and Absence." In *Reclaiming Genders: Transsexual Grammars at the Fin de Siècle*, edited by Kate Moore and Stephen Whittle, 173–92. London: Cassell, 1999.
Salamon, Gayle. *Assuming a Body: Transgender and Rhetorics of Materiality*. New York: Columbia University Press, 2010.
Samuels, Ellen. *Fantasies of Identification: Disability, Gender, Race*. New York: NYU Press, 2014.
Sandahl, Carrie. "Queering the Crip or Cripping the Queer: Intersections of Queer and Crip Identities in Solo Autobiographical Performance." *GLQ: A Journal of Lesbian and Gay Studies* 9, nos. 1–2 (2003): 25–56.
Scheman, Naomi. "Queering the Center by Centering the Queer: Reflections on Transsexual and Secular Jews." In *Feminists Rethink the Self*, edited by Diana Tietjens Meyers, 124–62. Boulder, CO: Westview, 1996.
Scholinski, Dylan. "After-Wards: Possible Side Effects Include." *Art of Dylan Scholinski*. Accessed August 17, 2020. https://dylanscholinski.weebly.com/after-wards.html.
Scholinski, Dylan. *The Last Time I Wore a Dress*. New York: Riverhead Books, 1997.
Scholinski, Dylan. *72 Hour Hold*. Accessed August 17, 2020. https://dylanscholinski.weebly.com/72-hour-hold.html.
Schuller, Kyla. *The Biopolitics of Feeling: Race, Sex, and Science in the Nineteenth Century*. Durham, NC: Duke University Press, 2017.
Schweickart, Patrocinio P. "Reading Ourselves: Toward a Feminist Theory of Reading." In *Readers and Reading*, edited by Andrew Bennett, 66–93. London: Longman, 1995.
Schweik, Susan. *The Ugly Laws: Disability in Public*. New York: NYU Press, 2009.
Sears, Clare. *Arresting Dress: Cross-Dressing, Law, and Fascination in Nineteenth-Century San Francisco*. Durham, NC: Duke University Press, 2014.
Sears, Clare. "Electric Brilliancy: Cross-Dressing Law and Freak Show Displays in Nineteenth-Century San Francisco." In *The Transgender Studies Reader 2*, edited by Susan Stryker and Aren Z. Aizura, 554–64. New York: Routledge, 2013.
Sedgwick, Eve Kosofsky. *Epistemology of the Closet*. Berkeley: University of California Press, 1990.
Sedgwick, Eve Kosofsky. *Touching Feeling: Affect, Pedagogy, Performativity*. Durham, NC: Duke University Press, 2003.

Serano, Julia. "Op-Ed: An Open Letter to the *New Yorker*." *Advocate*, August 5, 2014. http://www.advocate.com/commentary/2014/08/05/op-ed-open-letter-new-yorker.

Serano, Julia. *Whipping Girl: A Transsexual Woman on Sexism and the Scapegoating of Femininity*. Berkeley, CA: Seal, 2007.

Shipley, Ely. "Boy with Flowers." In *Boy with Flowers*, 8–9. New York: Barrow Street, 2008.

Shipley, Ely. *Boy with Flowers*. New York: Barrow Street, 2008.

Shipley, Ely. "In the Film." In *Boy with Flowers*, 21–22. New York: Barrow Street, 2008.

Shipley, Ely. *Some Animal*. New York: Nightboat, 2018.

Shrier, Abigail. *Irreversible Damage: The Transgender Craze Seducing Our Daughters*. Washington, DC: Regnery, 2020.

Siebers, Tobin. *Disability Theory*. Ann Arbor: University of Michigan Press, 2008.

Snorton, C. Riley. *Black on Both Sides: A Racial History of Trans Identity*. Minneapolis: University of Minnesota Press, 2017.

Snorton, C. Riley. "'A New Hope': The Psychic Life of Passing." *Hypatia: A Journal of Feminist Philosophy* 24, no. 3 (2009): 77–92.

Snorton, C. Riley, and Jin Haritaworn. "Trans Necropolitics: A Transnational Reflection on Violence, Death, and the Trans of Color Afterlife." In *Transgender Studies Reader 2*, edited by Susan Stryker and Aren Z. Aizura, 66–76. New York: Routledge, 2013.

Solomon, Andrew. *The Noonday Demon: An Atlas of Depression*. New York: Scribner, 2001.

Spade, Dean. *Normal Life: Administrative Violence, Critical Trans Politics, and the Limits of Law*. Rev. ed. Durham, NC: Duke University Press, 2015.

Spade, Dean. "Resisting Medicine, Re/modeling Gender." *Berkeley Women's Law Journal* 18, no. 1 (2003): 15–39.

Spillers, Hortense J. "Mama's Baby, Papa's Maybe: An American Grammar Book." *Diacritics* 17, no. 2 (1987): 64–81.

Stallings, L. H. *Funk the Erotic: Transaesthetics and Black Sexual Cultures*. Champaign: University of Illinois Press, 2015.

Steinbock, Eliza. "Groping Theory: Haptic Cinema and Trans-curiosity in Hans Scheirl's *Dandy Dust*." In *The Transgender Studies Reader 2*, edited by Susan Stryker and Aren Z. Aizura, 101–18. New York: Routledge, 2013.

Steinbock, Eliza. *Shimmering Images: Trans Cinema, Embodiment, and the Aesthetics of Change*. Durham, NC: Duke University Press, 2019.

Steinmetz, Katy. "The Transgender Tipping Point: America's Next Civil Rights Frontier." *Time*, May 29, 2014.

St. John, Leith. "Interview with Stephanie Brill and Rachel Pepper." *Lambda Literary*, January 20, 2010. http://www.lambdaliterary.org/interviews/01/20/the-transgender-child-by-stephanie-brill-rachel-pepper/.

Stockton, Kathryn Bond. *The Queer Child, or Growing Sideways in the Twentieth Century*. Durham, NC: Duke University Press, 2009.

Stoller, Robert. "Etiological Factors in Female Transsexualism: A First Approximation." *Archives of Sexual Behavior* 2, no. 1 (1972): 47–64.

Stone, Sandy. "The *Empire* Strikes Back: A Posttranssexual Manifesto." *Camera Obscura: Feminism, Culture, and Media Studies* 10, no. 29 (1992): 150–76.
Stryker, Susan. "(De)subjugated Knowledges: An Introduction to Transgender Studies." In *The Transgender Studies Reader*, edited by Susan Stryker and Stephen Whittle, 1–17. New York: Routledge, 2006.
Stryker, Susan. "Institutionalizing Trans* Studies at the University of Arizona," *TSQ: Transgender Studies Quarterly* 7, no. 3 (2020): 354–66.
Stryker, Susan. "My Words to Victor Frankenstein above the Village of Chamounix: Performing Transgender Rage." *GLQ: A Journal of Lesbian and Gay Studies* 1, no. 3 (1994): 237–54.
Stryker, Susan. "Portrait of a Transfag Drag Hag as a Young Man: The Activist Career of Louis G. Sullivan." In *Reclaiming Genders: Transsexual Grammars at the Fin de Siècle*, edited by Kate Moore and Stephen Whittle, 62–82. London: Cassell, 1999.
Stryker, Susan. *Transgender History*. Berkeley, CA: Seal, 2008.
Stryker, Susan. "Transgender Studies: Queer Theory's Evil Twin." *GLQ: A Journal of Lesbian and Gay Studies* 10, no. 2 (2004): 211–12.
Stryker, Susan, and Nikki Sullivan. "King's Member, Queen's Body: Transsexual Surgery, Self-Demand Amputation, and the Somatechnics of Sovereign Power." In *Somatechnics: Queering the Technologisation of Bodies*, edited by Nikki Sullivan and Samantha Murray, 49–63. Farnham, UK: Ashgate, 2009.
Sullivan, Louis. *From Female to Male: The Life of Jack Bee Garland*. Boston: Alyson, 1990.
Sullivan, Louis. *We Both Laughed in Pleasure: The Selected Diaries of Lou Sullivan, 1961–1991*. Edited by Ellis Martin and Zach Ozma. New York: Nightboat, 2019.
Thom, Kai Cheng. "Someone Tell Me That I'll Live: On Murder, Media, and Being a Trans Woman in 2015." *XOJane*, February 28, 2015. http://www.xojane.com/issues/someone-tell-me-that-ill-live-murdered-trans-women-2015.
Tolbert, TC. "Open, and Always, Opening—An Introduction in 3 Parts." In *Troubling the Line: Trans and Genderqueer Poetry and Poetics*, edited by TC Tolbert and Trace Peterson, 7–14. New York: Nightboat, 2013.
Tompkins, Jane P. "An Introduction to Reader-Response Criticism." In *Reader-Response Criticism: From Formalism to Post-structuralism*, edited by Jane P. Tompkins, ix-xxvi. Baltimore, MD: Johns Hopkins University Press, 1980.
Toomey, Russell B., Amy K. Syvertsen, and Maura Shramko. "Transgender Adolescent Suicide Behavior." *Pediatrics* 142 no. 4 (2018): 1–8. https://doi.org/10.1542/peds.2017-4218.
Tremain, Rose. *Sacred Country*. New York: Atheneum, 1993.
Tremain, Shelley. "Educating Jouy." *Hypatia: A Journal of Feminist Philosophy* 28, no. 4 (2013): 801–17.
Truitt, Jos. "Why the *New Yorker*'s Radical Feminism and Transgenderism Piece Was One-Sided." *Columbia Journalism Review*, August 6, 2014. http://archives.cjr.org/minority_reports/new_yorker_feminism_transgenderism_jos_truitt.php.
Vaccaro, Jeanne. "Felt Matters." In *The Transgender Studies Reader 2*, edited by Susan Stryker and Aren Z. Aizura, 91–100. New York: Routledge, 2013.

Valentine, David. *Imagining Transgender: An Ethnography of a Category*. Durham, NC: Duke University Press, 2007.
Valentine, David. "Sue E. Generous: Toward a Theory of Non-transexuality." *Feminist Studies* 38, no. 1 (2012): 185–211.
van der Hart, Onno, and Martin J. Dorahy. "History of the Concept of Dissociation." In *Dissociation and the Dissociative Disorders*, edited by Paul F. Dell and John A. O'Neil, 3–26. New York: Routledge, 2009.
van der Hart, Onno, Elert R. S. Nijenhuis, and Kathy Steele. *The Haunted Self: Structural Dissociation and the Treatment of Chronic Traumatization*. New York: Norton, 2006.
Vitulli, Elias. "Racialized Criminality and the Imprisoned Trans Body: Adjudicating Access to Gender-Related Medical Treatment in Prisons." *Social Justice* 37, no. 1 (2010–2011): 53–68.
Wanzo, Rebecca. *The Suffering Will Not Be Televised: African American Women and Sentimental Political Storytelling*. Albany, NY: SUNY Press, 2015.
Ward, Jane. "Gender Labor: Transmen, Femmes, and Collective Work of Transgression." *Sexualities* 13, no. 2 (2010): 236–54.
Wendell, Susan. "Unhealthy Disabled: Treating Chronic Illnesses as Disabilities." *Hypatia: A Journal of Feminist Philosophy* 16, no. 4 (2001): 17–33.
West, Issac. *Transforming Citizenships: Transgender Articulations of the Law*. New York: NYU Press, 2014.
White, Barbara A. "Loss of Self in *The Member of the Wedding*." In *Modern Critical Views on Carson McCullers*, edited by Harold Bloom, 125–42. New York: Chelsea House, 1986.
Wiegman, Robyn. *Object Lessons*. Durham, NC: Duke University Press, 2012.
Wilkerson, Abby L. "Normate Sex and Its Discontents." In *Sex and Disability*, edited by Robert McRuer and Anna Mollow, 183–207. Durham, NC: Duke University Press, 2012.
Williams, Cristan. "Fact Checking Janice Raymond: The NCHCT Report." *TransAdvocate*, September 18, 2014. http://www.transadvocate.com/fact-checking-janice-raymond-the-nchct-mreport_n_14554.htm.
Winnicott, D. W. "Dreaming, Fantasying, and Living: A Case-History Describing a Primary Dissociation." In *Playing and Reality*, 35–50. London: Routledge, 2005.
Withers, A. J. *Disability Politics and Theory*. Halifax, Nova Scotia: Fernwood Publishing, 2012.Kindle Edition.
Yergeau, M. Remi. *Authoring Autism: On Rhetoric and Neurological Queerness*. Durham, NC: Duke University Press, 2018.

INDEX